MY EXPERIENCES IN MANIPUR AND THE NAGA HILLS

MY EXPERIENCES IN MANIPUR AND THE NAGA HILLS

FOUNDER OF KASHMIR

JAMES JOHNSTONE

GYAN

Published by

GYAN

Gyan Publishing House
5, Ansari Road
Daryaganj, New Delhi-110002
Phone: 011-47034999, 9811692060
E-mail: books@gyanbooks.com

Distribution Network
gyanbooks.com
India, USA, Canada, UK, Australia

ISBN: 978-93-7447-260-6 (PB)

First Published, 1896

2nd Impression 2026

Printed at: Gyan Press, Delhi.

MY EXPERIENCES IN MANIPUR AND THE NAGA HILLS
Author: JAMES JOHNSTONE

Graham, Photo. Leamington Spa. Walker & Boutall Ph. Sc.

*Major-General
Sir James Johnstone, K.C.S.I.*

MY EXPERIENCES

IN

MANIPUR AND THE NAGA HILLS

BY THE LATE

MAJOR-GENERAL SIR JAMES JOHNSTONE

K.C.S.I.

WITH AN INTRODUCTORY MEMOIR

ILLUSTRATED

LONDON

SAMPSON LOW, MARSTON AND COMPANY

LIMITED

St. Dunstan's House

FETTER LANE, FLEET STREET, E.C.

1896

I DEDICATE

THESE PAGES TO THE MEMORY OF

My Wife,

WHO SHARED IN MANY OF MY LABOURS AND ANXIETIES

IN MANIPUR, AND THE NAGA HILLS,

AND WHOSE SPIRIT INSPIRED ME IN MY LAST ENTERPRISE,

AND WHO, HAD SHE LIVED,

WOULD HAVE WRITTEN A BETTER RECORD OF

OUR EXPERIENCES THAN I HAVE

BEEN ABLE TO DO.

AUTHOR'S PREFACE.

When I first brought my wife out to India in 1873, I was struck by the comments she made on things which had so long been part of my daily life. I had almost ceased to observe them. Every day she noted something new, and her diary was so interesting that I advised her to write a book on her "First Impressions of India," and she meant to do so, but never had time. Had she lived, this would have been a pleasure to her, but it was otherwise ordained. I feel now that I am in some way carrying out her wishes, by attempting a description of our life in India, though I am fully sensible that I cannot hope to achieve the pleasant chatty style in which she excelled.

I have also striven to give a fair record of the events with which I was connected; and perhaps, as they include a description of a state of things that has passed away for ever, they may not be devoid of interest. I am one of those old-fashioned Anglo-Indians who still believe in personal government, a system by which we gained India, solidified our rule, and made ourselves fairly acceptable to the people whom we govern. I believe the machine-like system which we have introduced and are endeavouring to force into every corner of India, till all personal influence is killed out, to be ill-adapted to the requirements of these Oriental races, and blighting in its effects. Not one native chief has adopted it in its integrity, which is in itself a fair argument that it is distasteful to the native mind; and we may be assured that if we evacuated India to-morrow, personal rule would again make itself felt throughout the length and breadth of the land, and grow stronger every day. I have always striven to be a reformer, but a reformer building on the solid foundations that we already find everywhere in India. Wherever you go, if there is a semblance of native rule left, you find a system admirably adapted to the needs of the population, though very often grown over with abuses. Clear away these abuses, and add a little in the way of modern progress, but always building on the foundation you find ready to hand, and you have a system acceptable to all.

We are wonderfully timid in sweeping away real abuses, for fear of hurting the feelings of the people; at the same time we weigh them down with unnecessary, oppressive, and worrying forms, and deluge the country with paper returns, never realising that these cause far more annoyance than would be felt at our making some radical change in a matter which, after all, affects only a minority. Take, for instance, the case of suttee, or widow-burning. It was argued for years that we could not put it down without causing a rebellion. What are the facts? A governor-general, blessed with moral courage in a great degree, determined to abolish the barbarous custom, and his edict was obeyed without a murmur. So it has been in many other cases, and so it will be wherever we have the courage to do the right thing. An unpopular tax would cause more real dissatisfaction than any interference with bad old customs, only adhered to from innate conservatism. The great principle on which to act is to do what is right, and what commends itself to common sense, and to try and carry the people with you. Do not let us have more mystery than is necessary; telling the plain truth is the best course; vacillation is fatal; the strongest officer is generally the most popular, and is remembered by the people long after he is dead and gone.

Personal rule is doomed, and men born to be personal rulers and a blessing to the governed, are now harassed by the authorities till they give up in despair, and swim with the stream.

The machine system did not gain India, and will not keep it for us; we must go back to a better system, or be prepared to relax our grasp, and give up the grandest work any nation ever undertook—the regeneration of an empire!

The House of Commons has to answer for much. No Indian administration is safe from the interference of theorists. To-day it is opium that is attacked by self-righteous individuals, who see in the usual, and in most cases harmless, stimulant of millions, a crying evil; while they view with apparent complacency the expenditure of £120,000,000 per annum on intoxicating liquors in England, and long columns in almost every newspaper recording brutal outrages on helpless women and children as the result.

Then the military administration is attacked, and in pursuance of another chimera, an iniquitous bill is forced on the Government of India calculated to produce results, which will probably sap the efficiency of our army at a critical moment. So it goes on, and it is hardly to be wondered at that the authorities in India give up resistance in sheer disgust, knowing all the while that, as the French say, *le deluge* must come after them.

It may be said, "What has all this to do with Manipur and the Naga Hills?" Nothing perhaps directly, but indirectly a great deal. The system which I decry carries its evil influence everywhere, and Manipur has suffered from it. I describe the Naga Hills and Manipur as they were in old days. I strove hard for years to hold the floods back from this little State and to preserve it intact, while doing all I could to introduce reforms. Now the floods have overwhelmed it, and if it rises again above them it will not be the Manipur that I knew and loved. May it, in spite of my doubts and fears, be a better Manipur.

CONTENTS.

CHAPTER VI.

CHAPTER VII.

CHAPTER VIII.

CHAPTER IX.

CHAPTER X.

CHAPTER XI.

CHAPTER XII.

CHAPTER XIII.

PAGE

CHAPTER XX.

CHAPTER XXI.

CHAPTER XXII.

CHAPTER XXIII.

CHAPTER XXIV.

CHAPTER XXV.

LIST OF ILLUSTRATIONS.

INTRODUCTORY MEMOIR.

THESE experiences were written in brief intervals of leisure, during the last few months of the author's busy life, which was brought to a sudden close before they were finally revised. Only last March when his nearest relations met at Fulford Hall to take leave of the eldest son of the house, before he sailed for India, the manuscript was still incomplete, and Sir James read some part of it aloud. His health had suffered greatly from over-fatigue in the unhealthy parts of India, in which his lot had been chiefly cast, but it was now quite restored and a prolonged period of usefulness seemed before him.

Improvements on the farms on his estate, a church within reach of his cottagers, to be built as a memorial to his late wife, and the hope of being once more employed abroad, probably as a colonial governor, were all plans for the immediate future, while the present was occupied with the magisterial and other business (including lectures on history in village institutes), which fill up so much of an English country gentleman's life. He had saved nothing in India. What the Lieutenant-Governor of Bengal wrote in 1872 of his early work at

Keonjhur, applied to everything else he subsequently undertook: "Captain Johnstone's schools, twenty in number, continue to flourish, attracting an average attendance of 665 children. Captain Johnstone's efforts to improve the crops and cattle of Keonjhur have before been remarked by the Lieutenant-Governor. His sacrifices for this end and for his charge generally, are, His Honour believes, almost unique."* But in 1881 by the death of his late father's elder brother, he inherited the Fulford estate on the boundaries of Worcestershire and Warwickshire, as well as Dunsley Manor in Staffordshire. The old Hall at Fulford, a strongly built, black and white, half-timbered erection of some centuries back, had been pulled down a few years before, and Sir James built the present house close to the old site. It was here that he was brought back in a dying state on June 13th, 1895, about 10 A.M., after riding out of the grounds only ten minutes before, full of life and energy. No one witnessed what occurred; he was a splendid horseman, but there was evidence that the horse, always inclined to be restive, had taken fright on passing a cottager's gate and tried to turn back, and that, as its master's whip was still firmly grasped in his hand, there had been a struggle.

He was engaged to assist the next day at the annual meeting of the Conservative and Unionist Association at Stratford-on-Avon. The Marquis of Hertford, who presided, when announcing the catastrophe in very feeling terms, spoke of the excellent work that Sir James Johnstone had done for

* Resolution. Political Department, No. 87, 1872.

the Unionist cause in Warwickshire. At Wythall Church (of which he was warden) the Vicar alluded, the following Sunday, to "the striking example he had set of a devout and attentive worshipper."

A retired official who had been acquainted with him in India for over thirty years, wrote on the same occasion to Captain Charles Johnstone, R.N.: "Your brother was a type of character not at all common, high-principled, fearless, just, with an overwhelming sense of duty, and restless spirit of adventure. It is by characters of his type, that our great empire has been created, and it is only if such types continue that we may look forward and hope that it will be maintained and extended."

Although the family from which Sir James Johnstone sprang is of Scottish origin, his own branch of it had lived in Worcestershire and Warwickshire for nearly a century and a half. "It has taken a prominent part in the social and public life of the Midlands, and has produced several eminent physicians." * He was the eleventh in direct male descent from William Johnstone of Graitney, who received a charter of the barony of Newbie for "distinguished services" to the Scottish crown in 1541. A remnant of the old Scottish estates was inherited by his great-grandfather, Dr. James Johnstone, who died at Worcester in 1802, and who, being the fourth son of his parents, had left Annandale at the age of twenty-one to settle in Worcestershire as a physician, but who always kept up his relations with Scotland, and meant to return there in his old age. His anxiety to secure this estate—Galabank—in the male

* *Birmingham Daily Post*, June 15, 1895.

line, really defeated his purpose; for he bequeathed it to his then unmarried younger son, the late Dr. John Johnstone, F.R.S., whose daughter now possesses it, to the exclusion of his elder sons who seemed likely to leave nothing but daughters. One of these elder sons was Sir James's grandfather, the late Dr. Edward Johnstone of Edgbaston Hall, who had married the heiress of Fulford, but was left a widower in 1800. Dr. Edward Johnstone was re-married in 1802 to Miss Pearson of Tettenhall, and of their two sons, the younger, James, born in 1806, practised for many years as a physician, and was President of the British Medical Association when it met in Birmingham in 1856. His eldest son, the subject of this notice, was born in a house now pulled down in the Old Square, Birmingham, on February 9th, 1841. Brought up in the midst of the large family of brothers and sisters, whose childhood was passed between their home in the Old Square and their grandfather's residence at Edgbaston Hall, where they spent the summer and autumn: he used also to look back with particular pleasure on his visits to his maternal grandfather's country house, where he first mounted a pony. His mother was his instructor, except occasional lessons from the Rev. T. Price, till at the age of nine he entered King Edward's Classical School, of which his father was a governor. The head master at that time (1850), was the Rev. (now Archdeacon) E. H. Gifford, D.D., and in the school list for 1852, Johnstone senior is placed next in the same class to Mackenzie (now Sir Alex.), the present Lieutenant-Governor of Bengal.

In 1855, young James Johnstone went to a military college in Paris, which was swept away before 1870, with a great part of the older portion of the city. After a year and a half in Paris he was transferred to the Royal Naval and Military Academy, Gosport, and a few months later qualified for one of the last cadetships given under the old East India Company. Without delay he proceeded to India, which was at that period distracted by the Indian Mutiny, so that his regiment the 68th Bengal Native Infantry, consisted only of officers attached to different European regiments, or acting in a civil capacity. With the 73rd (Queen's Regiment) he marched through the country, and was actively employed in the suppression of the insurgents, after which he was stationed for some time in Assam where he also saw active service. There, in 1862, he met with the accident he alludes to on pp. 3 and 20. It came in the course of his duty, as the population of a village which had been disarmed had sent to the nearest military post to ask for assistance against a tiger (panther), causing destruction in the neighbourhood; but he was very much hurt, and the weakening effects of this accident, seem to have predisposed him to attacks of the malaria fever of the district, from which he frequently suffered afterwards.

His next post was at Keonjhur, where there had been an outbreak against the Rajah by some of the hill-tribes and the chief insurgent had been executed. Lieutenant Johnstone was appointed special assistant to the superintendent of the Tributary Mehals at Cuttack, in whose official district Keonjhur lies. The

Superintendent wrote to the Lieutenant-Governor (Sir William Grey) of Bengal in 1869: "Captain Johnstone has acquired their full confidence, and hopes very shortly to be able to dispense with the greater part of the Special Police Force posted at Keonjhur. He appears to take very great interest in his work, and is sanguine of success." The same official when enclosing Captain Johnstone's first report, wrote: "It contains much interesting matter regarding the people, and shows that he has taken great pains in bringing them into the present peaceable and apparently loyal condition," and a little further on, when describing an interview he had with the Rajah: "From the manner in which he spoke of Captain Johnstone, I was exceedingly glad to find that the most good feeling exists between them." He also adds, apropos of a recommendation that the Government should pay half the expense of the special commission instead of charging it all on the native state: "Nearly one half of Captain Johnstone's time has been occupied in Khedda (catching wild elephants) operations, which have been successful and profitable to Government, and totally unconnected with that officer's duty in Keonjhur."*

A year later the superintendent (T. E. Ravenshaw, Esq.) reports: "Captain Johnstone, with his usual liberality and tact, has clothed two thousand naked savages, and has succeeded in inducing them to wear the garments;" and again, "Captain Johnstone's success in establishing schools has been most marked, and there are now nine hundred children receiving a rudimentary education. . . . Captain Johnstone

* Printed official reports.

has very correctly estimated the political importance of education and enlightenment among the hill people, and it is evident that he has worked most judiciously and successfully in this direction." And again: "In the matter of improvement of breed of cattle, Captain Johnstone has, at his own expense, formed a valuable herd of sixty cows and several young bulls ready to extend the experiment. . . . Captain Johnstone's experiments on rice and flax cultivation have been very successful" (two years later this is attributed to his having superintended them himself). The official report sums up, "Of Captain Johnstone I cannot speak too highly; his management has been efficient, and he has exercised careful and constant supervision over the Rajah and his estate, in a manner which has resulted in material improvement to both."

Subsequently, when Captain Johnstone was on leave in England, the Keonjhur despatches show that he sent directions that the increase of his herd of cattle should be distributed gratis among the natives. They were at first afraid to accept them, hardly believing in the gift.

"Keonjhur," says the Government report of India for 1870–1, "continues under the able administration of Captain Johnstone, who, it will be remembered, was mainly instrumental in restoring the country to quiet three years ago."

Captain Johnstone was too good a classic not to remember the Roman method of conquering and subduing a province; and as far as funds would permit, he opened out roads and cleared away jungle. But he suffered again from the malaria so prevalent in the forest districts of India, and took three months' furlough in 1871, which meant just one month in England. Although he had lost his father in May, 1869, and his absence from home that year gave him some extra legal expense, he would not quit his work till he could leave it in a satisfactory state; yet the Lieut.-Governor of Bengal (Sir George Campbell) twice referred to this furlough as being "most unfortunate," particularly as it had to be repeated within a few months. The superintendent wrote from Cuttack in his yearly report to the Lieut.-Governor: "Captain Johnstone's serious and alarming illness necessitated his taking sick leave to England in August, 1871. He had only a short time previously returned from furlough, and with health half restored, over-tasked his strength in carrying out elephant Khedda work in the deadly jungles of Moburdhunj."

In the spring of 1872, Captain Johnstone was married to Emma Mary Lloyd, with whose family his own had a hereditary friendship of three generations. Her father was at that time M.P. for Plymouth, and living at Moor Hall in Warwickshire. Their first child, James, died of bronchitis when six months old, and they returned to India a short time afterwards, at which point the experiences begin. Their second child, Richard, was born at Samagudting, and is now a junior officer in the battalion of the 60th King's Own Royal Rifles, quartered in India. The third son, Edward, was born at Dunsley Manor, and two younger children in Manipur.

Manipur, to which Colonel Johnstone was appointed

in 1877, was called by one of the Indian secretaries the Cinderella among political agencies. "They'll never," he said, "get a good man to take it." "Well," was the reply, "a good man has taken it now." The loneliness, the surrounding savages, and the ill-feeling excited by the Kubo valley (which so late as 1852 is placed in Manipur, in maps published in Calcutta) having been made over to Burmah, were among the reasons of its unpopularity. Colonel Johnstone's predecessor, Captain Durand (now Sir Edward) draws a very glaring picture in his official report for 1877, of the Maharajah's misgovernment; the wretched condition of the people, and the most unpleasant position of the Political Agent, whom he described as "in fact a British officer under Manipur surveillance. . . . He is surrounded by spies. . . . If the Maharajah is not pleased with the Political Agent he cannot get anything—he is ostracised. From bad coarse black atta, which the Maharajah sells him as a favour, to the dhoby who washes his clothes, and the Nagas who work in his garden, he cannot purchase anything." Yet, well knowing all this, Colonel Johnstone readily accepted the post, confident that with his great knowledge of Eastern languages, and of Eastern customs and modes of thought, he should be able to bring about a better state of things, both as regarded the oppressed inhabitants and the permanent influence of the representative of the British Government. Whether this confidence was justified, the following pages will show.

EDITOR.

MY EXPERIENCES

IN

MANIPUR AND THE NAGA HILLS.

CHAPTER I.

Arrival in India—Hospitable friends—The Lieutenant-Governor—Journey to the Naga Hills—Nigriting—Golaghat—A Panther reminiscence—Hot springs—A village dance—Dimapur—My new abode.

I LEFT England with my wife on November 13th, 1873, and after an uneventful voyage, reached Bombay, December 9th. We proceeded at once to Calcutta, where some of my old servants joined me, including two bearers, Seewa and Keptie, wild Bhooyas from the Cuttack Tributary Mehals, whom I had trained, and who had been with me for years in all my wanderings, in that wild territory. Thanks to the kindness of my friends the Bernards (now Sir C. and Lady Bernard), we spent only a day at an hotel, and remained under their hospitable roof till we left Calcutta.

My old appointment in Keonjhur had been abolished, and I had to wait till another was open to me. I had several interviews on the subject with the Lieutenant-Governor of Bengal, Sir G. Campbell.

Finally it was decided that I should go to Assam (then about to be made into a Chief Commissionership) and act as Political Agent of the Naga Hills, while the permanent official—Captain Butler—was away in the Interior, and subsequently on leave. I knew a large part of the district well, as one of the most malarious in India, and when asked if I would take the appointment, said, "Yes, I have no objection, but just hint to the Lieutenant-Governor that unless he wants to kill me off, it may be better policy to send me elsewhere, as the Medical Board in London said, I must not go to a malarious district, after the experience I have had of it in Keonjhur." The Secretary conveyed my hint, and when I next saw him, said, "The Lieutenant-Governor says, that is all stuff and nonsense." Later on Sir G. Campbell asked if my wife would go with me. I quietly replied that she would go anywhere with me.

Finally, on December 30th, we left Calcutta, and after a night in the train, embarked in one of the I. G. S. N. Co.'s steamers at Goalundo, for Nigriting on the Burrhampooter, where we had to land for the Naga Hills. The steamers of those days, were not like the well-appointed mail boats now in use. The voyage was long, the steamers uncomfortable, and the company on board anything but desirable. All the same, the days passed pleasantly, while we slowly wended our way up the mighty river, amid lovely and interesting scenery all new to my wife, to whom I pointed out the different historic spots as they came in view.

We halted at Gowhatty for the night, and early in the morning I swam across the river for the second time in my life, a distance of about three miles, as the current carried me in a slanting direction.

At last we reached Nigriting, and were landed on a dry sandbank five or six miles from the celebrated tea gardens of that name, and the nearest habitations. Fortunately, I had brought a tent and all things needful for a march; and my servants, well accustomed to camp life, soon pitched it and made us comfortable, and my wife was charmed with her first experience. We had a message of welcome from Mr. Boyle, of Nigriting Factory, and the next day went to his house in canoes, whence we set out for Golaghat.

It was to Nigriting that I was carried for change of air nearly twelve years before, when, in April, 1862, I was desperately wounded in an encounter with a large panther near Golaghat, where I had been stationed. I then lived for a week or so in a grass hut on a high bank, and the fresh air made my obstinate wounds begin to heal. Thus it happened that all the people knew me well, and I was long remembered by the name of "Baghé Khooah" literally the "tiger eaten," a name which I found was still familiar to every one. Loading our things on elephants, and having a pony for my wife, and a dandy (hill litter) in case she grew tired, we set off for Golaghat, and had a picnic luncheon on the way. How delightful are our first experiences of marching in India, even when we have, as in this case, to put up with some discomfort; the cool, crisp air in the morning; the good appetite that a ten-mile walk or ride gives; the feeling that breakfast has been earned, and finally breakfast itself; and such a good one. Where indeed but in India could we have a first-rate meal of three or four courses, and every dish hot, with no better appliances in the shape of a fireplace, than two or three clods of earth? Often have I had a dinner fit for a king, when heavy rain had been falling for hours, and there was no shelter for my men, but a tree with a sheet thrown over a branch.

We breakfasted at a place called "Char Alleé" and the march being long (nearly twenty miles), the sun was low long before reaching Golaghat. As we passed some road coolies, I began a conversation with the old Tekla (overseer) in charge, and asked him if he could get me a few oranges. He said, "Oh no, they are all over." He then asked me how I came to speak Assamese so well. I said, "I have been in Assam before." He said, "Oh yes, there have been many sahibs in my time," and he named several; "and then long ago there was a 'Baghé Khooah' sahib, I wonder where he is now?" I looked at him and said, "Ami Baghé Khooah" (I am the Baghé Khooah). The old man gazed equally hard at me for a moment and then ran in front of me and made a most profound obeisance. Having done this, he smilingly said, "I think I can find you some oranges after all," and at once ran off, and brought me some for which he refused to take anything. The good old man walked about a mile farther before he wished me good-bye; and my wife and I went on, greatly pleased to find that I was so well remembered.

We did not get to Golaghat till long after dark,

and pitched our tent on the site of the lines of my old detachment, which I had commanded twelve years before. What a change! Trees that I had remembered as small, had grown large, and some that were planted since I left, already a fair size.

In the morning we received a perfect ovation. People who had known me before, crowded to see me and pay their respects, many of them bringing their children born since I had left. All this was pleasant enough and greatly delighted my wife, but we had to proceed on our way, and it is always difficult to get one's followers to move from a civilised place, where there is a bazaar, into the jungle, and henceforth our road lay through jungle, the Nambor forest beginning about five miles from Golaghat. At last coolies to carry my wife arrived, and I sent her on in her "dandy" with her ayah, charging the bearers to wait for me at a village I well knew, called "Sipahee Hoikeeah." The men replied, "Hoi Deota" (Yes, deity*) and started. The elephants were a great difficulty, and it was some hours before I could get off, and even then some had not arrived. However, off I started, and hurried on to "Sipahee Hoikeeah" so as not to keep my wife waiting, but when I reached the spot, I found to my amazement that the village had ceased to exist, having, as I subsequently learned, been abandoned for fear of the Nagas. I hurried on in much anxiety, as my wife did not speak Hindoostani, and neither ayah nor bearers spoke English. At

* One of the witnesses at the trial of the Regent and Senaputty of Manipur, in 1891, stated that Mr. Quinton was partly induced to enter the palace from which he never emerged alive, by the Manipuris saying, "Are you not our deity?"—Ed.

last I caught them up at the Nambor hot springs, called by natives the "Noonpoong" where we were to halt.

The Noonpoong is situated in a lovely spot amidst fine forest. The hot water springs out of the ground, at a temperature of 112 degrees and fills a small pool. It is similar in taste to the waters of Aix-la-Chapelle, and is highly efficacious in skin diseases, being resorted to even for the cure of severe leech bites, which are easily obtained from the land leech infesting all the forests of Assam. Fortunately some of our cooking things, with chairs and a table arrived, also a mattress, but no bed and no tent. We waited till 9 P.M., and finding that no more elephants came up, I made up a bed for my wife on the ground under a table, to shelter her from the dew, but while sitting by the camp fire for a last warm, we heard the noise of an elephant, and saw one emerging from the forest. Fortunately he carried the tent which was quickly pitched, and we passed a comfortable night.

The hot springs are not the only attraction of the neighbourhood, as about two miles off in the forest, there is a very pretty waterfall, not high, but the volume of water is considerable, and it comes down with a thundering sound heard for some distance. The natives call it the "phutta hil," literally "rent rock." The Nambor forest is noted for its Nahor or Nagessur trees (*Mesua Ferma*) a handsome tree, the heart of which is a fine red wood, very hard and very heavy, and quite impervious to the attacks of white ants. Europeans call it the iron wood of Assam. It is very plentiful in parts of the forest

CAMPING OUT.

[Page 6.

between the Noonpoong and Golaghat, and also grows in the lowlands of Manipur.

The next morning we set out for Borpathar, a village with a fine sheet of cultivation on the banks of the Dunseree, and took up our quarters in the old blockhouse, which had been converted into a comfortable rest house. Here again we received a perfect ovation, the people, headed by my old friend Hova Ram, now promoted to a Mouzadar, coming in a body, with fruit and eggs, etc., to pay their respects. The population had sadly diminished since my early days, the people having in many cases fled the country for fear of Naga raids.

The march having been a short one, all our baggage had time to come up. In the evening the girls of the village entertained us with one of their national dances, a very pretty and interesting sight. After a good night's rest we again started, our march lying through the noble forest, where buttressed trees formed an arch over the road, showing plainly that Gothic architecture was an adaptation from nature. I had never marched along the road since it was cleared; but I was there in 1862, in pursuit of some Naga raiders, when it would have been impassable, but for elephant and rhinoceros tracks. Even then I was struck by its great beauty, and now it was a fairly good cold weather track.

We halted at Deo Panee, then at Hurreo Jan, and Nowkatta, and on the fourth day reached Dimapur, where we found a comfortable rest house, on the banks of a fine tank about two hundred yards square. This, with many others near it, spoke of days of civilisation that had long since passed away, before the Naga drove the Cacharee from the hills he now inhabits, and from the rich valley of the Dunseree. Near Dimapur we passed a Meekir hut built on posts ten or twelve feet high, and with a notched log resting against it, at an angle of about seventy degrees by way of a staircase, up which a dog ran like a squirrel at our approach. The Meekirs occupy some low hill ranges between the Naga hills and the Burrhampooter.

The country round Dimapur is exceedingly rich, and everywhere bears the marks of having been thickly populated. It is well supplied with artificial square tanks, some much larger than the one already referred to, and on the opposite bank of the river we crossed to reach our halting place, are the remains of an old fortified city. Mounds containing broken pottery made with the wheel, abound, though the neighbouring tribes have forgotten its use. At Dimapur, in those days, there were three or four Government elephants and a few shops kept by "Khyahs," an enterprising race of merchants from Western India.

The ruined city is worth describing. It was surrounded originally by solid brick walls twelve feet in height and six in thickness, the bricks admirably made and burned. The walls enclosed a space seven hundred yards square; it was entered by a Gothic archway, and not far off had a gap in the wall, said to have been made for cattle to enter by. Inside were tanks, some lined with brick walls, and with brick steps leading to the water. Though I carefully explored the interior, I never saw any other traces of brickwork, except perhaps a platform; but I found one or two sacrificial stones, for offerings of flowers, water and oil. One corner of the surrounding wall had been cut away by the river. The enclosure is covered with forest. Near the gateway are some huge monoliths, one eighteen feet in height. All are covered with sculpture, and some have deep grooves cut in the top, as if to receive beams. It is difficult to conjecture what they were brought there for, and how they were transported, as the nearest rocks from which they could have been cut, are at least ten miles away. If the Assam-Bengal Railway passes near Dimapur as is, I believe, arranged, this interesting old city wall will probably be used as a quarry for railway purposes, and soon none of it will remain. Alas, for Vandalism!

History tells us little about the origin of Dimapur, but probably it was once a centre of Cacharee civilisation, and as the Angami Nagas advanced, the city wall was built, so as to afford a place of refuge against sudden raids. It is a strange sight to see the relics of a forgotten civilisation, in the midst of a pathless forest.

On our march up, we frequently came upon the windings of the river Dunseree. At Nowkatta it runs parallel for a time with the road, and we took our evening walk on its dry sandbanks, finding many recent traces of tigers and wild elephants. From that time till we finally left the hills, the roar of tigers and the trumpeting of elephants were such common sounds, that we ceased to pay attention to them, and my wife, though naturally timid, became devoted to the wild solitude of our life.

At Dimapur we enjoyed the luxury of fresh milk, which, of course, the forest did not supply. The night was delightfully cold, and the next morning crisp and invigorating, and we set off at an early hour, for our last march into Samagudting.

For the first eight miles our road was through a level forest country, with the exception of a piece of low-lying grass land, and at a place called Nichu Guard the ascent of the hill commenced. This entrance of the gorge through which the Diphoo Panee river enters the low lands is very beautiful, the stream rushing out from the hills over a pebbly bottom, and it was a favourite encamping ground for us in our later marches. Now, we had not time to halt, so hurried on. The road up the hill was in fair condition for men and elephants, but did not admit of wheeled traffic, had there been any carts to use. We accomplished the ascent, a distance of four miles, in about two hours, obtaining several lovely views of the boundless forest, on our way.

The vegetation on the hill itself had been much injured by the abominable practice hillmen have, of clearing a fresh space every two or three years, and deserting it for another, when the soil has been exhausted. This never gives it time to recover. At last we reached the summit, and took possession of the Political Agent's house, a large bungalow, built of grass and bamboo, the roof being supported by wooden posts, on the highest point of the hill. A glance showed me that the posts were nearly eaten through by white ants, and that the first high wind would level it with the ground. It had been built by a man who never intended to stay, and who only wanted it to last his time.

Later in the day, I took over the charge from Mr. Coombs, who was acting till my arrival, and thus became, for the time, chief of the district. My staff consisted of Mr. Needham, Assistant Political Agent, and Mr. Cooper, in medical charge, the usual office establishment, and one hundred and fifty military police. Most of these, together with Captain Butler, for whom I was acting, were away in the Interior with a survey party. Mr. Coombs left in a day or two, and I then occupied his bungalow lower down the hill, and in a more exposed position, so as to allow of the larger house being rebuilt. Besides the Government establishment, we had a fair-sized Naga village on the hill, and just below the Political Agent's house. These people had long been friendly to us, and were willing, for a large recompense, to do all sorts of odd jobs, being entirely free from the caste prejudices of our Hindoo and degenerate Mussulman fellow-subjects.

CHAPTER II.

Samagudting—Unhealthy quarters—A callous widower—Want of water—Inhabitants of the Naga Hills—Captain Butler—Other officials—Our life in the wilds—A tiger carries off the postman—An Indian forest—Encouragement.

MY first impressions of Samagudting, were anything but favourable. It was eminently a "make-shift place." It had been occupied by us as a small out-post, from time to time, between 1846 and 1851, but it was never fit for a permanent post of more than twenty-five men, as the water supply was bad, there being no springs, and only a few water holes which were entirely dependent on the uncertain rainfall. A small tank had been constructed, but it was 500 feet below the summit, so that water was sold at an almost prohibitive rate. All articles of food were scarce, dear and bad, wood was enormously dear, and to crown all, the place was unhealthy and constantly enveloped in fog.

Samagudting* ought never to have been occupied, and would not have been, had the Government taken ordinary precautions to verify the too roseate reports of an officer who wished to see it adopted as the headquarters of a new district, as a speedy road

* The Assam Administration Report of 1877-8 writes of it as "notoriously unhealthy, and it had long been proposed to move the troops to a higher and less feverish spot."—ED.

to promotion, and subsequent transfer to a more favoured appointment. The report in question which, among other things, mentioned the existence of springs of water, that existed only in imagination, having once been accepted by the authorities, and a large expenditure incurred, it became a very invidious task for future Political Agents to unmask the affair, and proclaim the extreme unsuitability of Samagudting for a station.

Many other good and healthy sites were available, and I believe that our dealings with the Nagas were greatly retarded, by the adoption of such an unsuitable post. As it was, having made our road over the hill, it was necessary to climb an ascent of over two thousand feet, and an equal descent, before entering the really important portion of the Angami Naga country. I at once saw that the right entrance lay by the Diphoo Panee Gorge, and I recommended its adoption. I began to make this road during the Naga Hills Campaign of 1879-80, and it has since been regularly used.

Having said all that there was to say against Samagudting, it is only fair to mention its good points. First, though never so cold in the winter, as the plains, the temperature was never so high in the hot and rainy seasons; and when the weather was fine, it was very enjoyable. The views from the hill were magnificent. To the south, the Burrail range, from which a broad and undulating valley divided us. To the west, a long stretch of hills and forests. To the east, the valley of the Dunseree, bordered by the Rengma and Lotah Naga hills, a vast forest, stretching as far as the eye could reach, with here and there a large patch of high grass land, one of which many miles in extent, was the Rengma Putha, a grand elephant catching ground in old times, where many a noble elephant became a victim to the untiring energy of the Bengali elephant phandaits or noosers, from the Morung.* To the north, the view extended over a pathless forest, the first break being the Doboka Hills. Behind these, a long bank of mist showed the line of the Burrhampooter, while on clear days in the cold weather, we might see the dark line of the Bhootan Hills, with the snowy peaks of the Himalayas towering above them.† Altogether, it was a sight once seen, never to be forgotten.

There was a footpath all round the hill, which, after a little alteration of level here and there, and a little repairing, where landslips had made it unsafe, was delightful for a morning or evening walk or ride. As my wife was fond of botany, she found a subject of never-ending interest in the many wild flowers, ferns, and climbing plants, and soon grew accustomed to riding along the edge of a dizzy precipice.

Our private establishment consisted of ten or twelve servants in all, including a girl of the Kuki tribe, named Bykoout, who assisted the ayah; a very small establishment for India. Servants in Assam are bad and difficult to keep. Most of mine were imported, but, with the exception of my two faithful Bhooyas, Seewa and Keptie, and a *syce* (groom), by name

* When I first went to Assam almost all elephant-catching was done by noosing.

† The country bordering on the Bhootan Dooars in the Ringpore district.

SAMAGUDTING.

[Page 14.

Peewa, they were all soon corrupted, though some had been with me for years. Seewa once said to me, "The influence here is so bad, that we too shall be corrupted if we stay long." Seewa was quite a character. One day I got a letter from one of his relations, asking me to tell him that his wife was dead. I remembered her well; it was a love match, and she had run away with him. I feared it would be such a blow, that I felt quite nervous about telling him, and put it off till the evening, when, with a faltering voice, I broke the news as gently as I could. Instead of the outburst of grief I had looked for, he quietly asked, "What did she die of?" I said, "Fever." He replied, "Oh, yes, I thought it must be that. Will you write and see that all her property is made over to my brother, otherwise some of her people may steal it?"

The state of things at Samagudting was very discouraging. I resented seeing the Government and the establishment being charged famine prices for everything, by the Nagas and Khyahs; also the general squalor which prevailed, and which I felt need not exist. It was the inheritance of the hand-to-mouth system in which everything had been commenced in early days. However, my wife set me an example of cheerfulness, and I made up my mind to remedy all the evils I could. First, the supply system was attacked, and I made arrangements with some old Khyah friends at Golaghat, to send up large supplies of rice and other kinds of food, and as the season advanced, I encouraged such of the military police as could be spared to take up land at Dimapur, and cultivate. For ourselves, I bought two cows at Borpathar, and established them at Nichu Guard, whence my gardener brought up the milk every day. In a short time we were more comfortable than could have been expected, and there was the additional satisfaction of seeing that the arrangements for cheaper food for the establishment proved successful. Water was the standing difficulty; we had to depend upon the caprice of the Naga water-carriers, and frequently my wife's bath, filled ready for the next morning, had to be emptied in the evening to provide water for cooking our evening meal! Sometimes I got clean water for drinking from the Diphoo Panee, otherwise what we had was as if it had been taken from a dirty puddle. The want of water prevented our having a garden near our house; we had a few hardy flowers, including the shoe-flower—a kind of hibiscus—roses, and passion-flower. Such vegetable-garden as we had was at Nichu Guard, where the soil was good, and water plentiful.

Our house was watertight, and that was the best that could be said for it. It was thatched, with walls of split bamboos and strengthened by wooden posts; there were no glass windows, and the doors and shutters were of split bamboo tied together; the mud floor was also covered with thin split bamboos, and had to be swept constantly, as the dust worked through. We had one sitting-room, a bed-room, bath-room, pantry, and store-room, the latter full of rats. Snakes occasionally visited us, and a day or two after we had settled in, a cat rushed in while we were at breakfast, jumped on my knee and took away the meat from my plate, and bit and scratched me when I tried to catch her. My dressing-room was the shade of a tree outside, where I bathed Anglo-Indian camp fashion, substituting a large hollow bamboo for the usual *mussuk*, or skin of water.

We arrived at Samagudting on January 23rd, 1874, and by the beginning of February felt quite old residents; hill-walking no longer tired me, and we had made acquaintance with all the Nagas of the village, and of many others, and were on quite friendly terms with "Jatsolé," the chief of Samagudting, a shrewd far-seeing man, with great force of character.

I have mentioned the Burrail range, and the valley separating us. Besides Samagudting there were two other villages on our side, Sitekima, on the opposite bank of the Diphoo Panee Gorge, and Tesephima, on outlying spurs of Samagudting. I say Samagudting, as it has become the common appellation, but correctly speaking it should be Chumookodima.

On the side of the Burrail facing us, were villages belonging to a tribe we call Kutcha Nagas, a race inferior in fighting power to the Angamis, but not unlike them in appearance, though of inferior physique. These villages were formerly inhabited by Cacharees.*

On February 4th, I had a letter from Captain Butler, saying that he would be at Kohima in a day or two, and asking me to meet him there. He said that three of the police would be a sufficient escort. I accordingly took three men, and started on the

* See subsequent sketch of Naga tribes in Chapter III.

6th, marching to Piphima twenty-one miles, and the next morning another twenty-one into Kohima, two very hard marches. I was glad to renew my acquaintance with Butler, whom I had known when he first landed in India in 1861, and I was in Fort William, studying for my Hindustani examination. He was a fine manly fellow, admirably fitted to conduct an expedition, where pluck and perseverance were required. Here, I also met Dr. Brown, Political Agent of Manipur, and Captain (now Colonel) Badgley and Lieutenant (now Colonel C.B.) Woodthorpe, R.E., of the survey, also Lieutenant (now Major V.C.) Ridgeway, 44th N.I.), I spent a pleasant evening, discussing various subjects with Captain Butler, and early on the 8th started on my return journey.

Captain Butler had done the whole forty-two miles into Samagudting in one day, and I determined to attempt it, and succeeded, though the last 2000 feet of ascent to my house was rather hard, tired as I was. My wife did not expect me, but I had arranged to fire three shots from my rifle as a signal, if I arrived at any time by night; this I did about 500 feet below my house, and I at once saw lanterns appear far above me, and in a quarter of an hour, or twenty minutes, I was at my door. The sound of firing at 9 P.M. created quite a sensation among the weak-nerved ones on the hill, but it was good practice for the sentries to be kept on the alert. Ever after, three shots from a rifle or a revolver, were always my signal when I neared home, and often in after years were they heard in the dead of night, when I was thought to be miles away. My wife used to say that it kept the people in good order, never knowing when to expect me. I think it did.

Life was never monotonous. I took long walks, after our morning walk round the hill, to inspect roads and bridges—a very important work. Then I attended Cutcherry (the court of justice) and heard cases, often with a loaded revolver in my hand, in case of any wild savage attempting to dispute my authority; then I finished off revenue work, of which there was little, and went home, had a cup of tea, visited hospitals and gaol, if I had not already done so; and afterwards went for an evening walk with my wife, round the hill or through the village.

Sometimes duty took me to the plains, and we had a most delightful march to the Nambor hot springs, when I arranged to have a rest house built at Nowkatta, between Dimapur and Hurreo Jan. We reached the last place, just after a dreadful catastrophe had occurred. The rest house was raised on posts, six foot above the ground. One night when the man carrying the dak (post) had arrived from Borpathar, he hung up the letter bag *under the house* on a peg, and having had his evening meal, retired to rest in the house with one or two other travellers. Suddenly a huge tiger rushed up the steps, sprang through the open door, and seizing one of the sleepers, bounded off into the forest with him. One of my police who was there snatched up his rifle, pursued the tiger and fired, making him drop the man, but life was extinct, and when we arrived, there was a huge bloodstain on the floor, at least a yard long. Strange to say, the letter bag was on one occasion carried off by a tiger, but afterwards recovered, uninjured save by tooth marks. The policeman was promoted for his gallantry.

The day after leaving Hurreo Jan, we met a party of Rengma Nagas coming to see me, with some little presents. They were the men who helped to kill the panther, that wounded me in 1862,* and they brought with them the son of one of their number, who was killed by the infuriated beast, a fine lad of fifteen; needless to say, that I rewarded these friendly people, whom I had not seen for twelve years. We halted a day or two at the springs, as I had to visit Golaghat on business, and unfortunately missed seeing a herd of wild elephants caught, a sight I had wished my wife to see. She did see the stockade, but the elephants had been already taken out. I hope farther on to describe an elephant drive.

I do not know a more agreeable place to halt at than the hot springs in former days. In cold weather before the mosquitoes had arrived it was perfect rest. A little opening in the tall dark forest, in the centre some scrub jungle, including fragrant wild lemons and citrons, with the pool in the midst; a babbling stream flowed all round the opening, on the other side of which was a high bank. The

* Sir James (then Lieut.) Johnstone headed a party to clear an Assamese village from a panther that had killed several natives and was terrifying the district. It retreated into a house which he ordered to be pulled down, and as his men were thus engaged it sprang from a window on to his shoulder. With his other arm—the left—he fired at it behind his back and wounded it sufficiently to make it loose its hold, and rush off into the jungle, where it was killed in the course of the afternoon. His arm was terribly injured, and he always considered that he owed complete recovery of the use of it to the kindness and skill of an English medical friend who came from a great distance to attend him. Every one else who was wounded by the same panther died.—Ed.

bathing was delightful, and could be made quite private for ladies, by means of a cloth enclosure, well known to the Assamese by the name of "Âr Kapôr." Then the occasional weird cry of the hoocook ape, and the gambols of numerous monkeys in the tall trees on the high bank, gave plenty of interest to the scene, had the general aspect of the place failed in its attractions.

Soon after our return to headquarters, the survey party arrived from the interior of the hills, and after a few days' rest, departed for their summer quarters. Captain Butler then started for England, and Mr. Needham came in to Samagudting.

Thus left in charge for a considerable period, I felt justified in doing more than I should have done, had my stay only been of a temporary nature, and I went most thoroughly into all questions connected with the hills and their administration. My long experience in charge of a native state full of wild hill tribes, and my personal knowledge of many of the Naga and other wild tribes of Assam (a knowledge that went back as far as 1860), were a great help to me, as I was consequently not new to the work. The eastern frontier had always been to my mind the most interesting field of work in India, and now it was for me to learn all I could.

CHAPTER III.

Historical events connected with Manipur and the Naga Hills—Different tribes—Their religion—Food and customs.

SHORTLY after my arrival at Samagudting, I received a cheering letter, just when I most needed it, from my old friend Wynne, then Acting Foreign Secretary, saying, "Don't be too disappointed at not receiving a better appointment than the Naga Hills. You will have plenty of good work to do, and you will increase your already very extensive knowledge of wild tribes." It was the last letter I ever received from him, as cholera quickly carried him off, and I lost in him one of the kindest friends I ever had, one who had constantly interested himself in my work, and given me advice. Such a friend would have been invaluable now. Our position in the Naga Nills was an anxious one, and can only be properly realised by knowing the course of previous events.

Our first acquaintance with the Nagas practically began in 1832, when Captain Jenkins and Lieutenant Pemberton escorted by Rajah Ghumbeer Singh's Manipur troops, forced a passage through the hills with a view to ascertaining if there were a practicable route into Assam. They came *viâ* Paptongmai and Samagudting to Mohong Deejood. There is every

KOHIMA STONE. [*Page* 23.

reason to believe that the Manipuris in former days did penetrate into the Naga Hills, and exacted tribute when they felt strong enough to do so. All the villages have Manipur names in addition to their own. But during the period of her decadence, just before and during the Burmese War of 1819–25, any influence Manipur may have possessed fell into abeyance. At that time it was re-asserted, and Ghumbeer Singh reduced several villages to submission, including the largest of all, Kohima, at which place he stood upon a stone and had his footprints sculptured on it, in token of conquest. This was set up in a prominent position, together with an upright stone bearing carved figures and an inscription.

The Nagas greatly respected this stone and cleaned it from time to time. They opened a large trade with Manipur, and whenever a Manipuri visited a Naga village he was treated as an honoured guest, at a time when a British subject could not venture into the interior without risk of being murdered.

Even up to the Naga Hills campaign of 1879–80, the Nagas regarded Manipur as the greater power of the two, because her conduct was consistent; if she threatened, she acted. One British subject after another might be murdered with impunity, but woe betide the village that murdered a subject of Manipur. A force of Manipuris was instantly despatched, the village was attacked, destroyed, and ample compensation exacted. The system answered well for Manipur; many of the Nagas began to speak Manipuri, and several villages paid an annual tribute. Still, up to 1851, we considered that we had some shadowy claim to the hills, though we never openly asserted it.

I may as well give a short account of the different tribes inhabiting the Naga Hills district when I took charge. The oldest were—

Cacharees.

Their origin is obscure. They are first met with in the north-east portion of the Assam Valley between the Muttuk country and Sudya. Round the last in the vast forests, there are numerous ruins ascribed by the people to the Cacharee Rajahs, built of substantial brickwork. I have not seen any sculptured stonework, but it may exist. The traditions give no clue to their original home, which was probably in Thibet. From the neighbourhood of Sudya they penetrated down the valley, leaving buildings and remnants of their tribes here and there, notably in the Durrung district. The main body were, for a time settled in the nighbourhood of Dimapur, and the country lying between it and Doboka, the Cachar district, but when they arrived or how long they stayed we have no means of ascertaining. They occupied the first two or three ranges of the Burrails and stoutly contested possession with the Naga invaders, and after they had been dispossessed made a gallant attempt to retrieve their affairs by an attack on Sephema. They entered the hills by the Diphoo gorge and constructed a paved road up to the neighbourhood of Sephema where they would probably have succeeded in their operations, but that the Sephema Nagas, skilful then as now, in the use of poison, poisoned the waters and destroyed a large portion of the invaders; the rest retreated to Dimapur, and eventually left the neighbourhood and settled in Cachar, to which they gave their name. There are still a good many Cacharees on the banks of the Kopiti, in the neighbourhood of Mohung-dee-jood. They are a fine hardy race, and in my time the Naga Hills police was largely recruited from them. Under Captain Butler they did good service, and would have gone anywhere when led by him.* The Cacharees were governed formerly by a race of despotic chiefs.

Kukis.

The Kukis are a wandering race consisting of several tribes who have long been working up from the South. They were first heard of as Kukis, in Manipur, between 1830 and 1840; though tribes of the same race had long been subject to the Rajah of Manipur. The new immigrants began to cause anxiety about the year 1845, and soon poured into the hill tracts of Manipur in such numbers, as to drive away many of the older inhabitants. Fortunately, the political agent (at this time Lieutenant afterwards Colonel McCulloch)† was a man well

* Captain Butler was struck by a spear from a Naga ambuscade, near the village of Pangti in the Naga Hills on December 25, 1876. He died on January 7. He had held the appointment of Political Agent for seven years, and was the son of Colonel Butler, the author of 'Scenes in Assam' and 'A Sketch in Assam,' the earliest accounts of that eastern border.—Ed.

† "The influence exercised by Colonel McCulloch as a political agent at Manipur was most beneficial," wrote the *Times*, April 1, 1891, "and

able to cope with the situation. Cool and resolute, he at once realised and faced the difficulty. Manipur in those days, owing to intestine quarrels, could have done nothing, and the Rajah Nur Singh gladly handed over the management of the new arrivals to him.

Seeing that the Kukis had been driven north by kindred but more powerful tribes, and that their first object was to secure land for cultivation; McCulloch, as they arrived, settled them down, allotting to them lands in different places according to their numbers, and where their presence would be useful on exposed frontiers. He advanced them large sums from his own pocket, assigning different duties to each chief's followers. Some were made into irregular troops, others were told off to carry loads according to the customs of the state. Thus in time many thousands of fierce Kukis were settled down as peaceful subjects of Manipur, and Colonel McCulloch retained supreme control over them to the last. So great was his influence, that he had only to send round his silver mounted dao (Burmese sword) as a kind of fiery cross, when all able-bodied men at once assembled at his summons.

Colonel McCulloch's policy of planting Kuki settlements on exposed frontiers, induced the Government of Bengal to try a similar experiment, and a large colony of Kukis were settled in 1855 in the neighbourhood of Langting, to act as a barrier for North Cachar against the raids of the Angami Nagas. The

---

since his time no one has been more successful than Colonel Johnstone, who took charge in 1877, and rendered conspicuous service by raising the siege of Kohimas by the Nagas in 1879."—Ed.

experiment answered well to a certain extent, and would have answered better, had we been a little less timid. The Kukis are strictly monarchical, and their chiefs are absolutely despotic, and may murder or sell their subjects into slavery without a murmur of dissent. Their original home cannot be correctly ascertained, but there seem to be traces of them as far south as the Malay peninsula. They are readily distinguishable from the Nagas, and are braver men. Their women are often very fair, and wear their hair in a long thick plait down the back. The men are mostly copper coloured, and have often good features.

Kutcha Nagas.

The tribe we call Kutcha Nagas, very much resemble the Angamis, though of inferior physique. They are closely allied to the Nagas in Manipur, as well as to the Angamis, and probably were pushed in front of the latter from the Northern North-East, as the Kukis were forced in by the pressure of stronger tribes to their South. They have always been less warlike than their powerful neighbours, though they could be troublesome at times.

Angami Nagas.

A strong built, hardy, active race, the men averaging 5 feet 8 inches to 6 feet in height, and the women tall in proportion. In colour they vary from a rich brown to a yellowish or light brown. They have a manly independent bearing, and are bred up to war from their earliest years. While the Kukis are monarchists, the Nagas are republicans, and their Peumahs, or chiefs, are elected, and though they often have great influence, they are in theory, only *primus inter pares*, and are liable at any time to be displaced. Practically they often remain in office for years, and are greatly respected.

Where the Angamis came from must be uncertain till the languages of our Eastern frontier are scientifically analysed. The late Mr. Damant, a man of great talent and powers of research, had a valuable paper regarding them in hand, but it perished in the insurrection of 1879. The probability is, that they came originally from the south-eastern corner of Thibet.

Some of the Maories of New Zealand reminded me of the Angamis. The well-defined nose is a prominent characteristic of the last, as it is of some of the inhabitants of Polynesia. The people of Samagudting—that is, the adults in 1874—told me that they had come from the north-east, and were the seventh generation that had been there. When they first occupied their village, the site was, they said, covered with the bones and tusks of elephants which had come there to die.

Had I lived longer among the Nagas, I should have liked to have made deeper researches into their language and past history; as it was, all my time was taken up with my active duties, and I had not a moment to spare.

Their dress is a short kilt of black cotton cloth, ornamented, in the case of warriors, with rows of cowrie shells. They have handsome cloths of dark blue and yellow thrown over their shoulders in cold weather. Their arms are spears and heavy short swords, called by the Assamese name of *dao* ; helmets and shields of wicker work (used chiefly to cover the more vulnerable parts of the body) and sometimes clothed with skins of tigers or bears. They have also tails of wood decorated with goats' hair dyed red. The warspears are plain ; the ornamental ones are covered with goats' hair dyed red, and are sometimes used in battle. Their drill is of a most complicated style, and requires much practice. An Angami in full war paint is a very formidable-looking individual. They are divided into many clans. Several clans often inhabit one village, and it frequently happened that two clans thus situated were at deadly feud with each other.

Blood feuds were common among all the hill tribes, but the system was carried to excess among the Angamis. Life for life was the rule, and until each of the opposing parties had lost an equal number, peace was impossible, and whenever members of one village met any belonging to the other, hostilities were sure to result. Sometimes an attempt was made to bring about a reconciliation, but then it frequently happened that the number of slain to the credit of each were unequal. Mozuma and Sephema might be at war, and Mozuma killed five, whereas Sephema had killed only four. Sephema says, "I must kill one more to make the balance, then I will treat for peace," so war continues. Some day Sephema has a chance, but kills two instead of the *one* that was required ; this gives her the advantage, and Mozuma refuses to treat. So it goes on interminably. The position of a small village at war with a large one, was often deplorable as no one dared to leave the village except under a strong escort. I once knew a case of some Sephema men at feud with Mozuma, hiring two women of the powerful village of Konoma to escort them along the road as thus accompanied no one dare touch them.

Once at Piphima, when my assistant Mr. Needham was encamped there, parties from two hostile villages suddenly met each other and rushed to arms. He was equal to the occasion and stopped the combat. I made it a criminal offence to fight on our road called the "Political Path," and it was generally respected as neutral ground.

No Angami could assume the "toga virilis," in this case the kilt ornamented with cowrie shells, already described, until he had slain an enemy, and in the more powerful villages no girl could marry a man unless he was so decorated. The cowrie ornaments were taken off when a man was mourning the death of a relation.

To kill a baby in arms, or a woman, was accounted a greater feat than killing a man, as it implied having penetrated to the innermost recesses of an enemy's country, whereas a man might be killed anywhere by a successful ambush. I knew a man who had killed sixty women and children, when on one occasion he happened to come upon them after all the men had left the village on a hunting expedition.

Every Naga who was able to murder an enemy did so, and received great commendation for it by all his friends. Later, when I was in Manipur, I had a pleasant young fellow as interpreter. He often took my boys out for a walk when he had nothing else to do, and was a careful, trustworthy man. Once I asked him how many people he had killed (he wore the cowrie kilt, a sure sign he had killed some one). A modest blush suffused his face as if he did not like to boast of such a good deed, and he mildly said, "Two, a woman and a girl!"

The Angamis when on friendly terms are an agreeable people to deal with, polite, courteous, and hospitable. I never knew any one take more pains or more successfully not to hurt the susceptibilities of those they are talking to, indeed they show a tact and good feeling worthy of imitation. My wife and I soon knew all the villagers well, and often visited them, when we were always offered beer, and asked to come into their verandahs and sit down, and just as we were leaving, our host would search the hen's nests to give us a few eggs. The beer we never took, but many Europeans like it and find it wholesome. It is made of rice and has rather a sharp taste. Their houses are large substantial structures built of wood and bamboo thatched with grass, and the eaves come low down. Houses with any pretensions always have verandahs. Besides the houses, there are granaries, often at a distance for fear of fire. The Angamis bury their dead in and about their villages, and for a time, decorate them with some of the belongings of the deceased. Naturally they strongly object to the graves being disturbed, and in making alterations I was careful not to hurt their feelings.

The more powerful villages in the interior of the hills have a large area of cultivation on terraces cut out of the hillside, and carefully irrigated. Some of the terraces go up the hillsides to a great height, and show considerable skill in their formation. On these terraces lowland rice is grown and is very productive. Some of the smaller outlying villages like Samagudting have only ordinary hill cultivation, where upland rice is grown. The terrace land used to be greatly valued, and was often sold at prices equal to £22 to £25 per acre!

The Angamis, in common with most hill-tribes that I have come across, have a vague indefinite belief in a supreme being, but look on him as too great and good to injure them. They believe themselves also to be subject to the influence of evil spirits, whom it is their constant endeavour to appease by sacrifices. Every misfortune is, as a rule, ascribed to evil spirits, and much money is spent on appeasing them, the usual way being to offer fowls, of which the head, feet, and entrails are offered to the demon, with many incantations. The other parts are eaten by the sacrificer.

All kinds of animals are readily eaten by the Angamis, and those dying a natural death are not rejected. Dogs' flesh is highly esteemed. When a man wants to have a delicate dish, he starves his dog for a day to make him unusually voracious, and then cooks a huge dish of rice on which he feeds the hungry beast. As soon as the dog has eaten his fill, he is knocked on the head and roasted, cut up and divided, and the rice being taken out, is considered the *bonne bouche.* The Manipur dogs are regularly bred for sale to the hill-tribes, Nagas included, and a portion of the bazaar, or market, used to be allotted to them. I have seen a string of nineteen dogs being led away to be strangled. Poor things, they seemed to realise that all was not well.

The Naga women are not handsome but very pleasant-looking, and many of the girls are pretty, but soon age with the hard toil they have to perform; working in the fields and carrying heavy loads up endless hills. They have plenty of spirit and can generally hold their own. They do not marry till they are nearly or quite grown up. Divorce can be easily obtained when there is an equal division of goods. Often a young man takes advantage of this, and marries a rich old widow, and soon divorces her, receiving half her property, when he is in a position to marry a nice young girl. The tribal name of the Angámi Nagas is "Tengima." Naga is a name given by the inhabitants of the plains, and in the Assamese language means "naked." As some of the Naga tribes are seen habitually in that state, the name was abitrarily applied to them all. It is the greatest mistake to connect them with the snake worshippers, "Nag Bungsees" of India. Neither Nagas or Manipuris, or any tribes on the eastern frontier, are addicted to this worship, or have any traditions connected with it, and any snake, cobra (Nag) or otherwise, would receive small mercy at their hands. The slightest personal acquaintance with the Assamese and their language, would have dispelled this myth for ever.

The Nagas are skilful iron-workers and turn out very handsome spears. Their women weave substantial and pretty coloured cloths, and every man knows enough of rough carpentering to enable him to build his house, and make pestles and mortars for husking rice. They make rough pottery, but without the potter's wheel.

After Ghumbeer Singh's Expedition, our next dealings with the Angamis were in 1833, when Lieut. Gordon, adjutant of the Manipur Levy, accompanied the Rajah of Manipur with a large force of Manipuris into the Angami hills. On this occasion, Kohima and other villages were subdued, as already stated, and an annual tribute exacted by Manipur.

So far as the British territories were concerned, Naga raids went on as usual, but nothing was done till early in January 1839, when Mr. Grange, sub-Assistant Commissioner of the Nowgong District, was despatched with a detachment of the First Assam Sebundies (now 43rd Goorkha Light Infantry), fifty men of the Cachar Infantry, and some Shan Militia, with orders to try and repress these annual outrages. His expedition was ill supplied, but fortunately returned without any severe losses. His route lay through North Cachar to Berrimeh; thence, *viâ* Razepima to Samagudting and Mohung Deejood; beyond gaining local knowledge there was no result, except perhaps to show that a well-armed party could march where it liked through the hills.

In December 1839, Mr. Grange again visited the hills, and, excepting 1843, an expedition was sent into the hills every year till 1846 when a post was permanently established at Samagudting. None of these expeditions had any really satisfactory result. The Angamis submitted to our troops at the time, and directly we retreated, murder and the carrying

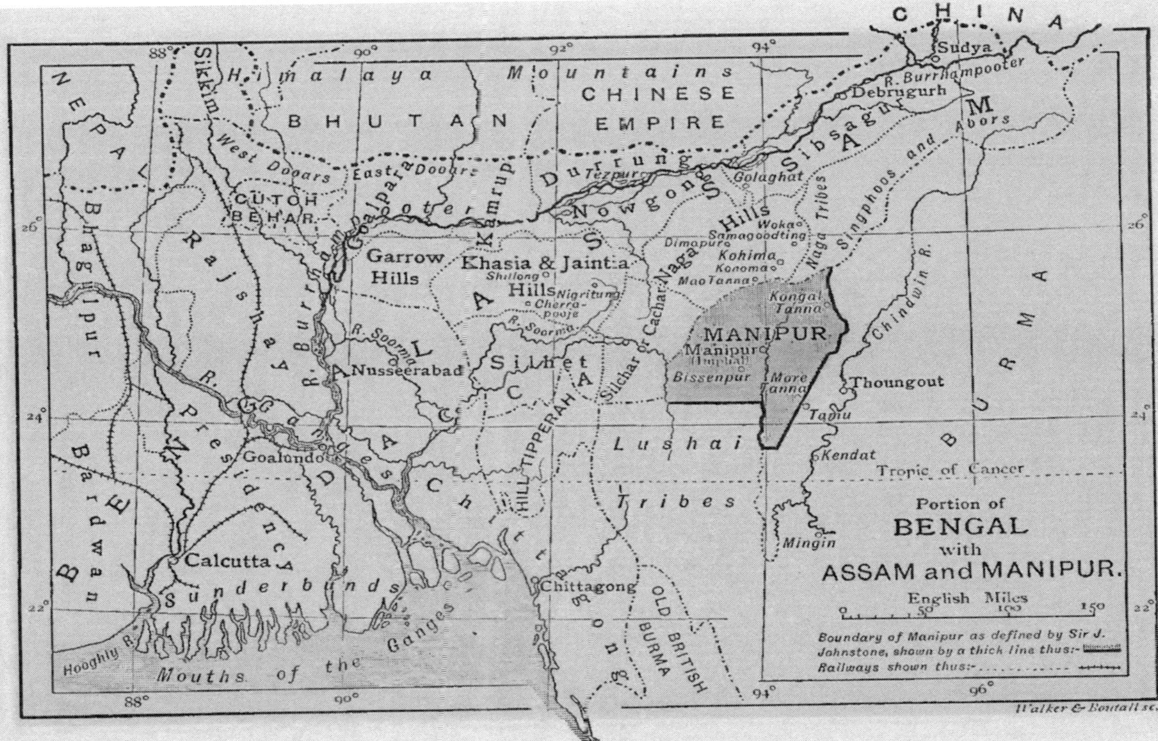

THE NAGA HILLS AND MANIPUR.

off of slaves re-commenced. The establishment of the post at Samagudting had the effect of improving our relations with the people of that village; and Mozuma was always inclined to be friendly; beyond this nothing was accomplished.

In August 1849, Bog Chand Darogal, a brave Assamese who was in charge of Samagudting, was murdered by one of the clans of Mozuma, owing to the rash way in which he interfered in a dispute with another clan, which latter remaind faithful to us, and thus led to another expedition on a large scale. Finally, in December 1850, a large force was sent up with artillery. Kohima, which had sent a challenge, was destroyed on February 11th, 1851. In this last engagement over three hundred Nagas were killed, and our prestige thoroughly established. We might then, with great advantage to the people and our own districts, have occupied a permanent post, and while protecting our districts that had suffered so sorely from Naga raids, have spread civilisation far and wide among the hill-tribes. Of course we did nothing of the kind; on such occasions the Government of India always does the wrong thing; it was done now, and, instead of occupying a new position, we retreated, even abandoning our old post at Samagudting, and only maintaining a small body of Shan Militia at Dimapur. The Nagas ascribed out retreat to fear, the periodical raids on our unfortunate villages were renewed, and unheeded by us; and finally, in 1856, we withrew the detachment from Dimapur and abandoned the post.

After that, the Nagas ran riot, and one outrage after another was committed. In 1862 the guard and village of Borpathar were attacked and, one Sepoy and thirteen villagers killed and two children carried off as slaves, but no notice was taken ; it was not till 1866 that, wearied out by repeated outrages and insults, we determined to establish ourselves in the hills, and once for all put down raiding.

A kind of vague boundary between Manipur and the Naga Hills had been laid down in 1842, by Lieutenant Biggs on our part, and Captain Gordon on the part of the Durbar, but in 1851, when utterly sick of Naga affairs, we determined on a policy of non-intervention, permission in writing was given to the Durbar to extend its authority over the Naga villages on our side of the border. This must be remembered later on. Failing any intention on our part to annex the hills, it would have been good policy to have re-organised the Manipur territory, and to have aided the Maharajah to annex and subdue as much as he could under certain restrictions. Had this been done we should have saved ourselves much trouble. Personally, I would rather see the Naga Hills properly administered by ourselves, but the strong rule of Manipur would have been far better than the state of things that prevailed for many years after 1851.

CHAPTER IV.

Value of keeping a promise—Episode of Sallajee—Protection given to small villages, and the large ones defied—"Thorough Government of India" views—A plea for Christian education in the Naga Hills.

ALMOST from the day I took charge, I let it be known that I was, as natives say, "a man of one word," and that if I said a thing, I meant it. If I promised a thing, whether a present or punishment, the man got it; and if I refused any request, months of importunity would not move me. This rule saved me much time and worry; instead of being pestered for weeks with some petition, in the hope that my patience would be worn out, I simply said Yes, or No, and the people soon learned that my decision was final. Later on, during the Naga Hills campaign, I found that my ways had not been forgotten, and this made dealing with the people much simpler than it might have been.

A certain number of the villages kept one or two men, as the case might be, constantly in attendance on me to represent them. These were called delegates, and received ten rupees each per mensem. I gave the strictest orders to these men not to engage in their tribal raids, but to remain absolutely neutral. Sephema had two delegates, Sejile and Sallajee by name, and, one day, it was reported to me that the last had joined in a raid by his village on Mozuma, and I instantly summoned him to attend and put him on his trial for disobeying a lawful order. Some wiseacres in the place shook their heads, and doubted if I were strong enough to punish, or the advisibility of doing so; but I held that an order must be obeyed, otherwise, it was no use issuing orders, also, that this was an opportunity of making an example. Of course it was an experiment, as no one had been punished before for a similar offence, and I well knew that resistance on his part would mean that to assert my authority I must attack and destroy Sephema, but I felt the time had come for vigorous action, and was prepared to go through with it. I tried Sallajee, found him guilty, and sentenced him to six months' imprisonment in Tezpore jail. In giving judgment, I said, "You have not been guilty of a disgraceful offence, therefore, I do not sentence you to hard labour, and shall not have you bound or handcuffed like a thief; but, remember, you cannot escape me, so do not be foolish enough to run away from the man in charge of you." I then sent him in charge of two police sepoys through one hundred miles of forest, and he underwent his imprisonment without attempting to get away. Right thankful I was that my experiment succeeded. Sallajee lived to fight against us, during the campaign in the Naga Hills in 1879-80.

The orders of the Government of India were strictly against our responsibilities being extended. We took tribute from Samagudting, but it was the only village we considered as under our direct rule, and that only so long as it suited us. Before leaving

Calcutta, the Foreign Secretary said to me emphatically, when I urged an extension of our sway—" but those villages (the Angami Nagas) are not British territory, and we do not want to extend the 'red line.' "

However, Government may lay down rules, but as long as they are not sound, they cannot be kept to by artificial bonds, and sooner or later events prove stronger than theories. The fact is, that no Government of late years had ever interested itself in the Eastern Frontier tribes, except so far as to coax them or bribe them to keep quiet. The Abors on the banks of the Burrhampooter had long been paid "blackmail," and any subterfuge was resorted to, that would stave off the day of reckoning which was nevertheless inevitable.

As regards the Nagas, this timidity was highly reprehensible. We had acquired such a prestige, that the least sign of vigorous action on our part was sure to be crowned with success, so long as we did not make some foolish mistake.

The people in the hills knew that we objected to the system of raiding, and could not understand why, such being the case, we did not put it down, and ascribed our not doing so to weakness, wherein they were right, and inability wherein they were wrong. The less powerful villages would at any time have been glad of our protection, and one of the most powerful—Mozuma, was anxious to become subject to us. Offers of submission had been made once or twice, but no one liked to take the responsibility of going against the policy and orders of the Government. At last an event occurred which brought things to a crisis, and forced us either to adopt a strong policy, or make ourselves contemptible by a confession of weakness, and indifference.

Towards the end of March 1874, a deputation came to me from the village of Mezeffina begging for protection against Mozuma, with whom they had a feud, and from whom for some reason or other they daily expected an attack. They offered to become British subjects and pay revenue in return for protection. I considered the matter carefully, and before I had given my decision, crowds of old people, and women carrying their children, came in asking me to save their lives. I at once decided to grant their request, and promised them what they asked, on condition that they paid up a year's tribute in advance. This they at once did, and I immediately sent a messenger to proclaim to Mozuma that the people of Mezeffina were British subjects, and to threaten them or any one else with dire vengeance if they dared to lay hands on them. Our new subjects asked me and my wife, to go out and receive their submission in person, an invitation which we accepted, and next day a large number of men turned up to carry my wife, and our baggage, and that of our escort, consisting of twenty men.

The Mezeffina men rested for the night in Samagudting, and early on the following morning we started, and reached the village in good time, where we were received with great demonstrations of respect. We spent the night there, and then were conveyed back to Samagudting, after a very pleasant visit.

I did not underrate the grave responsibility that I

incurred in going against the policy of Government, but I felt it was utterly impossible that I, as their representative, could quietly stand by, and see a savage massacre perpetrated, within sight of our station of Samagudting. There is no doubt that this would have speedily followed had I sent the people away without acceding to their wishes. Of course, I might have used my influence with Mozuma to prevent a raid in this particular instance, but that *would have been giving protection*, and, I argued, if we give protection, let us get a little revenue to help to pay for it. Why should all the advantage be on one side? Besides a half-and-half policy would never have succeeded. "Thorough" should be the motto of all who deal with savage and half-civilised races; a promise to refer to Government is of little avail when people are thinking of each other's blood. Action, immediate action, is what is required. A failure to realise this, brought on later the Mozuma expedition of 1877–78, in which a valuable officer lost his life.

Besides the obvious objections I have pointed out, any attempt to make terms in favour of one village after another by negotiations with their adversaries, would have involved us in so many complications, that it would probably have ended in a combination against us.

I reported the matter to Government, and before I could receive any answer, the village of Sitekima which had a feud with Sephema came in and asked for the same favour to be accorded to it, as had been granted to Mezeffina. I accordingly took them over on the same terms, and again issued a proclamation calling on all people to respect their rights as British subjects.

Soon after I heard from the Chief Commissioner of Assam, directing me to take over no more villages without a reference. However, this could not be, there was no telegraph in those days, and the tide in favour of asking for our protection had set in in earnest, and must be taken at the flood. "*Vestigia nulla retrorsum*" there was no retreat; and having acted according to my judgment for the best interests of the State, I felt bound to take further responsibility on myself, when necessary. Accordingly when the little village of Phenina applied for protection and offered revenue, I at once acceded, and accepted their allegiance as British subjects, with the result that they were left in peace by their powerful neighbours, and had no more anxiety as to their safety. Phenina was followed by several other villages, to whom I granted the same terms.

The Mozuma Nagas were always an intelligent set of men, and liked to be in the forefront of any movement. Seeing the part that other villages were taking, they came forward and offered to pay revenue, if we would establish a guard of police in their village, and set up a school for their children to attend. This was a question involving a considerable expenditure of money, and as they were not in need of protection, I felt that I could not accede to their request without further reference, but I sent on the proposal to Government with a strong recommendation that it should be adopted. The consideration of it was put off for a time, and when very tardily my recommendation was accepted, the

Mozuma people had, as I predicted, changed their minds. Such cases are of constant occurrence. When will our rulers take the story of the Sibylline books to heart?

The question of education generally, was one that greatly interested me, my success in Keonjhur* in the tributary Mehals of Orissa, where I had introduced schools, having been very great. In combination with other suggestions, I strongly urged the advisability of establishing a regular system of education, including religious instruction, under a competent clergyman of the Church of England. I pointed out that the Nagas had no religion; that they were highly intelligent and capable of receiving civilisation; that with it they would want a religion, and that we might just as well give them our own, and make them in that way a source of strength, by thus mutually attaching them to us. Failing this, I predicted that, following the example of other hill-tribes, they would sooner or later become debased Hindoos or Mussulmans, and in the latter case, as we knew by experience, be a constant source of trouble and annoyance, Mussulman converts in Assam and Eastern Bengal, being a particularly disagreeable and bigoted set. My suggestion did not find favour with the authorities, and I deeply regret it. A fine, interesting race like the Angamis, might, as a Christian tribe, occupy a most useful position on our Eastern Frontier, and I feel strongly

* As Assist-sup. of the tributary Mehals, Sir James (then Lieutenant) Johnstone endowed schools at Keonjhur and presented the Government with some land he had bought for the purpose. When the Rajah, during whose minority he had managed the affairs of Keonjhur as political officer, came of age, the agency was abolished for economy.—ED.

that we are not justified in allowing them to be corrupted and gradually "converted" by the miserable, bigoted, caste-observing Mussulman of Bengal, men who have not one single good quality in common with the manly Afghans, and other real Mussulman tribes. I do not like to think it, but, unless we give the Nagas a helping hand in time, such is sure to be their fate, and we shall have ourselves to thank when they are utterly corrupted.

The late General Dalton, C.S.I., when Commissioner of Chota Nagpure, did his utmost to aid Christian Mission among the wild Kols; his argument being like mine, that they wanted a religion, and that were they Christians, they would be a valuable counterpoise in time of trouble to the vast non-Christian population of Behar. In the same way it cannot be doubted, that a large population of Christian hill-men between Assam and Burmah, would be a valuable prop to the State. Properly taught and judiciously handled, the Angamis would have made a fine manly set of Christians, of a type superior to most Indian native converts, and probably devoted to our rule. As things stand at present, I fear they will be gradually corrupted and lose the good qualities, which have made them attractive in the past, and that, as time goes on, unless some powerful counter influence is brought to bear on them, they will adopt the vile, bigoted type of Mahommedanism prevalent in Assam and Cachar, and instead of becoming a tower of strength to us, be a perpetual weakness and source of annoyance. I earnestly hope that I may be wrong, and that their future may be as bright a one as I could wish for them.

CHAPTER V.

Dimapur—A terrible storm—Cultivation—Aggression by Konoma—My ultimatum—Konoma submits—Birth of a son—Forest flowers—A fever patient—Proposed change of station—Leave Naga Hills—March through the forest—Depredation by tigers—Calcutta—Return to England.

Once more before the weather began to be unpleasantly hot, we went down to Dimapur that I might inspect the road and a rest house being built at Nowkatta. Dimapur though hot, was pleasant enough in the evening, when I used to row my wife about on the large tank in a canoe which just held us both. We could see a few feet below the surface, the remains of the post set up when a tank is dedicated to the deity. This post is usually many feet above the water, but here it had rotted away from age. On a tree close to the rest house I shot a chestnut coloured flying squirrel.

One sultry afternoon I rode out alone to Nowkatta. About half-way I was stopped by a sudden storm, one of the most terrific I have ever seen; the wind howled through the forest, and the trees swayed to and fro literally like blades of grass. As the storm increased, trees were torn up by the roots right and left, and some that were very firmly rooted were shattered in pieces. Many of these trees were 80 to 120 feet in height, and large in proportion, but the wind was so high that I never heard the sound of the crash. I hardly expected to escape being crushed by a falling tree, and nothing but the extreme activity of my pony, a little Manipuri, saved me. I was at length enabled to get on to Nowkatta, but as I returned, I had much difficulty in making my way through the masses of fallen trees which formed an obstacle often six feet in height, and I could only pass them by penetrating the dense underwood, and riding round one end.

I returned to Dimapur later than I expected and drenched by the soaking rain. Next day we went back to Samagudting very glad to be again in a cooler atmosphere. We both paid for our visit to the lowlands in a sharp attack of intermittent fever. Luckily, my wife speedily recovered; but it told on my system, already saturated with malaria and was the forerunner of constant attacks.

Except for its unhealthiness, Dimapur was a nice place, and, if properly opened out, and cultivated, the country would be far more salubrious. For this reason I advocated families being induced to settle there as cultivators; and I had a scheme for establishing a Police Militia Reserve in that district. I thought that a certain number of the Naga Hills police might with advantage be discharged every year and enlisted as reserve men, liable to serve when needed in case of trouble; a reduced rate of pay to be given to each man, and a grant of land to cultivate. I believe the system would have worked well, but it was not sanctioned.

An incident occurred in the month of August which might have proved serious. A native of a

Kutcha Naga village within sight of Samagudting came to complain that, while gathering wild tea-seed for sale, he had been driven off by a Konoma Naga. Konoma, though not the most populous village, had long been considered the most powerful and warlike in the hills, and a threat from one of its members was almost a sentence of death to a man from a weak village. The Merema clan also, one of the worst in the hills for lawless deeds, had never made its submission to Captain Butler, though it had on one occasion to his predecessor. On hearing the man's complaint, I at once sent off a message by a Naga calling upon the chiefs of Konoma to come in to me, and also to cease molesting their neighbours; but the man returned, saying that they refused to come in, and intended to do as they liked with the tea-seed, as it was theirs. This was more than I could put up with, and I selected a particularly trustworthy man, a naik (corporal) in the police named Kurum Singh,* who knew the Naga language, and would, I was convinced, speak out fearlessly, and deliver my message. I sent him off at once to Konoma to call upon the head-men to come in without delay, and make their humble submission to me within a day and a half of receiving the summons, failing which I would attack and destroy their village. Kurum Singh left, and I felt rather anxious, as Konoma contained five times as many warriors as I had police all told, and it occupied a strong position; however, I felt I had done my duty. It was a great satisfaction when Kurum Singh returned, saying that the chiefs were coming in, and they did so

* I rewarded Kurum, and he distinguished himself later on.

within the stipulated time, and made their submission and presented me with a large state spear as a token of it. They also humbly apologised and promised never to molest that Kutcha Naga village again; and when I spoke of the Queen, begged me to write to her and say, that she must not believe any idle tales against the Konoma men, as they would be her humble servants. It was a satisfactory ending to what might have been a troublesome business. The state spear now ornaments my hall.

On the 23rd June, my wife presented me with a son, and he being the first child of pure European parentage born in the hills, the Nagas of Samagudting took great interest in the baby, and old Yatsolé the Péumah, said he should be their chief and named him "Naga Rajah." The friendly women and girls from the village constantly came to see him. We liked the hills and the people, and the work so much that we both felt we could willingly have passed our lives among them. All the same, our accommodation was really most wretched, and food was bad and scarce, and water scarcer. As the rainy season advanced the place grew more and more unhealthy, and having a baby to attend to, my wife never left Samagudting. I continued to go down to Dimapur occasionally, and sometimes rode out with my friend Needham to inspect the path that was being cut to Mohung Deejood and a rest house being built at a place in the forest on that road, called Borsali. It was pleasant to have a companion during a long lonely ride. Needham was an indefatigable worker, and always ready for a dash. He made a capital

FULFORD HALL. [*Page* 48.

frontier officer, and has since greatly distinguished himself on the N.-E. Frontier.

Towards the end of August, the Vauda Cærulea orchids began to come into flower. There was a magnificent plant of them in a large old tree on the summit of the hill, indeed the most splendid specimen of their kind that I ever saw; but wild flowers, many really beautiful, were generally procurable, especially a small snow-white flower rather like a periwinkle that grew in the jungle on a small ever-green bush. Ferns, including maidenhair, were very plentiful, and we made collections of them in our morning and evening walks. These walks often led us past stray huts, and once my wife was asked to come into one and prescribe for a sick Naga woman. We both entered it and finding that the woman had fever, we told her husband to keep her cool and quiet, and promised some medicine. When we again went to see her, the hut, about nine feet by seven feet in size, was full of little fires on the floor, over which several Nagas were drying strips of flesh from an elephant that had been killed a few miles away. The temperature must have been about 110 degrees, so little wonder that the poor woman was no better. The husband said she would not take her medicine, and when in our presence he attempted to give it she hit him on the head; yet he wore the warrior's kilt, so had taken at least one life. When my wife sat down by her and gave her the medicine she took it readily. Towards the end of the rainy season many were laid low by fever. Natives of other parts of India until thoroughly acclimatised, suffer greatly from the diseases peculiar to jungle districts, and our servants were not exceptions to the rule. Once acclimatised, a Hindoostani seems able to stand anything. It used to be said in my regiment, the 1st Assam Light Infantry Battalion, now 42nd, that Hindoostani recruits spent their first three years' service in hospital! I am sure that something of the same kind might have been said of those who came to the Naga Hills before the headquarters were removed to Kohima.

Captain Butler, recognising the unsuitableness of Samagudting for a station, had recommended the removal of the headquarters to Woka, in the Lotah Naga country, and about sixty-three miles from Kohima. I spoke to him on the subject, and pointed out the superior advantages of Kohima as a central position, dominating the Angami Naga country. He quite agreed with me, but said he had advocated Woka as being nearer the plains, nearer water carriage, and altogether a more comfortable situation, especially for the officers. I went into the whole subject most carefully, and before leaving the Naga Hills I thought it right to record my opinion in a memorandum to the Government of Assam. This I did, pointing out as forcibly as I could the very superior advantages of Kohima, and urging most strongly that it should be adopted as our headquarters station in the Naga Hills. As I was only the officiating agent, I could not expect my views to carry as much weight as Captain Butler's, but convinced as I was, I was bound to state them. The question was not settled for some years when Kohima was the site selected, and it has ever since been the headquarters station.

I had never got over the attack of fever I had in April, and as the rainy season advanced, and we were for days together enveloped in mist, I had constant attacks, with other complications, and as Captain Butler was coming out in November, and the doctor strongly recommended me to go to England again, I determined to apply for leave. My friend Needham had gone on leave to Shillong, so I could not think of starting till he returned. He was due at Samagudting early in November, and I prepared to leave then. It was with most sincere regret that we made arrangements for starting. We had got used to the discomforts of the place and had been very happy there and liked the people, and felt that they liked us; the cold weather too was just beginning and everything around us looked beautiful.

I had determined to march straight through the forest to Doboka, and thence take boat down the Kullung river to Gowhatty. It was a dreadful march to undertake, along a mere track untraversed by any European for years, but my wife liked the idea of it, and it was shorter than the route *viâ* Nigriting. On November 6th, we reluctantly said "good-bye" to all our kind friends at Samagudting and marched to Dimapur, where we halted next day to get all our things into order. Some of the chiefs of Samagudting accompanied us so far on our way and bade us a sorrowful adieu on the 7th. One old fellow took quite an affectionate farewell of our baby Dick. When I saw him again in 1879, he was blind, and one of his pretty little girls was dying.

We marched through dense forest on the 8th to

Borsali, my wife riding and carrying the baby in her arms, there being no other mode of progression along such a bad road. On the 9th after seven hours' actual marching, we reached Mohung Deejood, a place prettily situated on the banks of the Jumoona river with the last speck of the Rengma Hills standing out in high relief behind the village, but at some distance from it. Next day we again had a tiring march of eleven hours, including a halt for breakfast at a place called "Silbheta" where there are splendid waterfalls, and did not reach our halting place, Bokuleea, till 6 P.M. The last two marches had been through a country devastated by tigers which had literally eaten up the population; each day we passed deserted village sites. At Bokuleea we made rafts and floated down the river to Doboka, which we reached on November 13th.

Doboka is situated close to the hill of the same name and was a prominent object from Samagudting. There we took boats, and travelled in them down the Kullung river. We reached the junction with the Burrhampooter at daybreak on November 17th, and Gowhatty at midday. I was most thankful to see my wife and child safe in the Dak Bungalow after what was for delicate people a perilous journey, though an interesting and enjoyable one, through a country hardly ever traversed by European officials, and never by women and children. After a few days at Gowhatty to rest ourselves, we departed by steamer for Goalundo, arriving there early on November 29th, and immediately left for Calcutta, which we reached the same evening and went to stay with our kind friends the Rivers Thompsons, with whom we had travelled out to India in 1873. Glad as we were to be in civilised quarters once more after all our wanderings, we could not help regretting the kindly genial people we had left, and the beautiful scenery of the forest and mountain land, where we had lived so long and so happily.

On arrival in Calcutta, I went before the Medical Board, but not liking to go to England again so soon, I applied for three months' leave to visit the North-West Provinces for change of air, and we visited Benares, Lucknow, Cawnpore, and other towns. I do not attempt to describe them, as it has been often done by abler pens than mine. The after symptoms of malaria increased, and it was vain to prolong my stay in India in the hope of a cure. The Medical Board said my appearance was sufficient without examination, so we left Calcutta by the next steamer, going by "long sea" to avoid the fatiguing journey across India to Bombay. After unusually rough weather in the Mediterranean and off the coast of Spain, we landed at Southampton, on March 9th, at 9 P.M., and went on to London next morning.

CHAPTER VI.

Return to India—Attached to Foreign Office—Imperial assemblage at Delhi—Almorah—Appointed to Manipur—Journey to Shillong—Cherra Poojee—Colonel McCulloch—Question of ceremony.

MALARIA, and all the evils that follow in its train, are more easily acquired than got rid of. Possibly two years in England, including four visits to Carlsbad, which high medical authorities seem to consider, and very justly, a *sine quâ non*, might give a man a good chance if he never again visited a malarious district, otherwise, my own experience shows me that two years are nothing. Every time I have gone before a Medical Board in London, preparatory to returning to duty, their last charge has been, "You must never again go to a malarious district!" Medical Boards propose, and Government and circumstances dispose.

I stayed at home in a high and healthy part of the Midlands, and left for India again in October. I arrived in Calcutta in November, where I again suffered from malarious symptoms; but I soon got better, and was attached to the Foreign Office, at my own request, extra attachés being required for the Imperial Assemblage.

I had the good fortune to see the whole of that gorgeous pageant, the like of which this generation will probably never witness again, under the most favourable auspices; and though I had on an average eighteen hours' work out of each twenty-four, I was well repaid by being able to take part in it. I met many old friends, and also became acquainted with Salar Jung, Maharajahs Scindiah and Holkar, Sir Dinkur Rao, Madhava Rao, and several other now historical celebrities. The Viceroy's reception-tent at night was a grand sight, filled with gallant soldiers, European and native, and great statesmen.

Among the new arrivals was the Khan of Khelat, an intelligent but savage-looking chief, with eyes all about him. I was being constantly deputed to carry polite messages from the Viceroy to different chiefs and celebrities and to meet them at the railway stations. Among those whom I met were the envoy from the Chief of Muscat, also the Siamese Ambassador and his suite, a highly intelligent and sensible set of men. I remember well the rough-and-ready way in which the younger Siamese officers looked after their luggage and effects. They were provided with a handsome set of tents, and all dined together at one table in European fashion, in the most civilised way, with the British officer attached to them.

I stayed at Delhi till the assemblage broke up, and after a few days in Calcutta with the Foreign Office, went to Bombay to meet my wife, who, with our two boys, arrived there on February 2nd. We at once set out on our way to Almorah in the Himalayas, where I was permitted to reside for a year and compile Foreign Office records.

We were delayed at Moradabàd for a few days, as the passes were covered with snow. At last we started, and found Nynee Tal deep in snow, and the lake frozen. Next day we marched across the track of an avalanche, and the following afternoon reached the Almorah Dak Bungalow, or rest house. The ground was covered with snow, and the cold intense, the bungalow draughty and very uncomfortable. After a few days we got into a house, which Sir H. Ramsey, who was then out on duty in the district, had kindly taken for us, and I dived deep into my records, consisting of early documents relating to Assam and the Singpho tribes.

As the weather grew warmer, Almorah became very pleasant. I pined for active work, but our stay here gave my wife experience in the mode of life in India, for which she was afterwards very thankful, and she obtained hints on housekeeping subjects from other ladies, which were a help to her later on. Life in the Naga Hills was of course very different to what it is in more civilised parts of India.

The Foreign Office had my name down in their list for an appointment. I could have gone to Manipur when I landed in Calcutta, but was not well enough. In July, I had a telegram to say that Lieut. Durand, who had lately been appointed, was ill, and must be relieved. Would I go? I at once replied in the affirmative, and off we started on July 16th. It was very short notice, but changing quarters at short notice is part of an Indian official's life, and the prospect of work was delightful to me. We had a trying journey down to Calcutta, as the rains had not begun in the North-West Provinces, and the heat was tremendous. However, we arrived none the worse for it, and stayed for a day or two with our kind friends, the Medlicotts.

As Colonel Keatinge, the Chief Commissioner of Assam, wished to see me before I went to Manipur, I was ordered to join at Shillong, so we proceeded by rail to Goalundo, one night's journey from Calcutta, and thence by river steamer to Chuttuk, on the Soorma, where we changed into country boats, and proceeded up a smaller river and across great jheels or shallow lakes, often passing for miles through high grass growing in the water, which hid us from everything, till we reached a place called Bholagunj, situated on a river rapidly becoming narrower, where we again changed, this time into small canoes, the only conveyances that could take us up the rapids, with which the river abounds.

From Chuttuk we had come through a country mostly covered with grass jungle, twelve to fifteen feet in height; now we passed through forest scenery, very lovely fine trees, with festoons of creepers and flowers overhanging the stream. At last we reached Thuria Ghât, where the ascent of the hills commenced, and there we halted for the night in the Dak Bungalow, or rest house. Most places situated as Thuria Ghât is, would be deadly on account of malaria, but it seems to be an exception, and, as far as I have seen, healthy.

Knowing the servant difficulties in the province of Assam, we had brought servants with us from Almorah, men who had implored us to take them. When I consented to do so I voluntarily raised their wages from fifty to eighty per cent. above what they had been receiving, but with the exception of a Dhobee (washerman), and a bearer (a compound of housemaid and valet), they all became corrupted by the other servants they met at Shillong, and who spoke of Manipur in very disparaging terms, so before going farther I let them go, as they demanded an enormous increase of wages.

The Dhobee Nunnoo, and the bearer Horna, stuck to me to the very last, and proved admirable servants. It was fortunate that we had servants, as there were none at Thuria Ghât rest house; as it was, we managed very well, and were prepared to march in the morning before the coolies were ready to take up our luggage. We had a tiring march up the hill to Cherra Poojee; my wife and the children were in baskets on men's backs, but I was on foot and felt the march in the intense heat to be very fatiguing, though we halted to rest half-way. However, when we reached the plateau of Cherra Poojee, 4000 feet above Thuria Ghât, the cool air speedily set me right, and we all enjoyed the scenery, hills, plains, waterfalls in abundance, deep valleys, and the lowlands of Sylhet, covered with water, as far as the eye could reach. We had a comfortable bungalow to rest in, and a cool night at last.

Next day we marched to Moflung, 6000 feet above the sea, and then to Shillong, where for the next few days we were hospitably entertained by the Chief Commissioner, Colonel (now General) Keatinge, V.C., C.S.I., who kindly sent a carriage to meet us on the road. As Colonel Keatinge wished me to remain at Shillong for a time, and meet Mr. Carnegy, political officer in the Naga Hills, who was coming there later on, I arranged to stay, and took a house; so we settled down comfortably till the early part of October—a very pleasant arrangement for us instead of facing the intense heat of the Cachar Valley in August. It gave me a good opportunity of looking over the records of the Chief Commissioner's office, where I found much relating to Manipur, but I fear that it was lost when the Record Office was burnt down some years ago, the copies also having been destroyed in Manipur during the rebellion of 1891. At last the day for leaving came, and we packed up our things and prepared once more to set off on our travels.

Before leaving, I paid several visits to Colonel McCulloch, who, since retiring from the service, had established himself at Shillong, and asked his advice on many points, and learned much from him regarding Manipur. He very kindly gave his opinion freely on all questions, telling me where some of my predecessors had failed, and pointing out the pitfalls to be avoided. He added to all his kindness by writing to the Maharajah, and telling him that, from what he had seen of me, he was sure it would be his fault if we did not get on together.

CHAPTER VII.

Start for Manipur—March over the hills—Lovely scenery—View of the valleys—State reception—The Residency—Visitors.

LOWREMBA SUBADAR, an excellent old fellow, formerly in the service of Colonel McCulloch, was sent to Shillong to be in attendance on me, and of course to find out all he could about me and report the result. Before I left, he sent a note to the Maharajah of my requirements in the way of coolies, etc., for our long journey of ten days between Cachar and Manipur, and I also intimated that, as the representative of the British Government, and as one who well knew what was due to me as such, I should expect to be received with proper ceremony.

This was a point on which I laid much stress, as my experience had taught me that in a native state so tenacious of its dignity and ancient customs as Manipur, my future success depended in a great measure on my scrupulously requiring all that I was entitled to, and as much more as I could get. It had been a complaint against one of my predecessors that he had been discourteous, and I determined that the Manipuris should not have to complain of me on that score, and in my letters I took care to be as courteous and considerate as possible.

On former occasions it had been the custom for a new political agent to enter the capital unattended, and to call on the Maharajah the next day, the latter repaying the visit a day later. This I did not consider sufficient, and I determined that he should come out to meet me in state. When Colonel McCulloch returned to Manipur the second time, this had been done, Colonel McCulloch being an old and intimate friend of the Maharajah. I quoted this as a precedent. I tried in vain to get the Foreign Department to back up my request, but could not induce them to interfere on my behalf, so I took the responsibility on myself, and sent a formal demand to the Maharajah to send a high officer—a major commanding a regiment—to meet me on the road, and to meet me himself in state at a suitable distance from the capital. The result will be described.

All being ready we left Shillong, my wife, nurse and children on men's backs as before, for Cherra Poojee, where we arrived the second day; thence, on the third day, we went to Thuria Ghât, on by boat *viâ* Bholagunj, to Sylhet and Cachar. We reached Cachar on October 17th, after passing the historical fort of Budderpore, where a battle was fought with the Burmese in 1825, and settled down in the bungalow of our kind friend Major Boyd who was away. Our coolies arrived on October 18th, and we again packed our things and prepared to depart on our final march.

We left Cachar for Manipur on October 20th, my wife and the nurse and boys in "doolies," a kind of tray four feet long by two in width, with sides and ends eight inches in height, supported by two long poles running along the bottom of each side, and slung at each end to loose bars of wood carried on men's shoulders. The passenger sits inside as best he can, and there is a light matting roof thrown over to protect him from the weather. To begin with, it is an uncomfortable and shaky conveyance, but in time one gets accustomed to it.

Our baggage was carried mostly on men's backs, each load varying from sixty to seventy pounds in weight. Altogether we had, I daresay, one hundred coolies, as everything we required for a ten days' journey had to be carried, in addition to personal baggage and stores for our use on arrival. I had provided a tent in case of need, but did not use it, as rude huts were provided for us at all the stages along the road. Our first halt was at Luckipore, in British territory, and, as usual, the first march was the most trying; for servants, coolies, etc., have to learn each other's ways. I had an escort of one hundred men of the 35th Native Infantry, under a subadar, as it was expected that I might have to go on an expedition soon after my arrival, and these men had their own special coolies, so we were a large party altogether.

We halted at Luckipore, as I have said, a few miles from the Hoorung Hills and at Jeree Ghât. Next day we left British territory and entered Manipur, where we found some huts built for our accommodation. At Jeree Ghât the really interesting part of the journey commenced; thence, till Bissenpore in the valley of Manipur is reached, the traveller marches day after day over hills and across rivers. The first day from Jeree Ghât we crossed the Noonjai-bang range, the summit of which is 1800 to 1900 feet above the sea from whence a fine view of the next range, Kala Naga or in Manipuri, Wy-nang-nong, is obtained. The road which was made under the superintendence of Captain (afterwards Colonel) Guthrie, of the Bengal Engineers between 1837 and 1844, at the joint expense of the British and Manipuri Governments, the former paying the larger share, was excellent for foot passengers and pack animals, but not wide enough and too steep for wheeled traffic on a large scale.

After descending from Noong-jai-bang we halted on the banks of the Mukker river amidst splendid forest, and next day ascended the Kala Naga range and halted on the crest close to a Manipuri guard house at a height of 3400 feet.

From this spot a magnificent view of the plains of Cachar is obtained, and in fine weather, far beyond them the Kasia hills in the neighbourhood of Cherra Poojee may be descried. The scene at sunset is sometimes magnificent. In the foreground the dark forests, and in the far distance a huge bank of golden clouds with their reflection in the watery plain, and a mingled mass of colours, green fields, purple, crimson, red and gold, all mixed up in such a way as no painter would ever attempt to copy. As the sun sinks those colours change and re-arrange themselves every minute in quick succession, and when at last night closes in, the impression left on the mind is one of never-ending wonder and admiration.

From Kala Naga to the Barâk river is a very stiff descent, calculated to shake the knees of an in-experienced hill-walker, and many is the toe-nail lost by the pressure of one's boots. Here as at the Mukker and other rivers farther on, the Barâk is crossed by cane suspension bridges, which vibrate and move at every step. In the dry season these rivers are crossed by very cleverly constructed bamboo pontoon bridges, but when the rainy season has commenced, they become raging torrents, which nothing but a fish could live in, and but for the suspension bridges, all communication with the outer world would be cut off. The bridge over the Eerung river was one hundred yards in length, and like all the others, was, when I first went to Manipur, constructed entirely of cane and bamboo, and could by great exertions, be finished in three days. During my period of office, wire ropes were substituted for the two main cables on which all rested, and the strength of the bridges greatly increased thereby. It was an important part of my duty to see that both roads and bridges were kept in order.

Our march was interesting but uneventful. We started after breakfast and generally reached our halting place in time for a late luncheon or afternoon tea. Wherever we halted we had a hut to live in, generally in some picturesque spot, one day giving a splendid view of hill and valley with nothing but forests in view, on another we were perched on a hill overlooking the beautiful Kowpoom valley, a sheet of cultivation. At last, on the ninth day after crossing the Lai-metol river, and ascending the Lai-metol, we had our first view of the valley of Manipur* spread out like a huge map at our feet. Seen as it was by us at the end of the rainy season, and from a

* The name means beautiful garden.—Ed.

height of 2600 feet above it, is a vast expanse of flat land bordered by hills, and mostly covered with water, through which the rice crops are vigorously growing. To the south the Logtak lake is visible, with several island hills in it, while far away to the north-east might be seen the glittering roofs of the temples of Imphal, the capital. It requires time to take in the view and to appreciate it. In the dry season it looks very different with brown, dried-up hills in the place of green.

The valley of Manipur possesses a few sacred groves, left, according to the universal aboriginal custom, throughout all parts of India that I have visited, for the wood spirits, when the land was first cleared; but no natural forest. These groves are little isolated patches of forest dotted here and there; the villages have plenty of planted trees, many of great antiquity, and from the heights above they have the appearance of woodland covered with grass. Besides this, all is one sheet of cultivation or waste covered with grass. It was once entirely cultivated, that is, before the Burmese invasion of 1819, when the population of the valley, was from 500 to 1000 per square mile.

We halted to rest on the summit of the Lai-metol, and then descended, passing sometimes under a kind of wild apple tree with very eatable fruit, and once through a lovely grove of oak trees, called "Oui-ong-Moklung," and then, still far below us, saw some elephants sent for us by the Maharajah. These elephants were posted at Sebok Tannah,* a

* Tannah means outpost.—Ed.

police station where the ground begins to grow level, and a mile farther brought us to Bissenpore, where there was a rude rest house. Here we halted for the night.

I have mentioned my demand that I should be met with proper ceremony. It was of course stoutly resisted, every argument founded on old custom, etc., being used against it. However, I stood firm, and absolutely refused to go beyond Bissenpore, till the Maharajah gave me an assurance that he would do all I required. In the end he gave in, and a day before reaching that place, his uncle met me on the road with a letter saying that all should be done as I wished. This official, by name Samoo Major, became a great friend of mine, and remained so till I finally left; he is, alas, I believe, now a prisoner in the Andamans, having been supposed to be implicated in the rising in 1891.

The next day we left Bissenpore in good time, and marched the seventeen miles to the capital, halting half-way at Phoiching, where I was met by some officials. Farther on, some of still higher rank came to greet me, and finally, at the entrance to the capital, I was met by the Maharajah himself, surrounded by all his sons. A carpet was spread with chairs for him and myself, we both of us having descended from our elephants, advanced and met in the centre of the carpet, and having made our salutations (a salute of eleven guns was fired in my honour), we sat and talked for two minutes. We then mounted, the Maharajah's elephant being driven by his third son, the master of the elephants; and we rode together through the great bazaar, till our roads diverged at the entrance to the fortified enclosure to the palace, where we took leave of each other, and he went home, and I went to the Residency, which I reached at four o'clock, my wife and children having made a short cut.

The Residency then was a low and dark bungalow built of wattle and daub, and thatched. It had one large room in the centre, and a bedroom on either side with a small semicircular room in front and rear of the centre room; there was one bathroom (I speedily added more), and verandahs nearly all round. There were venetians to the windows, but no glass, and the house was very dark and very full of mosquitoes. However, all had been done by the Residency establishment to make the place comfortable, and we were too old travellers and too accustomed to rough it, to grumble. The house might be rude and uncomfortable, but some of my happiest days were spent in it. The building was at the end of a garden, with some nice mango, and other trees here and there, and had a little more ground attached to it, but we were on all sides surrounded by squalid villages and filthy tanks and cesspools, and the situation was very low, though well drained. Our English nurse grumbled incessantly, but we had engaged in advance, a nice pleasant Naga woman, named Chowkee, to help her, and soon made everything right for the night, but the mosquitoes were terrible, and though my life has been spent in countries swarming with them, I give Manipur the palm, it beats all others!

No European lady or children of pure blood had ever before been seen in Manipur, and at first there was great excitement wherever we went, all the population turning out to look at us. By degrees they became accustomed to the novelty, but still occasionally people from distant villages coming to the capital stopped to stare. Every now and then my wife had visits from strange old ladies, often from the Kola Ranee, the widow of the last Rajah of Assam, and by birth a Manipuri princess, daughter of Rajah Chomjeet, and first cousin of the Maharajah Chandra Kirtee Singh. Once an old woman of 106 years of age, with a daughter of 76, were visitors, and once or twice some other relic of a bygone age called on us. Among the latter was old Ram Singh, the last survivor of Wilcox's famous survey expeditions in Assam, in 1825–26–27–28. Wilcox was one of the giants of old, men who with limited resources, did a vast amount of work among wild people, and said little about it, being contented with doing their duty. In 1828, accompanied by Lieutenant Burton, and ten men belonging to the Sudya Khamptis (Shans), he penetrated to the Bor Khamptis country, far beyond our borders, an exploit not repeated till after our annexation of Upper Burmah. Ram Singh had a great respect for his former leader, and loved to talk of old days.

CHAPTER VIII.

Visit to the Maharajah—His minister—Former revolutions—Thangal Major.

AFTER a day's rest I paid a visit to the Maharajah, having first stipulated as to my proper reception. I was received by the Jubraj (heir apparent) at the entrance to the private part of the palace, and by the Maharajah a few paces from the entrance to the Durbar room (hall of reception), and conducted by him to a seat opposite to his own, with a table between us, his sons and officials being seated on either side. I read the Viceroy's letter, informing the Maharajah of my appointment, and, after a short conversation, during which my age was asked (a question invariably put to European officers by Manipuris of rank), I took my leave, and was escorted back to the place where I was met on my arrival. I was favourably impressed by what I saw, but I at once realised that I was on no bed of roses, and that I would have to make a good fight to obtain and maintain my just influence with the Durbar. The Maharajah had undoubtedly grievances against us, and I felt that it was folly and injustice not to acknowledge these. At the same time, he and his ministers had on some occasions taken advantage of this state of affairs to behave in an unseemly way, and for this a sharp rebuke had to be administered. The natural sense of injustice is strong in mankind, and I saw that chafing under slights they had received, and often magnifying them, it was necessary for me first to acknowledge these, and try as far as possible to make amends, and then to come down on them very sharply for having forgotten their position.

The Maharajah returned my visit, and we had one or two interviews when we discussed affairs. I pointed out the extreme gravity of resisting the British Government in any way, and we soon became very friendly. Colonel McCulloch's introduction had been a great advantage to me, and every one was inclined to give me credit for good intentions, at the same time that every effort was made to restrict my authority and influence.

The Maharajah was a rather thick-set man of about five feet five inches in height and forty-five years of age. In India he would have been called fair. He had the features of the Indo-Chinese race, and the impassive face that generally goes with them, but which is often not so marked in the Manipuris. He was far the ablest man in his dominions, and a strong and capable ruler. He had a great taste for mechanical arts of all kinds, and a vast fund of information which he had acquired by questioning, for he questioned every one he met. English scientific works were explained to him, and his researches extended even to the anatomy of the human body, of which he had a very fair knowledge. He had a taste for European articles, and owned a large assortment. He had glass manufactured in his workshops, and once sent me a petroleum lamp, every portion of which was made by his own artificers. His rule, for such a strong man, was mild as compared with that of his predecessors, and he thoroughly realised that his prosperity depended on his loyalty to the British Government. At the same time, he was most tenacious of his rights, and earnestly desired to preserve his country intact, and to give us no excuse for annexing it.

The fear of tempting us to annex was so great that, once when I thought of growing a little tea for my own consumption, he was much agitated. I, as a matter of courtesy, first sent to ask him if he had any objection to my growing a little, and, in reply, he sent an official to beg me not to think of it. This man said, "The Maharajah will supply you with all the tea you want free of cost, but begs you not to think of growing it." The officer went on to explain, that it was feared that, if I successfully demonstrated that tea could be grown in Manipur tea planters would come up, and there would be a cry for annexation! Certainly our annexation of the Muttuk country in 1840 justified the suspicion, and we cannot blame people for having long memories.

The Jubraj, or heir apparent, was an amiable young man of twenty-six or twenty-seven, with a pleasant smile which was wanting in his father. He was of a weak character, although possessing some ability. Like his father, he could speak Hindoostani, but both were ignorant of English. Backed up and influenced by an honest and capable Political Agent, he would probably have made an excellent ruler, and, had we done our duty by him, he might now be at the head of a flourishing little state, instead of having died an exile in Calcutta.

The next son, Wankai Rakpar, afterwards known as the "Regent" during the recent troubles, was an ignorant, uncouth boor, who knew no language but his own, and was quite unfitted for any responsible work; he took little part in public affairs. The third known as Samoo Henjaba (Master of the Elephants), was a clever, pleasant, sensible young man, said by Thangal Major, no mean judge of character, to be the ablest of the ten sons of the Maharajah. He died during my tenure of office.

The fourth son, Kotwal Koireng, who afterwards acquired an infamous reputation as the "Senaputtee," was always a bad character, cruel, coarse, and low minded. From early childhood he was given to foul language, and was absolutely dangerous when he grew up. His mother had been unfaithful to the Maharajah, who used to say that the son was worthy of her. Colonel McCulloch had always disliked him as a boy.

None of the other six sons of the Maharajah were in my time mixed up in public affairs, so I need not describe them, except that Pucca Senna was the champion polo player, though not otherwise worthy of notice. The practical ministers were Bularam Singh, or Sawai Jamba Major, and Thangal Major. They were both faithful adherents of the Maharajah, although the first who had once had much influence had married the daughter of the former Rajah Nur Sing. He was nominally the first in rank, but

Thangal Major was rapidly gaining ground, and viewed with increasing favour by the Maharajah.

I quote the following description of the Government of Manipur from an article I wrote for *The Nineteenth Century*, by kind permission of the editor. "The government of Manipur has always been a pure despotism tempered by assassination and revolution. While he occupies the throne the rajah is perfectly absolute. A minister may be all powerful, and all the princes and people may tremble before him; for years he may practically rule the rajah; but he is after all a cipher before his sovereign, a single word from whom may send him into exile, make him an outcast, or reduce him to the lowest rank. Yet with all this power an obscure man may suddenly spring up, as if from the ground, to assert himself to be of the blood royal, and gathering a large party round him place himself on the throne. All this happened not unfrequently in days gone by, when many were the rajahs murdered or deposed. History tells us of rajahs being deposed, re-elected, and deposed again."

There can be no doubt that in old days the people benefited by the system of constant revolutions, as a rajah was obliged to keep in touch with his subjects if he wished to occupy the throne for any length of time, and many concessicns were made to gain a strong following. The average intelligence of the Manipuris being higher than that found among the cultivators of many other native states, the people knew what reforms to ask for, and often insisted on their being granted.

Nothing can be harder on the people of a native

state, than for the paramount power to hold a ruler on the throne with a firm grasp, and protect him against internal revolution, and at the same time to refrain from insisting on needful reform.

Chandra Kirtee Singh's long reign and strong government, were in many ways a great benefit to the people, because he was a man of sound sense, and though selfish and unscrupulous, naturally of a kindly disposition, a fact proved by the few executions that took place in his reign. In his earlier years he had the benefit of Colonel McCulloch's good advice, enforced by his great influence. All the same there can be no doubt that a little more interference judiciously applied, would have vastly improved the state of affairs during the time he occupied the throne. Of course an individual Political Agent might bring about improvements in the administration, but these all rested on his personal influence and lasted only while he remained. Had the Government of India stepped in and exerted its authority they would have been permanent.

Bularam Singh was a typical Manipuri in face and had good manners, but he had no force of character, and gradually yielded to his more able colleague. He was generally known as the Toolee-Hel major, *i.e.*, the major or commander of the Hel regiment.

Thangal Major was a remarkable character, and had a chequered history. His uncle had saved the life of Rajah Ghumbeer Singh (Chandra Kirtee Singh's father), then a child, when his older brother Marjeet attempted the murder of all his relations. Thangal Major was one of the props of the throne when Ghumbeer Singh ascended it. He had been introduced at Court at an early age, and accompanied the Rajah in an expedition against the village of Thangal inhabited by a tribe of Nagas. He was given the name Thangal in memory of the event. He accompanied the old Ranee with her infant son Chandra Kirtee Singh into exile, when she fled after attempting the Regent Nursing's life while he was engaged in worship in the temple of Govindjee in 1844; had stayed with him and carefully watched over his childhood and youth. When in 1850 the young Rajah came to Manipur to assert his rights, Thangal accompanied him and greatly contributed to his success. This naturally made him a favourite, and his bold, active, energetic character always brought him to the front when hard or dangerous work had to be done. For a time he fell into disfavour, but Colonel McCulloch, recognising his strong and useful qualities, and the fact that he was an exceedingly able man, interceded for him with the Maharajah, and he again came to the front. In person he was short and thickset, darker than the average of Manipuris, with piercing eyes and rather a prominent nose, a pleasant and straightforward but abrupt manner, and, though a very devoted and patriotic Manipuri, was extremely partial to Europeans. He knew our ways well, and soon took a man's measure. He was acquainted with every part of Manipur, and, though ignorant of English, could point out any village in the state, on an English map. In fact, he had studied geography in every branch to enable him to defend the cause of Manipur against the survey officers who were suspected by the Manipuris of wishing to include all they could within British territory. He knew all our technical terms such as "watershed" in English, and had gained much credit for enabling the survey to carry on their work in 1872, when the patriotic but ill-judged zeal of an older officer, Rooma Singh, nearly brought about a rupture. Thangal Major's knowledge of us and our customs, as well as of our moral code, was astonishing. He realised the power of the British Government, and though he would resist us to the utmost in the interests of Manipur, nothing would have induced him to join in any plot against our rule in India. When I say that he was unscrupulous and capable of anything, I only say that he was what circumstances and education had made him, and would make any man under similar conditions. He had not the polish of a native of Western India, and had not had the advantage of English training that many ministers in other states have. The internal administration of Manipur had never been interfered with by us, and Thangal Major was the strong able man of the old type. A strong and capable political agent might do well with him, but a weak one would soon go to the wall. He commanded the Toolee Nehah, and was often called by that title, but was better known as Thangal Major.

One of my predecessors had quarrelled with Thangal Major, and this had led to recrimination, and very unseemly conduct on the part of the Durbar. This conduct I had rebuked as directed, but it was a question as to how Thangal Major was to be dealt with. I was authorised to demand his dismissal from office, and for some time he had not been received by my two immediate predecessors. I made careful inquiries, and feeling convinced that there was a good deal to be said on Thangal's side, and that by careful management I should be able to keep him well in hand, I sent for him. The old man, he was then sixty, having been born in 1817, came in a quiet unostentatious way, and after a severe rebuke, and receiving an ample apology from him, I forgave him, and restored him to the position of minister in attendance upon me; and thenceforth I saw him daily, generally for an hour or two.

In addition to the Minister, two Subadars, Lowremba and Moirang, were placed in attendance on me, but as time went on, and I and the Durbar became friends, we transacted business in a friendly way, through any one.

CHAPTER IX.

Manipur—Early history—Our connection with it—Ghumbeer Singh—Burmese war.

MANIPUR consists of about 8000 square miles, chiefly hills surrounding a valley 650 square miles in extent. This valley from north to south is about 35 miles, and from east to west 25. The capital Imphal, as it formerly existed, was a large mass of villages looking like a forest from the neighbouring heights, and covering about 15 square miles. Every house was in the centre of its own well-planted garden, and every garden contained a few forest trees. The census of 1881 gave the population of the capital as 60,000, that of the rest of the valley an equal number, while the hills were estimated to have 100,000. It was only in the capital that pure Manipuris lived, except the soldiers in the military posts which were scattered all over the country.

The valley itself is 2600 feet above the sea, and the hills rise on an average to an equal height above it, though here and there some of the distant peaks are 10,000 to 12,000 feet in height. Thus Manipur contains within its borders a variety of climate from almost tropical, to a greater cold than that of England. The heat is never very excessive in the valley, and for eight months in the year it is most enjoyable. Foreigners suffer much from bronchial affections, doubtless owing to the waterlogged soil, but these complaints are not more prevalent among the native population than elsewhere, and if sanitary laws were properly observed, the valley might be a most healthy place and the population would rapidly overflow.

The capital is almost intersected by the 25th parallel north latitude, and 95° east longitude, and is 132 miles by road from Silchar, the capital of Cachar, and 70 from Tamu in the Kubo valley. The valley of Manipur forms the centre of a chain of valleys, viz., Cachar, Manipur, and Kubo, connecting Bengal with Burmah proper. The sides of the hills facing the valley of Manipur are generally covered with grass or scant jungle which rapidly dries up as the cold season advances, but when once the crest is passed, a fine forest is reached; except where the hill-tribes have destroyed it, to raise one crop and then let it relapse into grass and scrub. Alas, I have seen noble oak forests laid low and burned for this purpose. It is an abominable custom, and nothing can justify our permitting it where we hold sway. That it is not necessary is shown by the Angamis and some of the Tankhool tribes, who though they do occasionally indulge in this wasteful cultivation are quite independent of it, as they terrace their hill-sides and cultivate the same tract for generations. The forests of Manipur are plentifully supplied with fine timber trees; several varieties of oak and chest-nut exist, and many others unknown in England such as Woo-Ningtho, an excellent timber said to resist the ravages of white ants; wang, which can be worked in its green state as it never warps; teak, etc. Fir trees are found in abundance to the south, east, and north-east of the valley, and bamboos of many kinds, including the giant, are plentiful.

Rhododendrons and wild azaleas of several kinds, as well as many species of brilliant orchids, add greatly to the beauty of the forests, and in some parts tree ferns are abundant. I know nothing more lovely in the world, than some of the forest scenery of Manipur with its solemn stillness.

The early history of Manipur is lost in obscurity, but there can be no doubt that it has existed as an independent kingdom from a very early period. In the days when the Indian branch of the Aryan race was still in its progressive and colonising stage, this district was repeatedly passed over by one wave after another of invaders, intent on penetrating into the remotest parts of Burmah. We have no means of ascertaining what government it had before the year 700 A.D., but it is believed that a monarchy prevailed at that era. About the year 1250 A.D., a large Chinese force invaded the country, and was signally defeated; all who were not killed being made prisoners. These taught the Manipuris silk culture, and a number of them were settled at Susa Rameng in the valley, where they have still descendants. The Chinese also taught the art of brick-making, and erected two solid blocks of masonry in the palace, between which the road to the Lion Gate passed. These blocks were levelled with the ground by the Burmese invaders, but rebuilt on the old foundations by Ghumbeer Singh.

Manipur in old days possessed a famous breed of ponies, larger and better bred that the so-called Burmese ponies that come from the Shan states. On these ponies were mounted the formidable cavalry that in the last century made Manipur feared throughout Upper Burmah, and enabled her rulers on more than one occasion, to carry their victorious arms within sight of Ava, where their Rajah Pamheiba erected a stone pillar to commemorate the event. The cavalry used the regular Manipuri saddle protecting the legs, and were armed with spears and two quivers of darts. These darts in a retreat were grasped by a loop and swung round in a peculiar way, when the shaft formed of peacock feathers with an iron head suddenly became detached, and flying with great force inflicted a fatal wound wherever it struck. A skilful man could throw them with great precision.

The territories of Manipur varied according to the mettle of its rulers. Sometimes they held a considerable territory east of the Chindwin river in subjection, at other times only the Kubo valley, a strip of territory, inhabited, not by Burmese, but by Shans, and lying between Manipur proper and the Chindwin. Again they were driven back into Manipur proper. For the greater part of the last century, the Kubo valley unquestionably belonged to Manipur, and it was never in any sense a Burmese province, being, when not under Manipur, a feudatory of the great Shan kingdom of Pong.

In the middle of the last century one of those extraordinary men who appear from time to time in the East, destined to shine like a blazing meteor, imparting exceeding brilliancy to their country, and then as suddenly vanishing, so that it returns to its original obscurity, appeared in Burmah. His name, Along Pra, has been corrupted by us into Alompra, by which he is always known. He speedily raised Burmah to a commanding position. The kingdom of Pong was overthrown and its territories mostly annexed, Pegu was conquered, our district of Chittagong threatened, and Siam forced to relinquish several coveted possessions. The war fever did not die with Alompra, and in 1817 and 1819 Assam and Manipur were respectively invaded, internal dissensions having bred traitors, who, in both countries, made the path of the invaders easy. But the master spirit was gone, and when we appeared upon the scene, they could make no efficient stand. Had we then marched to Ava, the Burmese Empire would have collapsed like a house of cards, and the events of 1885 been anticipated by sixty years. As it was, we did not realise our strength and the Burmese weakness, and contented ourselves with annexing Assam and Cachar and protecting Manipur.

It is not very evident what the religion of Manipur was in early days, but we see no trace of Buddhism. Probably, whatever the belief in early years when the people may have been affected by the intermittent stream of Aryans passing through, for many centuries no religious rites were used before the recent rise of Hindooism, further than to appease evil spirits, as is the custom of the surrounding tribes. There can be little doubt that some time or other the Naga tribes to the north made one of their chiefs Rajah of Manipur, and that his family, while, like the Manchus in China and other conquerors, adopting the civilisation of the country, retained some of their old customs. This is shown in the curious practice at the installation of a Rajah, when he and the Ranee appear in Naga costume ; also that he always has in his palace a house built like a Naga's, and wherever he goes he is attended by two or three Manipuris with Naga arms and accoutrements. I once told a Manipuri what I thought on the subject, and he was greatly struck by it, and admitted the force of what I said.

Towards the middle of the last century, for some reason or other, a great Hindoo revival took place in the East of India. Assam was once Hindoo but had long become Buddhist under its Ahom kings, and now became converted to Hindooism, by Brahmins from Bengal. All difficulties were smoothed over, and converts were made by tens of thousands. It is to be regretted that it was so, as these "converts" quickly deteriorated. The easy conquest of Hindooised Assam by the Burmese, when Buddhist Assam had successfully resisted a powerful army sent by Arungzebe from India and composed largely of recruits from Central Asia, seems proof of it, if all other evidence were wanting.

The process of conversion in Manipur began a generation later than in Assam, and proceeded on somewhat different lines, but it was not less effective, and was still going on at a late date. It had not the same deteriorating effect, for the Rajahs assumed to themselves a position greater than that of High Pontiff, and could at any time by their simple fiat have changed the religion of the country and degraded all the Brahmins, in fact all admissions to the Hindoo pale from the outer world of unorthodoxy were made by the Rajah himself. Sometimes the inhabitants of a village were elevated *en masse* from the level of outcasts, to that of Hindoos of pure caste, but more often single individuals were "converted." A man belonging to a hill-tribe, for instance, could, if the Rajah chose, at any time receive the sacred thread of the twice-born castes, and on payment of a small sum of money be admitted as a Hindoo and was thenceforth called a Khetree.* This privilege was not accorded to Mussulmans. I once asked a Manipuri why they received hill-men and not Mussulmans, both being Mlechas,† according to Hindoo theory. He said it was because the hill people had sinned in ignorance, whereas Mussulmans knew the evil of their ways.

Of course, every one who knows anything of Hindooism is aware that theoretically a man must be born a Hindoo, and that proselytism is not admitted. Practically, however, this rule is ignored on the eastern frontier, and all along it from Sudya down to Chittagong, where conversions are daily taking place. I remember villages in Assam where caste was unknown thirty-five years ago, but where now the people live in the odour of sanctity as highly orthodox and bigoted Hindoos. Strange to say, the pure Hindoos of the North-West Provinces acknowledge the pretensions of these spurious converts sufficiently so as to allow of their drinking water brought by them. It is probably easier to take the people at their own valuation than to carry water one's self from a distance when tired. By the

* Probably a corruption of Khatyra.

† *I.e.* Unclean.

religious law of the Hindoos, it is forbidden to eat or drink anything touched by one of another tribe.

Our first relations with Manipur date from 1762, when Governor Verelst of the Bengal Presidency—with that splendid self-reliance and large-mindedness characteristic of the makers of the British Indian Empire, men who acted instead of talking, and were always ready to extend our responsibilities when advisable—entered into a treaty with the Rajah of Manipur. As this treaty came to nothing, practically our connection with the little state really dates from 1823. It had been invaded by the Burmese in 1819, and its people driven out or carried off into slavery in Burmah. The royal family were fugitives.

At that time Sylhet was our frontier station, and our relations with the Burmese, who were at the highest pitch of their power, were daily becoming more strained. On our side of the frontier we were ably represented by Mr. David Scott, agent to the Governor-General, and preparations were being made for the inevitable struggle. One day a young Manipuri prince waited on Mr. Scott and asked leave to raise a Manipuri force to fight on our side. He was short and slight, and of indomitable courage and energy, and the agent to the Governor-General recognising his ability, allowed him to raise 500 men. These were soon increased to 2000, cavalry, infantry and artillery. Two English officers, Captain F. Grant and Lieutenant R. B. Pemberton, were attached to the force, thenceforth called the Manipur Levy, to drill and discipline it.

In 1825 a general advance was made all along our line, Cachar was invaded and subdued, and we essayed to pursue the enemy into Manipur and thence into Burmah, but our transport arrangements failed. Hitherto we had been accustomed to wars in the arid plains of India, and our military authorities did not realise the necessities of an expedition into the eastern jungles. Hence, camels and bullocks were sent to dislocate their limbs in the tenacious mud and swamps of Cachar, and when the advance into Manipur was desired, our regular troops were powerless. At this crisis the Manipur Levy showed its immense value. The men could move lightly equipped without the paraphernalia of a regular army, and advance they did, and with such effect that in a short time not only was Manipur cleared, but the enemy driven out of the Kubo valley. Later on, Ghumbeer Singh was recognised as Rajah of Manipur, and the Kubo valley was included within his territories.

Manipur at this time contained only 2000 inhabitants, the miserable remnants of a thriving population of at least 400,000, possibly 600,000, that existed before the invasion. Ghumbeer Singh's task was to encourage exiles to return, and to attempt to rebuild the prosperity of his little kingdom. He was a wise and strong though severe ruler, and though he owed his throne greatly to his own efforts, he to the last retained the deepest feelings of loyalty and gratitude to the British Government, promptly obeying all its orders and doing his utmost to impress the same feeling on all his officers.

As is always the case, though we had carried all before us in the war, we began to display great weakness afterwards. We had an agent, Colonel Burney, at Ava, and the Burmese who were not disposed to be at all friendly, constantly tried to impress on him the fact that all difficulties and disputes would be at an end if we ceded the Kubo valley to them, that territory belonging to our ally Ghumbeer Singh of Manipur. Of course the proposal ought to have been rejected with scorn, and a severe snub given to the Burmese officials. The advisers of the Government of India, however, being generally officers brought up in the Secretariat, and with little practical knowledge of Asiatics, the manly course was not followed. It was not realised that a display of self-confidence and strength is the best diplomacy with people like the Burmese, and with a view to winning their good-will we basely consented to deprive our gallant and loyal ally of part of his territories. An attempt was made to negotiate with him, but Major Grant said, "It is no use bargaining with Ghumbeer Singh," and refused to take any part in it. He was asked what compensation should be given, and he said 6000 sicca rupees per annum.

When Ghumbeer Singh heard the final decision he quietly accepted it, saying, "You gave it me and you can take it away. I accept your decree." The proposed transfer was very distasteful to many of the inhabitants, including the Sumjok (Thoungdoot) Tsawbwa,* but they were not consulted. The Kubo valley was handed over to the Burmese on the 9th of January, 1834, and on that day Ghumbeer Singh died in Manipur of cholera. Perhaps he was happy in the hour of his death, as he felt the treatment of our Government most severely.

* Mentioned frequently later on. In August, 1891, he was a fugitive from the British Government, hiding himself on the Chinese frontier.—ED.

CHAPTER X.

Ghumbeer Singh and our treatment of him—Nur Singh and attempt on his life—McCulloch—His wisdom and generosity—My establishment—Settlement of frontier dispute.

GHUMBEER SINGH did much for Manipur during his comparatively short reign. He made all the roads in his territory safe, and subdued the different hill-tribes who had asserted their independence during the troubles with Burmah. Imphal, the old capital, had not been re-occupied, though the sacred spot where the temple of Govindjee stood was cared for; but a new palace had been built at Langthabal at a distance of three and a half miles from Imphal where several fine masonry buildings were erected, and a canal dug for the annual boat races. Langthabal* was deserted in 1844 and the old site re-occupied, and in my time, the buildings at Langthabal were picturesque ruins, having been greatly injured by time and the earthquakes of 1869 and 1880. Ghumbeer Singh left an infant son, Chandra Kirtee Singh who was two years of age at his father's death and a distant cousin, Nur Singh, was appointed Regent. Contrary to all precedent, the Regent was loyal to his charge and governed well and ably for the infant

* Here a British native regiment was stationed, after Sir J. Johnstone's retirement, but some time before the troubles of 1891.—ED.

prince, in spite of constant attempts to overthrow his government. In 1844, the Queen-Mother wishing to govern herself, attempted to procure Nur Singh's murder as he was at prayers in the temple. She failed and fled with her son the young Rajah Chandra Kirtee Singh to British territory. The Regent then proclaimed himself Rajah with the consent of all the people. The Manipur Levy had been maintained up till 1835 when the Government of India withdrew their connection from it, and ceased to pay the men. Major Grant left Manipur, and Captain Gordon, who had been adjutant since 1827, was made Political Agent of Manipur. Captain Pemberton had long since been on special survey duty.

Captain Gordon died in December 1844. He was much liked and long remembered by the people whom he had greatly benefited, among other ways by introducing English vegetables, and fruits. He was succeeded by Lieutenant (afterwards Colonel) McCulloch.

Rajah Nur Singh died in 1850, and was succeeded by his brother Debindro, a weak man, quite unfit for the position. In 1850, young Chandra Kirtee Singh invaded the valley with a body of followers, Debindro fled, and he mounted the throne without opposition. Up to this time the Government of India had always acknowledged the *de facto* Rajah of Manipur, and revolutions with much accompanying bloodshed were common. Now, however, McCulloch strongly urged the advisability of supporting Chandra Kirtee Singh, and he received authority to "make a public avowal of the determination of the British Government to uphold the present Rajah and to resist and punish any parties attempting hereafter to dispossess him." The Court of Directors of the East India Company, in a despatch dated May 5th, 1852, confirmed the order of the Government of India and commented thus: "The position you have assumed of pledged protector of the Rajah, imposes on you as a necessary consequence the obligation of attempting to guide him, by your advice, but if needful of protecting his subjects against oppression on his part; otherwise our guarantee of his rule may be the cause of inflicting on them a continuance of reckless tyranny."

These words of justice and wisdom were steadily ignored by successive governments. On no occasion did the Government of India ever seriously remonstrate with the Rajah, or make a sustained effort to improve his system of administration. The East India Company's order became a dead letter, but the resolution to uphold Chandra Kirtee Singh bore good fruit, and during his long reign of thirty-five years no successful attempt against his authority was ever made, and he on his part displayed unswerving fidelity to the British Government.

I have already mentioned the great work that Colonel McCulloch accomplished with regard to the Kukis. This added to his long experience, gave him great influence in the State, and when he retired from the service in 1861, it was amidst the regrets of the whole people. Able, high-minded, respected, and having accomplished a task few could even have attempted, he left without honour or reward from his Government. How many men of inferior capacity, and quite without his old-fashioned single-minded devotion to duty, are nowadays covered with stars! When he left he made every effort to hand over his vast power and influence intact to his successor, and to smooth his way as much as possible. Had the Government of India exercised the slightest tact and discretion in the selection of its agent, he might have carried on the good work so ably commenced, and brought Manipur by rapid strides into the path of progress. As it was it would have been difficult to find an officer more unfitted to succeed Colonel McCulloch than the one selected; he was soon involved in difficulties, and after a troubled period was ordered by Government to leave at three days' notice. For a time the agency remained vacant, but the Rajah applied for another officer, and Colonel McCulloch was requested by the Government to quit his retirement, and again assume charge. He did so, and was received with acclamations by Rajah and people, the whole State turning out to meet him. His first effort was to restore the confidence forfeited by the late political agent, and everything went on as smoothly as ever; but, towards the end of 1867, he finally retired, staying on a few days after his successor's arrival to post him up in his work. This time it would have been thought that some judgment would be shown in the selection of an officer for the post; but the next political agent was eminently unfitted and for some years before his death in 1876, was on very indifferent terms with the Durbar.

During the brief period that elapsed between the last event and my taking charge, two different officers held the post.

My Government establishment consisted of a head clerk, a most excellent man, Baboo Rusni Lall Coondoo; a native doctor, Lachman Parshad; native secretary and Manipuri interpreter; Burmese interpreter; Naga interpreter; Kuki interpreter; and latterly six chuprassies, *i.e.*, orderlies or lictors. As for private servants we had three Naga girls, a Mugh cook and assistant, who could turn out a dinner equal to any of the London clubs for one hundred people at a couple of days' notice, and under him I had four young Nagas learning their work, as I was determined to do more for my successors than my predecessors had done for me, viz., teach and train up a staff of servants so as to save the necessity of importing the scum of Calcutta. I had an excellent bearer, Horna, as I have already stated, and under him were two or three Nagas; washerman, syces, gardeners, water-carriers, etc., made up the number. All my interpreters, chuprassies, and servants, I clothed in scarlet livery which made a great impression, and gradually the air of squalor which prevailed when I arrived began to disappear. I had charge of a Government Treasury from which I used to pay myself and the Government establishment. The currency of the country was a small bell-metal coin called "Sel," of which 400 to 480 went to the rupee, also current, but copper pice were not used, and all Manipuri accounts were kept in "Sel."

At this time the Naga Hills were still under a political officer whose actual jurisdiction was limited to the villages which had paid tribute to me, as already described. He was supposed to exercise a certain influence over many of the large villages, but the influence was lessened by the feeling entertained by the Nagas that our stay in the hills was uncertain, and that for all practical purposes the Manipuris were the power most to be reckoned with, and from our point of view it was very desirable that our headquarter station should be removed to Kohima. A dispute with Mozuma, due chiefly to our vacillating conduct, was now going on, but its chiefs would not accept our terms, and an expedition to coerce them was in preparation in which I was to take part. Mr. Carnegy was political officer, a man of ability and determination, and very pleasant to deal with. During the dispute with Mozuma, the other villages held aloof, thinking Mozuma was able to hold its own, and waiting to see which side gained the day.

Burmah was still under its native rulers. There were constant frontier disputes going on between it and Manipur, but that state of things was chronic.

To the south of Manipur, the Chin and Lushai tribes were quiet.

There was a long standing boundary dispute between Manipur and the Naga Hills. The boundary had been most arbitrarily settled by us when the survey was carried out, so far as a certain point, beyond that it was vague. Manipur claimed territory which we certainly did not possess, and which she had visited from time to time, but did not actually hold in subjection. Other portions, as I afterwards proved, were occupied by her, though the fact had not been ascertained. Over and over again efforts had been made to bring the Durbar to terms, but without success. I determined to grapple with the question at once. I took a map and drew a line including all that I thought Manipur entitled to, in the neighbourhood of the Naga Hills, and advised the Maharajah to accept the arrangement on the understanding that when I visited the country claimed further eastward, I would recommend the Government of India to allow him to retain all that he actually held in his possession. This was agreed to by him and confirmed by Government, and I believe that substantial justice was done to both parties.

I should like to have seen Manipur get more, as a set-off against our unjust treatment in former years, but as we were sure eventually, to occupy all the Naga Hills, it was necessary to make such an adjustment as would not injure British interests in the future.

CHAPTER XI.

My early days in Manipur—The capital—The inhabitants—Good qualities of Manipuris—Origin of valley of Manipur—Expedition to the Naga Hills—Lovely scenery—Attack on Kongal Tannah by Burmese—Return from Naga Hills—Visit Kongal Tannah.

The first few weeks in Manipur were taken up in making acquaintance with the place and people, and doing all that was possible to disarm the fears of the Durbar. Never was there one so suspicious. At first all my movements were watched, and wherever I went spies, open or secret, followed; however, I encouraged it to the utmost, and told the officials to inquire into everything I did, and they very soon saw that there was no necessity for special espionage, though all my acts were still noted and reported. Several little difficulties cropped up regarding British subjects, and required some care in dealing with them. In one case, a man had taken upon himself to intrigue with some of the Nagas under Manipur, and urged them to declare themselves British subjects, and in another, a man had robbed the Maharajah. In both instances the Durbar had acted foolishly and precipitately, though under much provocation. However, I turned both men out of the country, with orders never to return.

The question of British subjects and their rights was one that gave me much trouble for years.

Judging by a decision of the High Court of Calcutta that all the descendants of European British subjects were European British subjects, I insisted on all descendants of British subjects being considered as such, and subject to my jurisdiction. After a long struggle I carried my point, and it very greatly strengthened my position.

A few more words about the capital and the Manipuris may not be amiss. Imphal, as has been said,* covered a space of fifteen square miles. On the north side it touches on some low hills, called Ching-mai-roong, and running westward is bounded by a shallow lake, which is partly enclosed by a continuation of the hills, here called Langol, on which grows a celebrated cane used for polo sticks. Then, running south, it is intersected by several roads, notably the road to Silchar, which enters the capital at a place called Kooak-Kaithel (*i.e.* crow bazaar). Here it is bounded by rice cultivation. Going farther south, and sweeping round in an easterly direction, it is bounded by the Plain of Lang-thabal, at one extremity of which lies the old capital; here two rivers intersect it. And going farther east, it is bounded by the lower slopes of a hill rising 2500 feet above the valley. Then turning to the northward and crossing two rivers, we come again to the place from which we started. The want of the town was a good water-supply; there were one or two fair-sized tanks, or ponds, as they would be called in England, and the afore-mentioned rivers, of which the water is not improved by re-

* Quoted by kind permission of editor from my article in *Nineteenth Century*.

ceiving the ashes of the dead burned on their banks. Beyond this, all the water obtainable was derived from small ponds, one or more of which was to be found in every garden enclosure. The ground on which the capital stands must at one time have been very low, probably a marsh, and it has been artificially raised from time to time by digging these tanks; every raised road, too, meant a deep stagnant ditch on either side. The people are not sanitary in their habits, and when heavy rain falls the gardens are flooded, and a fair share of the accumulated filth is washed into the drinking-tanks, the result being frequent epidemics of cholera.

The Manipuris themselves are a fine stalwart race descended from an Indo-Chinese stock, with some admixture of Aryan blood, derived from the successive waves of Aryan invaders that have passed through the valley in prehistoric days. It may be this, or from an admixture of Chinese blood, but certainly the Manipuris have stable and industrious qualities which the Burmese and Shans do not possess. Since then the race has been constantly fed by additions from the various hill-tribes surrounding the valley. The result is a fairly homogeneous people of great activity and energy, with much of the Japanese aptitude for acquiring new arts. The men seem capable of learning anything, and the women are famous as weavers, and in many cases have completely killed out the manufacture of cloths formerly peculiar to certain of the hill-tribes, over whom the Manipuris have obtained mastery by superior intellect. They are always cheerful, even on a long and trying march, and are good-humoured under any difficulties and never apparently conscious of fatigue. They are very abstemious, and live chiefly on rice and fish, which is often rotten from preference. Though rigid Hindoos outwardly, they have a curious custom by which a man of low caste, marrying a high-caste woman, can be adopted into her tribe, the exact reverse of what prevails in India, where a woman of high caste marrying a low-caste man is hopelessly degraded and her children outcasts.

It is impossible for those who have marched much in the hills with Manipuris to avoid liking them. Their caste prejudices, though rigid, give no trouble to others. Hungry or not, they are always ready to march, and march all day and all night, if necessary. Still, the Indo-Chinese races exceed even the ordinary Asiatic in reserve and sphinx-like characteristics, and the Manipuris are an inscrutable set. I had many intimate friends among them, yet, on the whole, prefer the pure Hindoo.

What is now the valley of Manipur was evidently once a series of valleys and ranges of hills, between the higher ranges which now border it and converge to the south. The rivers now flowing through the valley then flowed through it like the Barak, Eerung, and others, at a much lower level. One of the great earthquakes, to which these regions are so subject, closed the outlet and raised a permanent barrier; thus a lake was formed, and in the course of ages the alluvium brought down by the streams filled it up to its present level leaving the Logtak Lake in its lowest part, a lake which has constantly lessened and is still lessening in size. The crests of the sunken ranges are still to be seen running down the valley, and mostly parallel to the bordering ranges, such are Langol, Langthabal, Phoiching, Lokching, and others. Sometimes a river, as at a place called "Eeroce Semba," runs at the base of a hill, and cuts away the alluvium, showing the solid rock. This alluvium forms one of the deepest and richest soils in the world.

I have referred to the proposed expedition to the Naga Hills, to aid the troops there in the operations against the powerful village of Mozuma. In order to take part in this expedition I had brought up one hundred men of the 35th Native Infantry, from Cachar, and I started from Manipur on December 3rd, 1877, having sent on the 35th and a Manipuri force of over three hundred men under the Minister Bularem Singh. I rode out the first day to Mayang Khang, a distance of forty miles, where I caught up my men. I passed Songmai at a distance of thirteen miles on the border of the valley, and up to which the road is flat, and soon entered a broken country, first grass, then scrub, then forest. The road lay over a succession of spurs of the Kowpree Hills which run down into a very narrow valley, and was as bad as can be imagined—very steep ascents and descents. At last we reached Kaithemabee, the second stage, and fourteen miles from Sengmai. It is exceedingly picturesquely situated, having a splendid view of the Kowpree range, here rising to over 8000 feet. The outpost is situated on a high bank overlooking a stream, and beyond it a splendid rolling slope of grass extending for miles.

All this part of the country is covered with beehive-shaped cairns, built of well-selected stones. They are said to have been made by the Köereng Nagas, formerly a very powerful race, whose miserable remnants now inhabit the neighbouring hills. Farther on the bee-hives end suddenly, and a region of monoliths is entered. Probably both monoliths and bee-hives were erected to commemorate great events in the lives of the builders, the death of a chief, the birth of a son, the giving of a great feast when a bison, or possibly many, were killed. Monoliths are common, and exist all over the Naga Hills and among the Kolarian and Dravidian tribes, as well as all over Europe. Cairns also are common, but the beehive-shaped cairns are, I believe, unique, and found only in Manipur and in this neighbourhood.

I reached Mayung Khang at 4 P.M., having an hour before crossed the watershed, all the streams south of it falling into the tributaries of the Chindwin Irrawaddy, all to the north running into the tributaries of the Ganges and Burrhampooter.

Mayung Khang is a highly undulating grassy slope, the Kowpree rising to nearly nine thousand feet in the west, while after crossing a small stream a lower range closes it in on the east. We halted there for the night close to a monolith, and the next day marched to Mythephum.

Mythephum or Muphum (*lit.* Manipuri settlement) was a small military post, and we encamped below in a wide valley among recently cut rice fields, with a river rushing by us. The place is so named from having been a Manipuri settlement, in the old days before the Burmese invasion. High hills rose above us on all sides, the valley running in and out among them and following the course of the stream. To our north, and at a distance of a mile or two, was the once powerful village of Muram, still populous but submissive. I had a small but most comfortable straw-built hut, and well remember how delightful the early morning was next day, when I had breakfast at sunrise and saw my thermometer at thirty-two degrees. Only those accustomed to great heat realise the delights of a low thermometer. Mythephum is over 4000 feet above the sea, and being a low valley is often extremely cold. Sometimes in winter the stream is for a day quite choked by blocks of ice, and I have seen the thermometer at twenty-six degrees, 150 feet above the valley, which probably meant eighteen degrees at the lowest level on the grass.

It was my intention to march on Mozuma by a track which would avoid the powerful villages of Viswena, Kohima, Jotsuma and Konoma, and enable me to attack the enemy in the rear. Halfway I was delayed by receiving no letter from Mr. Carnegy, with whom I had to act in concert, and this prevented me from reaching the scene of operations, as I received the startling news that the Manipuri outpost of Kongal Tannah on the borders of the Kubo valley had been attacked on December 14th by a party of men sent by the Rajah of Sumjok or Thoungdoot, and eight men killed. This threw the whole population of Manipur into a state of commotion, and the Maharajah begged me to return at once, and I felt it my duty to do so, as my chief work was to protect Manipur and its interests.

I therefore returned to Manipur on December 17th, leaving my party on the frontier, where they remained some time longer, the Nagas being unwilling to submit; and making overtures instead to the Maharajah Chandra Kirtee Singh. He sternly declined their offers, and threatened that if they did not speedily yield to the British authorities, he would send a large force to our aid.

The Naga Hills Campaign of that year had no further interest for Manipur, and it had a sad ending for us, as Mr. Carnegy was accidently shot by a sentry.

The "Kongal outrage," as it was thenceforth called, was so serious and so evidently premeditated, that a most thorough inquiry was needed. It took some time to collect evidence as wounded men had to be brought in, and it was the end of the month before I was able to proceed to the spot. At last I started and crossed the Yoma range of hills for the first time. What a lovely march it was and what an anxious one, as I left my wife not at all well, and no one but an ignorant and not very sweet-tempered English nurse to look after her. However, duty must come first, and off I started, posting relays of ponies on the way to enable me to return quickly when the work was done. Thangal Major accompanied me.

The first part of our march lay across the valley, and we began the ascent of the hills at a place called Ingorok. After a wearisome ascent of 3500 feet and a more gradual one along the crest, we made a rapid descent of 4000 feet to the Turet river, where we encamped. The river runs at the bottom of an exceedingly narrow valley, and the ascent on both sides is one of the most wearisome I have ever made. On a dark night lights on the hillside above, appear as stars from the bed of the stream. The scenery was majestic, and the vegetation very fine. The next day we commenced with a steep ascent of 2500 feet, and ended with a descent of 3000 feet to the Maghung river. From the Maghung next morning we started for Kongal Tannah, which we reached in good time.

I carefully examined the place and saw the charred remains of the murdered men, and many bullets still sticking in the stockade. The evidence being complete, I turned homewards, and by travelling incessantly reached Manipur next morning to find that my wife had presented me with another son, the first pure European child born in Manipur. It had been an anxious time for me, and I was thankful to find both her and the baby well. We named the baby Arthur.

I sent a full report of the Kongal case to the Government of India, and a demand for reparation was made at the Court of Mandalay, but it was not backed up with sufficient vigour. The outrage was unprovoked, and nothing less than the execution of the ringleaders, who were well known, would have satisfied Manipur, and, indeed, the claims of justice, but though the case dragged on for years, no redress was ever given. I predicted at the time that failure to do justice would eventually lead to underhand reprisals on the part of Manipur, as the Durbar could not understand our Government tolerating an attack of this kind on a protected state, and naturally ascribed our forbearance to weakness. I shall have to refer to the case farther on.

CHAPTER XII.

Discussions as to New Residency—Its completion—Aunual boat races—Kangjoopkool—Daily work—Dealings with the Durbar.

I HAVE briefly described the old Residency which was rented from the Heir Apparent. Money had been sanctioned for a new Residency, to belong to the British Government, but there had been squabbles for a long time between my predecessors and the Durbar regarding a suitable site. Also such a building as was required could only be built with the help of the Durbar whom it was advisable to conciliate.

One of my predecessors wished to build on a small hill called "Chinga," about a mile from the palace. It was an admirable site, and had the position of the Political Agent been similiar to that in other Indian States, it could not have been better. But in Manipur, the representative of the Government of India was regarded by the Maharajah as a powerful prop and support in case of his throne being attacked, as was constantly the case in former years. On this ground the Durbar objected that it was too far off; also that the place was reported to be the residence of an evil spirit inimical to the Royal family, so that it was not a convenient spot for the Maharajah to visit. So, after many acrimonious disputes, the negotiation fell through.

Another Political Agent chose a site called Ching-mai-roong, which in many ways was very satisfactory, and the Durbar reluctantly consented to give it, but it was a mile and a half from the palace, and therefore much out of the way. The question was still in abeyance when I arrived. As soon as I had time, I discussed the matter with the Durbar, and found the Maharajah much averse to my removal from the old site. He said "Where you are now, I can call to you; but if you go to a distance, I shall be cut off entirely."

I quite saw the advisability of being on the spot, also in what I may call the fashionable quarter of the town; and, as from a sanitary point of view, the position was as good as any other, I agreed to stay, on condition that all the squalid houses and slums in the neighbourhood were cleared away, dirty tanks filled, and others deepened, and a fine largo space cleared and handed over to me. I further insisted that I should have all the assistance necessary in building a suitable Residency. My terms were agreed to, and the work put in hand. I determined to have a building worthy of the representative of the British Government, and sacrificed everything to suitable rooms, and sound construction, so that it was not till the end of 1880 that it was finished.

I was greatly indebted to my head clerk, Baboo Rusni Lall Coondoo, who acted as clerk of the works. The result was a charming residence. It was in the half-timber style of old English houses, modified to suit the climate, all on one floor, but raised on a solid brick foundation, which gave a lower storey seven feet in height, thus keeping us high and dry, the house being approached on four sides by flights of solid masonry steps. The lower storey was built so as to be shot proof, as I designed it as a place of retreat from stray shot for non-combatants, in the event of the Residency being again, as it had been before, subjected to a cross-fire from contending parties during one of the many revolutions so common to Manipur. Little did I dream that folly, and incompetency would ever lead to our being directly attacked!

The large compound, about sixteen acres in extent, was surrounded by a mud breastwork and ditch, quite capable of being defended, if necessary, and there were four entrances which I named respectively, the Great Gate, the Milking Gate, my cows'-shed being close to it, the Water Gate and the Kang-joop-kool Gate. I made a riding road all round to exercise ponies, and besides making a splendid kitchen garden, adding considerably to Colonel McCulloch's, we laid out flower beds, and had cool shady spots for the heat of the day. Deodars and other exotic trees were imported by me and throve wonderfully. One large sheet of water with an island in the centre was cleared, deepened, and the banks repaired, and as I never allowed a bird to be killed, it was covered in winter with water-fowls to the number of four hundred and fifty or five hundred of every kind, from wild geese downwards, and rare birds took refuge in the trees. In the north-east corner of the compound were the lines for my escort, with a tank of the purest drinking water, where formerly squalor and filth had held sway. Finally I covered most of the large trees with beautiful orchids, so that in the season we had a blaze of colour. I spared no expense on the garden, and we were rewarded. Altogether the Residency and its grounds formed a beautiful and comfortable resting-place.

The new building was also commodious and contained a handsome Durbar-room for receptions 24 feet square, fine dining and drawing-rooms, very airy and comfortable bedrooms, etc., with an office for myself. The pantry was so arranged that cold draughts of air, so great a drawback in Indian houses in cold weather, were avoided when dinner was being brought in. The bedrooms had fireplaces, and the sitting-rooms excellent stoves which in winter were very necessary. The shot-proof rooms in the basement were not used, except one for a storeroom, and the one under the verandah of the Durbar-room, used as a sleeping place by the men of my guard.

The Great Gate was a picturesque half-timber structure, with rooms on either side, one of which I built specially as a pneumonia hospital, so it was designed with a view to maintaining an equable temperature, pneumonia being a great scourge among newly arrived Hindoostani sepoys. Not long after I left, it was diverted to other purposes, being considered too good for a hospital!

"With the exception of the Residency, no house when I left Manipur, was built of brick, partly from fear of earthquakes, partly on account of expense. The ordinary houses of the people are huts with wattle and daub or mud walls, those of greater folks the same, but on a larger scale. Every house has a verandah in front with the main entrance leading from it, and a little side door on the north side close to the west end, the houses invariably facing east. The roofs are all of thatch, with the exception of the Rajah's, which was of corrugated iron. There were several temples built of brick stuccoed over. One in the palace had an iron roof, another a gilded one. I sent some models of these temples and several other buildings to the Indian and Colonial Exhibition of 1886, every beam and rafter being represented and made according to scale. The larger of the temples had bells of a fine deep tone. Some of the approaches to the Rajah's dwelling-house were made of brick. Formerly the palace enclosure was entered from the front by a quaint and picturesque old gateway, not beautiful, but characteristic of Manipur; the old Rajah Chandra Kirtee Singh substituted for it a tawdry and fantastic structure with a corrugated iron roof, a structure without any merit, and quite out of keeping with its surroundings. I remonstrated in vain; shoddy and vulgar tastes had penetrated even to Manipur, and the picturesque old building that spoke of bygone ages was doomed; but we who have destroyed so many fine buildings, have little right to criticise.

"Close to the gateway is the place where the grand stand is erected, from which the Rajah and his relations view the boat races on the palace moat. I say 'view,' as in old age, a Rajah sits there all the time; but in the prime of life he takes part in these races, steering one of the boats himself. These boat races generally take place in September when the moat is full, and are the great event of the year.

Every one turns out to see them, the Ranees and other female relations being on the opposite side of the moat, for in Manipur there is no concealment of women, while the side next to the road is thronged with spectators. The boatmen have a handsome dress peculiar to the occasion, and the whole scene is highly interesting. The boats are canoes hewn out of single trees of great size, and are decorated with colour and carving." *

The valley of Manipur is hot and steamy in the rainy season, and Colonel McCulloch built a small hut at a place called Kang-joop-kool, situated on a spur of the Kowpree range, to the west of the valley at a height of 5170 feet above the sea. The distance from the capital was fourteen miles, and four from the foot of the hills, and he lived there for the whole of the rainy season, except for a few visits to the capital. His successors till my time did not stay there much, but I bought a small hut from my immediate predecessor, and pulled it down, and built a new one far more commodious. I enclosed the land, and laid out a small garden, and planted a wood of Khasia pines, the land being quite bare, and in time it became a most charming place. It was pleasant to leave the ceremonial life at the capital, where I never walked out without a train of followers clad in scarlet liveries, and settle down quietly at Kang-joop-kool where we could roam about the hills as if we had been in England.

I spent little or no time in sporting, my eyes were never very good, and before I came to Manipur had

* Quoted by kind permission of editor from my article in *Nineteenth Century*.

become so deficient in what oculists call power of "accommodation," that, though formerly a fairly good shot, I was then a bad one. In one way this was an advantage, as all my interests were concentrated on my work, and nothing of greater interest could have been found. Somehow or other, there was subject for conversation with State officials and non-officials, to last me from early morning till night, and fill up every spare moment. My door was always open, and the guard at the great gate had orders to let every one pass. All the minor gates were unguarded.

No attempt was made by the Durbar, as in other native states, to bribe the Residency servants, except in one notable case that happened before my time. All negotiations were carried on with the Political Agent direct, and the penurious Manipuris would have thought it waste of money to bribe his servants. This was a very satisfactory state of things, and probably saved many unpleasant complications.

In my dealings with the Durbar, I always tried to bear in mind that I was the representative of the strong dealing with the weak, and so to ignore little silly acts of self-assertion, such as a native court loves to indulge in, and childish ebullitions, as unworthy of notice. Whenever it became necessary for me to interfere, I did so with great firmness, but always tried to carry the Maharajah and his ministers with me, and make any desired reform appear to emanate from him. Except on one occasion, I never experienced any rudeness from an official.

At the same time when any attempt was made to infringe on the rights of the British Government or its subjects, I spoke in very unmistakable language. I think the Durbar gave me credit for good intentions and appreciated my desire to work with them; of course they tried to get all they could out of me, and it was a daily, but, on the whole, friendly struggle between us. I knew perfectly well that to exalt themselves, the Court party spoke of me behind my back in disparaging terms, and boasted of what they could do, and of their independence of the British Government, but I was quite satisfied that they did not believe what they said, and that in all important matters they deferred to me on every point, and were always coming to me to help them out of difficulties. I kept in mind Colonel McCulloch's wise saying to the Rajah: "I don't care what you say of me, so long as you do as I tell you."

CHAPTER XIII.

Violent conduct of Prince Koireng—A rebuke—Service payment—Advantage of Manipuri system. Customs duty—Slavery—Releasing slaves—Chowba's fidelity—Sepoy's kindness to children—Visit to the Yoma range.

An incident occurred which might have caused some trouble, while it served to show the violent disposition of Kotwal Koireng, later known as the Senaputtee. One evening my Naga interpreter reported to me that an Angami Naga of Kohima had been cruelly assaulted by that prince, while he was passing along the road to the east of the palace enclosure. Soon after the man was brought in to me, and an examination by my native doctor proved that he was suffering from a severe contusion above the right eye, which might or might not prove fatal. Now, strictly speaking, the man was not a British subject, but some day or other he was sure to be one, and we had assumed an indefinite control over his people. This made me feel that passing over the offence as one not concerning us, would be to lose prestige with Manipur, as well as with the Naga tribes, who ought, I felt, to be assured of my sympathy. I therefore at once sent a strong remonstrance to the Durbar, claiming the man as a British subject, and demanding prompt recognition of, and reparation for the outrage. On further investigation it appeared, that the man was with some of his friends carrying a large joint of beef on his shoulder just as Kotwal Koireng was passing, and a few drops of blood fell on the ground; this enraged the Prince so much that he at once attacked the man with a thick stick which he carried, and beat him till he was almost senseless. There was no real provocation, as eating the flesh of cows that had died a natural death was always allowed, and any dead cow was at once handed over to the Nagas and other hill-tribes; it was simply an outburst of temper. The result was, that until the man's recovery was assured, Kotwal was held in a species of arrest; then he was released and sent with the Jubraj to make an apology to me; the man received a sum of money, and the affair ended amicably. I did not often come across the princes, though sometimes I met them out riding, and then we were very friendly. Once when I was walking out, I met one of the younger ones riding in state on an elephant, he forgot to make the usual salutation. This was reported to the Maharajah, who sent him with Thangal Major to apologize.

The Manipuris paid very little revenue in money, and none in direct taxes. The land all belonged to the Rajah, and every holding paid a small quantity of rice each year. The chief payment was in personal service. This system known by the name of "Lalloop," and by us often miscalled "forced labour," was much the same as formerly existed in Assam under its Ahom Rajahs. According to it, each man in the country was bound to render ten days' service out of every forty, to the Rajah, and it extended to every class in the community. Women were naturally exempt, but, among men, the blacksmith, goldsmith, carpenters, etc., pursued their different crafts in the Rajah's workshops for the stated time, while the bulk of the population, the field workers, served as soldiers, and made roads or dug canals, in fact executed great public works for the benefit of the state.

The system was a good one, and when not carried to excess, pressed heavily on nobody. It was especially adapted to a poor state sparsely populated. In such a state, under ordinary circumstances, where the amount of revenue is small, and the rate of wages often comparatively high, it is next door to impossible to carry out many much-needed public works by payment. On the other hand, every man in India who lives by cultivation, has much spare time on his hands, and the "Lalloop" system very profitably utilises this, and for the benefit of the community at large. I never heard of it being complained of as a hardship. The system in Assam led to the completion of many useful and magnificent public works. High embanked roads were made throughout the country, and large tanks, lakes, appropriately termed "seas," were excavated under this arrangement. Many of the great works of former ages in other parts of India are due to something of the same kind.

It was a sad mistake giving up the system in Assam, without retaining the right of the state to a certain number of days' labour on the roads every year, as is the custom to this day, I believe, in Canada, Ceylon, and other countries.

Unfortunately, our so-called statesmen are carried away by false ideas of humanitarianism, and a desire to pose in every way as the exponents of civilisation, that is the last fad that is uppermost, and the experience of ages and the real good of primitive people are often sacrificed to this *ignis fatuus.* I hear that "Lalloop" has been abolished in Manipur since we took the state in charge. We may live to regret it; the unfortunate puppet Rajah certainly will. Why cannot we leave well alone, and attack the real evils of India that remain still unredressed, evils that to hear of them, would make the hair of any decent thinking man stand on end? We have still to learn that the native system has much good in it, much to recommend it, and that it is in many cases the natural outgrowth of the requirements of the people.

Manipur in old days required very little to make it a model native state of a unique type, and its people the happiest of the happy. All it required was a better administration of justice, and a few smaller reforms, also more enlightened fiscal regulations such as many European states have not yet attained. Given these, no one would have wished for more. No one asked for high pay; enough to live on, and the system of rewards already in force from time immemorial, satisfied all aspirations. The people were contented and happy, and it should have been our aim and object to keep them and leave them so. Shall we have accomplished this desirable object when we hand over the state to its future ruler, that is if it ever does again come under a Native Government?

One of the standing grievances of the Government of India against Manipur, was the levying of customs duties on all articles imported into the state, and on some articles exported to British territory. These duties supplied almost the only money revenue the Maharajah had, and also to some extent protected Manipuri industries. During my tenure of office I did something towards regulating the system, and in the case of articles not produced in Manipur, induced the Durbar to lower the rates. In the case of cloths, however, I strongly advocated the duties being kept up, where, as in the case of coarse cloths the imports entered into competition with the excellent manufactures of Manipur, which I wished to see preserved in all their integrity.

Our system of free trade has done much to injure useful trades in India, and none more than those in cotton goods. Among an ignorant people the incentives of cheapness and outward appearance are so great, that the sudden importation of cheap and inferior foreign goods may kill out an ancient art, and the people only discover when too late what they have lost, and then lament having abandoned the really good for the attractive flimsy article. Thus, in many parts of India, the beautiful chintzes which were common thirty-five years ago, are now nowhere to be had, and every year sees the decay of some branch of manufacture. This was very noticeable in Assam, and the arts there lost were only kept up in Manipur, owing to its having a Native Court where tradition and taste encouraged them. Soon after I went to Manipur, I found that the valley had almost been drained of ponies by their exportation to Cachar. The ministers consulted me about it, and I gave my consent to the trade being stopped, and this was done for years until the numbers had again increased.

On the whole the duties on almost every article were lowered during my term of office, and the imports largely increased. Indeed, but for the cumbersome system of levying the custom charges, they would have been no grievance at all; and as it was they hardly added anything to the cost of the articles when sold in Manipur, many of which could be bought for little more than the price paid in Cachar, plus the charge for carriage.

Slavery of a mild form existed in Manipur, the slaves being hereditary ones, or people, and the descendants of people who had sold themselves for debt, their services being pledged as interest for the debt. For instance a Naga (a very common case), marries a girl of another Naga village, thereby incurring a debt of forty rupees to the father, that being the price of a Naga bride. The man not being able to pay, his father-in-law says, "Sell yourself, and pay me." This is done, and the man pays the forty rupees and has to work for his master till he can pay the debt, something being sometimes allowed for subsistence, or they agree upon a monthly payment, which if not paid is added to the principal. The wife probably works and supports the family, and, if the creditor is a fairly good fellow, things go smoothly, and the debtor never attempts to fulfil his obligations more than he can help. The law allows a man to transfer his services to any one who will take up the debt. Here and there great abuses crop up, and the master takes advantage of the corrupt courts to bind the slave more and more securely in the chains of debt, and then every effort is made to escape. I often paid the debts of slaves who came to me for help and let them work off the money. Once a little girl named Nowbee came to me. Her mother had sold her to pay her father's funeral expenses. She stayed with us, working in the nursery for years, and when I left I forgave her the remainder of her debt which was unpaid, as, of course, I did with all the others. I once offered to redeem the mother, who, in turn, had sold herself, but the old woman declined, as some one told her that we should take her to England, and she was afraid to go. Sometimes cases of very cruel ill-treatment came before me, or cases where people had been made slaves contrary to the laws, and then I made a strong remonstrance to the Durbar, and insisted on justice. Once or twice I took the complainants under my protection immediately, and insisted on keeping them. One day a young man and a small boy came to me for protection: the case was a bad one, and I at once took them into my service as the best way of settling the difficulty, the young man as a gardener and the boy to work in the kitchen and wait at table; both were named "Chowba," *i.e.* big; a name as common out there as John in England. We gave little Chowba clothes, and he stood behind my wife's chair at dinner, the first evening crying bitterly from fear. However, he learned his work, and became an excellent servant. When I went on leave in 1882, I offered to place him with my *locum tenens*, but the boy said, "No, sahib, you have been kind to me; I have broken your things and you have threatened to beat me, but have never done so; you have threatened to cut my pay, but have never done so; I will never serve any one but you!" The poor boy kept his word; he preferred hard toil, cutting wood and such-like work; but unfortunately died before I returned.

Another bad case I remember, in which a woman complained to me that her child had been stolen from her house while she was away. I ordered the child to be brought to me; the poor little thing was only four years old, and could hardly stand from having been made to walk a great distance by the man who had stolen her, and whose only excuse was, that her father, who was dead, owed him nine rupees. I gave her to her mother, and insisted on the Durbar punishing him. The story was a sad one. The father of the child, a debtor slave, had been told by his master to leave his home and go with him, and the man in desperation attempted to kill his wife and little girl, and then committed suicide.

While in Manipur I did all I could to afford relief in individual cases. It was a great abuse, but slavery in Manipur must not be put in the same rank as slavery in Brazil, the West Indies, or Turkey and Arabia. A thorough reform of the judicial system of Manipur would have entirely taken the sting out of it. All the same, I wish I could have abolished it.

My wife's nurse very speedily left us, and we were left to natives and did much better with them.

We always had three or four Naga girls who did their work well in a rough-and-ready way. Chowbee, Nembee, and Nowbee, just mentioned, were the best. Chowbee was the wife of a Naga bearer named Lintoo, and Nembee afterwards married our head bearer Horna. We engaged a tailor named Suleiman, brother of Sooltan, one of our chuprassies, as a permanent servant, to do the ordinary household sewing and mending. My two boys, Dick and Edward, became very friendly with all the people, and were drilled daily by a naick (corporal of my escort), and the good-natured sepoys used to allow themselves to be drilled by the boys. One afternoon, I met these two walking up the lines with my orderly. I asked what they were going for, and they replied that the sepoys had not done their drill well that day, and they were going to give them some more. Whenever a new detachment came, the boys were formally introduced to the new native officers and men. As they grew older they learned to ride, and rode out morning and evening when I went for a walk.

As the Burmese difficulty did not show signs of decreasing, I went out in February to Kongjang on the Yoma range, to reconnoitre and select a place for a new stockade, if necessary. At three and a half miles on my way, I passed Langthabal, the old capital of Ghumbeer Singh, a pretty place where the cantonment of the Manipur Levy used to be, and where Captain Gordon was buried under a tree. The ruined palace lies nestling under a hill, on a spur of which is a magnificent fir tree; behind the palace a garden run to waste and wood, with a few ponds, formed an admirable cover for ducks, which I saw in abundance. After leaving Langthabal, we passed a place called Leelong, the place of execution for members of the Royal family, who are sewn up in sacks and drowned in the river. Farther on is a great fishing weir, where a small lake discharges itself into a river. At last, after a march of thirty miles, I halted at Pullel, a village of low caste Manipuris. Next morning we ascended the Yoma range, reaching Aimole, a village picturesquely situated and inhabited by a tribe of that name. The head of the village was an intelligent old man, who remembered Captain Gordon and talked a good deal about him. I gave him a coat, and the girls and boys of the village got up a dance for my benefit, the most graceful and modest that I ever saw among a wild people.

I reached Kongjang in the afternoon, a place very picturesquely situated, with a fine view of the valley of the Lokchao and the hills beyond, and of a portion of the Kubo valley. I selected a spot for a stockade, and, after reconnoitring in the neighbourhood, marched back next day to Pullel, and thence to Manipur, again passing Langthabal. I never saw Langthabal without regretting its abandonment, there is something very charming about the situation, and it is nearer to Bissenpore on the Cachar road than Imphal; also a few miles nearer the Kubo valley. It has always had the reputation of being very healthy, which is not invariably the case with Imphal, and is, if anything, a little cooler. Before leaving in 1886, I strongly recommended it as the site for a cantonment, in the event of troops being stationed in the valley. My recommendation was adopted.

CHAPTER XIV.

An old acquaintance—Monetary crisis—A cure for breaking crockery—Rumour of human sacrifices—Improved postal system—Apricots and mulberries—A snake story—Search after treasure—Another snake story—Visit to Calcutta—Athletics—Ball practice—A near shave.

WE had not been dull in the Naga Hills, still less in Manipur, for I was always interested in native life. Something to vary one's work was constantly occurring.

One day some men in Shan costume came and asked me for a pass to enter Burmah. I inquired who they were, and one said he was the Chowmengti Gohain. I remembered him fourteen years before, at Sudya, in Assam, when he was but a boy. He was the son of a Khampti chief, long since dead. I asked him if he remembered me, and after a minute or two, he did. I managed to keep up a conversation in Singpho, though I had not spoken it for many years, and have never done so since. He was going to Mandalay to marry a daughter to the king.

Time went on fairly smoothly. I was occupied all day long, and used to talk for hours to the ministers and others who came to see me, while my wife looked after the house and children, and taught the Naga girls to knit and sew, and other useful things. When the weather grew too hot, we migrated to Kang-joop-kool, and enjoyed the change. About this time much dissatisfaction was caused by speculators in the capital hoarding "sel," the coin of the country. The usual rate at which they were exchanged for the rupee was 480 = 1 rupee, but there were occasional fluctuations; large sums were paid in rupees, but the amount was always reckoned in sel. Consequently, when the latter were hoarded, a man having only rupees in his possession found their purchasing power greatly diminished. On this occasion, almost all the "sel" in circulation were collected in a few hands and a panic was the result; the bazaar was in an uproar, and business ceased. I spoke to the Maharajah on the subject, and represented the very great injury to the country that would inevitably result if immediate steps were not taken to rectify the mischief done, and urged him to issue a large quantity of sel. This he did, and the exchange which had gone down to 240, at once rose to 400, and at this rate he fixed it, and so it remained all the time I was in Manipur.

Our Naga boys, though intelligent and willing to learn, were careless and often worse, as in playing and fighting with each other, they broke much crockery, and the loss was serious, as it took months to replace it. I threatened in vain, as I could not bear to make the poor lads pay. At last, in desperation, I hit upon a remedy; I said that the next time anything was broken, the breaker should pound it up to a fine powder with a pestle and mortar, and mix it with water and drink it. This threat had some effect, but at last one day the old cook brought up Murumbo, our musalchee (*i.e.* dishwasher) with a vegetable dish in pieces, broken, as usual, in play. I said very severely, "Very well, grind it to powder in a pestle and mortar, and then you shall mix it with water and drink it." So Murumboo sat for hours in the sun, pounding away. At last it was reduced to a fine powder, and I told him to mix it with water and drink it in my presence. Of course, what I had foreseen, happened, all the other servants headed by the old cook, Horna and Sultan, came up and humbly begged that he might be forgiven this time, a request which I graciously acceded to, and Murumboo went away very penitent. The result was excellent, as for the future I hardly lost any crockery. Poor Murumboo; he served me well, and became an excellent cook and got a good place when I finally left.

The summer and autumn passed quietly, except for a rumour that human sacrifices had been offered up, though no actual complaint was made. I believe the report to have been true. I had seen enough of countries where within a few years they had been undoubtedly offered, to know that such things did occasionally happen among ignorant people, where appeasing evil spirits is a common custom. I took such precautions as effectually prevented any recurrence of this horrible practice.

One reform carried out was in our postal arrangements. When I first arrived, the post, which came in every other day, frequently took eight days to reach us from Cachar, a distance of 132 miles. By altering the system, I reduced it to a maximum of four days, though it often came more quickly, and by constantly hammering at all concerned, I achieved the triumph of a daily post delivered in less than two days from Cachar before I left.

Once when riding between Manipur and Kang-joop-kool, I saw, in passing a small bazaar, a woman selling apricots. I made inquiries about them, and was told that they had existed from time immemorial, but that they would give me a violent internal pain if I ate them. I did try them, raw and cooked, but the statement was quite true, nothing made them agreeable, and I did suffer pain. They were probably introduced from China in early days, and having been neglected had degenerated. They blossom in January. I tried Himalayan apricots, and the trees throve wonderfully, but could never, while I was in Manipur, learn to blossom at the right time. They blossomed as they were accustomed to do in their native country, that is three months too late, and the fruit was destroyed by the early rains. Perhaps they have by this time adapted themselves to the climate. I introduced Kabulee mulberries and they did well, but those in the valley grew long like the Indian variety, while those at Kang-joop-kool were shaped like the common European mulberry, and very good to eat.

Another time when out riding in the evening, I witnessed a strange sight. I was near Kooak Kaithel when I saw a large number of sparrows assembled on the road in front, and perched on a clump of bamboos near; others were constantly joining them, and numbers were flying to the spot from all sides. They first joined the assemblage on the road, and then flew up to and around the bamboos, which were already covered with the first-comers. I asked one of my mounted orderlies what it all meant. He said that a snake was concealed among the bamboos, and that the birds were come to see him and try and drive him out. Whatever be the explanation, it was a very interesting sight, and I never at any time saw such a large number of small birds together. Once when riding along this same road, but farther on, in company with Thangal Major, I happened to see a deep hole freshly dug in the side of a hill, apparently without any object. I asked him what it was dug for, and he replied that it was probably some refugee returned to the land of his ancestors, who had dug it, in search for treasure buried during the Burmese invasion by a relation, who had left an exact description of the spot as a guide to any of his descendants who might return. He said that there were many cases of this kind. I used to hear the same story many years ago in Assam where the truth was never questioned, and many were the tumuli that bore the marks of having been opened by searchers "for buried gold." I never knew of an authentic case of the kind in Manipur, but doubtless old Thangal could tell of many such; possibly he had shared in the proceeds.

I have just related a story of birds attacking a snake, and I may as well tell another story in which one of his tribe was the aggressor. When returning from my cottage at Kang-joop-kool, after a day spent there in October, I saw an enormous python poised up on the high embanked road with its head erect, and body and tail in coils on the slope, ready to spring on some young buffaloes grazing near; it must have been at the lowest estimate thirty feet

SAMAGUDTING.

[*Page* 14.

long and of proportionate thickness. I was too near, and riding too fast, to stop my pony, so gave a loud shout, and urged him to speed, and the snake turned itself back and fell with a crash into a morass by the road side, and I saw no more of it. I spoke to Thangal Major about it, and he told me that pythons were known to exist about the place where I saw this. I once shot a young one on the Diphoo Panee river, near Sudya, which measured nine feet, and a sepoy of my old regiment shot one near Borpathar fifteen feet in length.

Several very deadly snakes abound in Manipur, notably the "Tanglei" and the "Ophiophagus," a terrible looking creature, eight to twelve feet in length. No house is safe from snakes, and in the old Residency one fell from the roof once in my bedroom, from where a few minutes previously the baby's bassinette had hung, so the child had a narrow escape. I never dare let the children play alone in the garden for fear of their being bitten.

The extreme loneliness of Manipur, and the necessity of leaving my wife and children quite alone sometimes, made me very anxious to get some trustworthy English nurse for her, but we quite failed in doing so. In this emergency, one of her sisters volunteered to come out, which was a great help and relief. As I had to go to Calcutta to see the Viceroy in December, we asked her to meet us there. We left Manipur on November 27th, 1878, and returned on January 23rd, bringing her with us. Kohima was occupied by the Political Agent of the Naga Hills (Mr. Damant), in November, and before leaving for Calcutta I had some correspondence with him, and, at his request, sent my escort—then consisting of Cachar Frontier Police; men, for service qualities in the hills, far superior to the Native Infantry I had—to his assistance.

In Calcutta, I met Sir Steuart Bayley, who had been lately appointed Chief Commissioner of Assam, and had interviews with the Viceroy, Lord Lytton, and the Foreign Secretary, Mr. (now Sir Alfred) Lyall.

Early in 1879, there was some discontent on account of the dearness of rice, owing to a deficient crop, but there was no real anxiety, as the stock of rice in hand was sufficient. I remember that during that time I was rather scandalised at hearing that the old Ranee had gone off to Moirang on the Logtak lake for change of air, accompanied by a retinue of over one thousand persons. Many people had been employed for weeks past in building a little temporary town for their accommodation, and all for five days' stay. I remonstrated with Thangal Major at this useless waste of resources at a time when food was scarce, and told him that he ought to prevent such thoughtlessness. He told me, and I believe sincerely, that he greatly regretted it, and promised to use his influence to amend matters, but said what was perfectly true, that if he gave good advice, there were plenty of people quite ready to offer the reverse, and contradict his statements. I often thought what an advantage it would have been, if we had insisted on all authority being in the hands of one powerful minister responsible to us. Under a strong man like Chandra Kirtee Singh there would have been some difficulty in arranging it, but under his weak, though amiable and intelligent successor, Soor Chandra, it would have been easy, and would have saved us one of the most painful and disgraceful episodes in our history.

Almost every day brought some exciting news from the frontier. One day, an incursion by Chussad Kukies on the Kubo side; another, an outrage committed by Sookti Kukies. Then a little later a report that the Muram Nagas were restless. All these reports came to me at once, and I had to decide what was to be done. Occasionally an expedition was the result, regarding the conduct of which I gave general instructions. Sometimes late at night a minister came to me in a high state of excitement at some outrage on the Burmese frontier, in which, of course, every one, from the Court of Mandalay downwards, was said to be implicated. Anything against Burmah was readily believed, and not without reason, perhaps, judging from past history, and I had, on the spur of the moment, to decide on the policy to be adopted, and calm down and convince my impulsive visitor.

Manipur is a great place for athletics, and some fine wrestling is to be seen there. Athletic sports are regularly held at stated periods, sometimes for Manipuris, at other times for Nagas. At the last there are races run by men, carrying heavy weights on their backs. At the conclusion of these exhibitions of strength and skill, four Manipuris, dressed in Naga costume, executed a Naga war dance. This I always thought the most interesting part of the performance, showing as in many other cases, the tacit acknowledgment of a connection with the hill-tribes surrounding them. It always reminded me of the same connection between the Rajahs in the hill tracts of Orissa, Sumbulpore and Chota Nagpore, and their aboriginal subjects. I am rather inclined to believe that in the case of Manipur some of the customs point distinctly to the Rajahs being descended from, or having been originally installed by, the hill-tribes, as was notably the case in Keonjhur one of the Cuttack Tributary Mehals. To this subject, however, I have already referred.

During each cold season, I insisted on the Manipuri troops being put through musketry practice with ball cartridge, and often attended for hours together, with the Maharajah, to see how the men acquitted themselves. Sometimes the firing went on all day, the targets being erected at one end of the private polo ground in the palace, with a mountain of rice straw in their rear to catch stray bullets. Sometimes the bullets went through everything, and one evening, as my wife and myself with the children, were taking our evening walk, we had ocular demonstration of this, as a shot passed close to my second boy's (Edward) head. I spoke to Thangal Major about it, suggesting that the pile of straw should be made thicker, but only elicited the reply, "Of course, if you go in the line of fire, you must expect to be shot." This reminded me of my early days in Assam, when my old regimental friend Ross shot another friend out snipe shooting. The latter complained, but all the satisfaction he got from Ross was, "Well, you must have been in the way."

CHAPTER XV.

Spring in Manipur—Visit to Kombang—Manipuri orderlies—Parade of the Maharajah's guards—Birth of a daughter—An evening walk in the capital—Polo—Visit to Cachar.

THE spring in Manipur is a charming time, the nights are still cool, though the days are hot, and abundance of flowering trees come into blossom; among them one that attains a considerable size, called in Manipuri "Chinghow." It has two kinds, one with pink and the other white and pink flowers. Out in the hills are wild pears and azaleas in abundance, and rhododendrons, while here and there are beautiful orchids. The oak forests too are splendid with the fresh young leaves, and every hill village has peach trees in flower, so that it is a delightful season for marching, and one can be out from morning till night. I took advantage of the fine weather, and early in April again visited the Yoma range, and went along the road to Jangapokee Tannah, as far as a place called Kombang, 4600 feet above the sea. On my way there and back I halted at Haitoo-pokpee, 2600 feet above the sea, where the thermometer at sunrise stood at 55 and 56 degrees respectively; but the day between, when I was at Kombang, it was 67 degrees at sunrise, the additional elevation raising the thermometer.

I noticed the phenomenon over and over again in Manipur, and in the cold weather generally found the sunrise temperature lower in the valley than in the hills. Upland valleys were sometimes colder than that of Manipur, and now and then to the north I found very great cold prevailing on high land, as at Mythephum. The day temperature in the hills was invariably lower than that in the valley, in short, it was more equable. The road to Kombang was pretty, but the place not particularly so. The night I was there I heard the loud crackling of a burning oak forest set on fire to clear the ground for *one crop*. It is difficult to speak with patience of this abominable system, which is gradually clearing the hills in Eastern India, and destroying valuable timber, while it encourages nomadic habits in the tribes.

Whenever I went on an expedition into the hills, besides the usual Manipuri Guard in attendance, four or five officers or non-commissioned officers were told off to accompany me. Jemadars Thamur Singh, Sowpa, Sundha, Thŭt-tôt, and Thûrûng were those generally sent, excellent men who never left me from morning till night, on the hardest march. Many was the adventure we had together, and any one of them could march fifty miles on end. They were well known throughout the hill territory of Manipur. A bugler always formed one of my party, and it was his duty to sound a lively quick march as we approached our camp in the evening. Of course, he always got a special reward from me on my return to headquarters.

One day the Maharajah invited me to attend a review of his regiment of guards called the "Soor Pultun."

I went, and he asked me whether he should put them through their manœuvres himself, or let one of his officers do it. Not wishing him, as I thought, to expose his ignorance, I suggested the last; but, to my surprise, he conducted the parade himself very creditably, giving the word of command in English with great clearness. The men's marching was poor, and the step not free enough, but otherwise they did well. They were fairly well up in the Light Infantry exercises of ten years back, and their drill generally was a slight modification of that of 1859. On this, as on most occasions, when an invitation was sent by the Maharajah, it was conveyed by two or three officers of not lower rank than that of subadar or captain, and generally by word of mouth. If I was away in camp all communications were by letter, sometimes accompanied by a verbal message.

On February 28th, 1879, we were gladdened by the birth of a little daughter. Being a girl, her arrival did not cause as much excitement as Arthur's, but when she was old enough to be carried out in a small litter, all the population turned out to see her, and passers-by would sometimes offer her a flower. How interesting our daily walks were. Turning to the left, after leaving our gate by the guard-house, we passed along by the wide moat surrounding the palace, and in which as has been said the great annual boat races were held. There, might be seen women washing their babies by the waterside in wooden tubs, cut out of a single block bought for the purpose. At every step, if in the evening, we passed or were passed by gaily clad women carrying baskets of goods to sell in the great bazaar, "Sena Kaithel," *i.e.*,

Golden Bazaar, assembled opposite the great gate of the palace, the picturesque structure already alluded to. In this bazaar the women sat in long rows on raised banks of earth, without any other covering in the rainy weather than large umbrellas. Here could be bought cloth of all kinds, ornaments, rice, etc., fowls and vegetables. Dogs were also sold for food. As a rule, articles of food other than fowls, were more plentiful in the morning bazaar. Blind people and other beggars would post themselves in different parts of the market, and women as they passed would give them a handful of rice, or any other article of food they possessed. Women are the great traders, and many would walk miles in the morning, and buy things in the more distant bazaars to sell again in the capital in the evening. It was not considered etiquette for men too often to frequent the bazaars, and few Manipuris did so, but crowds of hill-men were constantly to be seen there, and it presented a very gay and animated scene, the contrast between the snow-white garments of Manipuri men, the parti-coloured petticoats of the women, and the many-coloured clothes of the hill-men being very picturesque. Opposite the great gateway on the right-hand side, Royal proclamations were posted up. There, too, in presence of all the bazaar, offenders were flogged, generally with the utmost severity. This was, I am sorry to say, rather an attractive spectacle to foreigners. Going through the bazaar along a fine broad road, the only masonry bridge in the country was seen crossing the river, and on the opposite bank the road turned sharp to the left, and went off to Cachar. Before crossing it, and to the left was a piece of waste ground with a rather ill-looking tree in it, under which men were executed. Opposite, and to the right of the road, was the sight of the morning bazaar. Here I have seen boat-loads of pine-apples landed, fruit that would have done credit to Covent Garden.

Between the Residency grounds, the "Sena Kaithel" and the great road, was the famous polo ground, where the best play in the world might be seen. There was a grand stand for the Royal family on the western side, and one for myself on the north. Sunday evening was the favourite day, and then the princes appeared, and in earlier days the Maharajah. In my time one of the Maharajah's sons, Pucca Sena, and the artillery major, were the champion players. In Manipur, every man who can muster a pony plays, and every boy who cannot, plays on foot.

But to continue our walk. Passing the bazaar, we still skirt the palace, meeting fresh groups and turning sharp round at one of the angles of the moat, here covered with water lilies, come upon an exceedingly picturesque temple once shaded with a peepul tree (*Frecis religiosa*); this tree was torn off by the great earthquake of June 30th, 1880. Afterwards taking two turns to the right, and one to the left, and crossing a most dangerous-looking bamboo bridge, we came upon a piece of woodland on the opposite bank of the stream. This is the "Mah Wathee," a bit of forest left as it originally was for the wood spirits. It is now filled with monkeys, which are great favourites with my children who have brought rice for them which causes great excitement. But it is soon bedtime for the young monkeys, and the river being deep, they spring on to the backs of their mothers who swim across with them in the most human fashion. Saying good-night to the monkeys, we go homewards, passing Moirang Khung, a tumulus said to be the site of a battle between the Mungang and Moirang tribes; to this day a Moirang avoids it. We pass a couple of boys riding jauntily on one pony, determined to get as much pleasure out of life as they can. Finally, we reach home in time for a game with the children, and dinner.

I have alluded to the high esteem in which the game of polo was held in this, its native home, and of the splendid play that could be seen on Sundays. I never played myself, much as I should have enjoyed it. Had I been a highly experienced player, able to contend with the best in Manipur, I might have done so; but I did not think I was justified, holding the important position I did, in running the risk of being hustled and jostled by any one with whom I played: men whom I was bound to keep at arm's length. Had I done so I should have lost influence. I could not be hail-fellow-well-met, and though talking freely with all, I at once checked all disposition to familiarity, and people rarely attempted it.

Colonel McCulloch, it is true played, but he began life in Manipur as an Assistant Political Agent, and also did not succeed to office as I did, when our prestige had dwindled down to nothing.

In September 1879, hearing that Sir Steuart Bayley, Chief Commissioner and Acting Lieut.-Governor of Bengal, was about to visit Cachar, I went there to see him, performing the double journey including a night there, in less than seven days. It was the first time I had made the march in the rainy season, and I was greatly struck by the extreme beauty of the scenery which was much enhanced by the number of waterfalls, that a month later would have been dry. The masses of clouds and the clearness of the air when rain was not falling, added greatly to the effect, and I enjoyed the journey till I got to the low-lying land. There the mud, slush, and great heat were unpleasant. It was very satisfactory to be able to discuss the affairs of Manipur with the Chief Commissioner, as though I was not then directly under him, I was from my position very dependent on him, and was anxious to hear his views on many subjects.

CHAPTER XVI.

Punishment of female criminals—A man saved from execution—A Kuki executed—Old customs abolished—Anecdote of Ghumbeer Singh—The Manipuri army—Effort to re-organise Manipur levy—System of rewards—"Nothing for nothing"—An English school—Hindoo festivals—Rainbows—View from Kang-joop-kool.

MANIPUR professed to follow the old Hindoo laws, and accordingly no woman was ever put to death, or to very severe punishment. When one was convicted of any heinous or disgraceful offence she was exposed on a high platform in every bazaar in the country, stripped to the waist, round which a rope, one end of which was held by her guard, was tied and her breasts painted red. A crier at the same time proclaimed her crime, and with a loud voice called out from time to time, "Come and look at this naughty woman!"

Exposure on a platform was also a punishment inflicted occasionally on male offenders. Sometimes it was followed by death. Once I saved a man from this part of the sentence, his crime being one for which our law would not have exacted so severe a penalty. Fortunately, I heard in time, and a message to the Maharajah in courteous, but unmistakable terms, brought about a remission of the capital portion. The ministers generally consulted me before carrying out sentence of death. Once in a case of murder by a Kuki they asked my opinion, so I requested them to send the man to me that I might examine him myself. This was done, and as he confessed openly to being guilty, I told them they might execute him, and as an after-thought said "How shall you put him to death?" Bularaam Singh replied, "According to the custom of Manipur, in the way in which he committed the murder. As he split his victim's head open with an axe so will his head be split open." I said "I have no objection in this case on the score of humanity, but it is not a pretty mode of execution; some day there will be a case accompanied by circumstances of cruelty, when I shall be obliged to interfere; so take my advice, and on this occasion and all future ones, adopt decapitation as the mode of carrying out a death sentence. You can do it now with a good grace, and without any apparent interference on my part to offend your dignity." Old Bularaam Singh said, "Oh no, the laws of Manipur are unalterable, we cannot change; we must do as we have always done." I said, "Nonsense, my old friend, go with Chumder Singh (my native secretary and interpreter) and give my kind message to the Maharajah, and say what I advise, as his friend." In half-an-hour Chumder Singh returned with an assurance that my advice was accepted, and from that time decapitation was the form of capital punishment adopted.

I never knew a case of torture being employed, but otherwise the laws were carried out with severity. Ghumbeer Singh (reigned 1825–34) occasionally tore out an offender's eyes, but such things had been forgotten in the days of his son, and though the Government was strong, probably there were fewer acts of cruelty than in most native states. Once when Ghumbeer Singh had lately introduced tame geese into the country; he gave two to a Brahmin to take care of. It was reported that a goose was dead. "Tell the Brahmin to eat it," said the indignant Rajah. The severity of such an order to a Hindoo will be appreciated, by any one knowing what loss of caste entails. Ghumbeer Singh's orders were always implicitly obeyed, so I am afraid that the sentence was carried into effect.

The army consisted of about 5000 men at the outside, in eight regiments of infantry and an artillery corps. The famous cavalry was a thing of the past, and many of the infantry were quite unacquainted with drill. There were eight three-pounder brass guns, and two seven-pounder mountain guns given as a reward for services in the Naga Hills, one of which did admirable service in the Burmese war. Most of the infantry were armed with smooth-bore muskets, some being of the Enfield pattern. Besides the above, there were about 1000 to 12,000 Kuki Irregulars. A Manipuri military expedition was a strange sight, the men besides their arms and ammunition carrying their spare clothes, cooking vessels, food, etc., on their backs. All the same, they could make long and tiring marches day after day on poor fare and without a complaint, and at the end of a hard day would hut themselves and fortify their position with great skill, however great the fatigue they had undergone. It was a standing rule that in an enemy's country a small force should always stockade itself, and a Manipuri army well commanded was then able to hold its own against a sudden attack. On their return from a successful expedition the troops were greatly honoured, and the general in command accorded a kind of triumph, and it was an interesting sight to see the long thin line of picturesque and often gaily-clad troops, regulars and irregulars winding their way through the streets and groves of the capital bearing with them spoils and trophies gained in war. Here a party headed by banners, there some Kukis beating small gongs and chanting in a monotonous tone. Finally, after marching round two sides of the palace, they enter by the great gate, pass between the Chinese walls, and again between the two lions (so called), and being received by the Maharajah at the Gate of Triumph, their General throws himself at his feet and receives his chief's benediction, the greatest reward that he can have.

I realised from the first that it would be an immense advantage to reconstitute the Manipur Levy, and keep up a permanent force of 800 men under my direct orders, properly paid, armed, clothed and disciplined. I foresaw that a war with Burmah was a mere question of time, and wished to have a force ready, so as to enable the British Government to act with effect at a moment's notice through Manipur, on the outbreak of hostilities. Regular troops eat no more than irregular, and are ten times as valuable. My plan was to have 800 men enlisted, of whom 200 would have come on duty in rotation, according to the Manipur system, all being liable to assemble at a moment's notice. Thus a splendid battalion of hardy men could have been formed, with which I could have marched to Mandalay. Such a force would have been absolutely invaluable when the war broke out in 1885, men able to stand the climate, march, fight, row boats, dig, build stockades, in fact do all that the best men could be called upon to do. However, to my great disappointment, the idea did not commend itself to Government, and I never ceased to regret it. I often later on thought of the lives and money that might have been saved in 1885–86 had we been better prepared, the cost of the proposed levy would have been trifling.

One part of the Manipuri system ever struck me as very admirable, and I tried always to encourage it; that was the system of rewarding services by honorary distinctions. The permission to wear a peculiar kind of turban, coat, or feather, or to assume a certain title was more valued than any money reward, and men would exert themselves for years for the coveted distinction. It is charming to see such simple tastes and to aspire no higher than to do one's duty and earn the approval of our fellow-creatures.

One day the two ministers Thangal Major and Bularaam Singh came to see me, accompanied by old Rooma Singh Major. They looked rather uneasy, and I suspected something was coming out. Presently Thangal rose and saluted me, and said, "The Maharajah has promoted us to be generals." I received the intelligence without any enthusiasm, feeling assured that the act had been dictated by a desire to give them a more high-sounding title than my military one, I being then only a lieut.-colonel. It was in fact a piece of self-assertion. Any one understanding Asiatics will know what I mean, and that I knew instinctively it was a move in the game against me which I ought to check. I coldly replied that of course the Maharajah would please himself, but that I loved old things, old names, and old faces, and that I had so many pleasant associations with the old titles that I could not bring myself to use the new ones, and should continue to call them by the dear old name of Major. I then shook hands with them most cordially and said good-bye, and they left rather crestfallen, where they had hoped and intended to be triumphant. I may as well tell the remainder of the story. Time after time was I begged to address my three friends as "General," but I was inexorable, and the titles almost fell into disuse among the Manipuris who had at first adopted them. Old Thangal once had a long talk about it, and I said plainly, "I give nothing for nothing: some day when you do something I shall address you as General." Years passed. I went on leave, and my *locum tenens* too good-naturedly gave in, and addressed them as General, and even induced the Chief Commissioner of the day to do likewise. When he wrote to me and told me of it, I was naturally not very pleased, and mentioned it to an old Indian friend, who said, "Well, you will have to do the same now that the Chief Commissioner has." However, I was not going to swerve from my word. I returned to Manipur, and one of the ministers met me on the boundary river. I again greeted him as "Major Sahib," and immediately the new titles again began to fall into disuse. I told the Chief Commissioner my views when I next met him, and he approved, as I said I could not alter my word.

Some time after this I again renewed efforts that I had long been making for the establishment of an English school in Manipur. The Durbar naturally objected; wisely from their point of view, they knew as well as I did that the fact of their subjects learning English would eventually mean a better administration of justice, and a gradual sweeping away of abuses. I felt, however, that the time was come, and I urged the question with great force, and one day said to the ministers, "You have long wanted to be addressed as 'General,' and I told you that when you did something worthy of it I should do so. Now the day that the Maharajah gives his consent to an English school being established, I shall address you as General." A few days afterwards the Maharajah's consent was brought. I immediately stood up and shook hands most warmly with them, saying, "I thank you cordially, Generals." From that day the question was finally set at rest, after years of longing on the part of the old fellows. We had always understood each other, and they felt and respected the part I had taken, and, I believe, valued their titles all the more from my not having given in at once.

The Rath Jatra Festival, *i.e.*, the drawing of the Car of Juggernaut, is greatly honoured in Manipur, and every village has its Rath (car). The Dewali, the feast of lights, is also faithfully kept. Also the Rathwal, one of the feasts of Krishna, when there are many dances, and an enormous bird is cleverly constructed of cloth with a bamboo framework, and a man inside, who struts about to the delight of the children. The Koli Saturnalia is also duly celebrated; the red powder "Abeer," is thrown about amongst those who can get it, and the burning of the temporary shrines lights up the sky at night, and the holes where the poles stood, are a fertile source of danger to ponies and pedestrians for weeks afterwards. The Durga Poojah is kept, but is a feast of minor importance. At the Rath Jatra the number of people drawn together was enormous, and the white mass could be very distinctly seen from Kang-joop-kool with a telescope, when the weather was clear. This view was sometimes obscured by clouds, and often when staying there did I wake up to see the whole of the valley filled up with fog, like a vast sea of cotton-wool, stretching across to the Yoma range of hills many miles away.

Lunar rainbows were not uncommon in Manipur, and I often saw them from Kang-joop-kool. Often, too, from thence have I seen a complete solar rainbow, each end resting on the level surface of the valley. Once, in riding to Sengmai on a misty morning, I saw a white rainbow rising from the ground; a fine and weird sight it was.

The view over the valley at night from the surrounding hills was sometimes wonderful. I never shall forget one night in the rainy season, when the moon was shining brightly in the valley, but obscured from my view by an intervening cloud; the bright reflection on the watery plain sent out a long stream of light which brightened up the glistening temples of the Capelat. This, and the dim hills in the distance, and the whole amphitheatre enclosed by them lighted up faintly, while the dark threatening cloud hanging in air between me and the rising moon, that had not yet apparently reached my level (I was 2500 feet above the valley, and seemed to be looking down on the moon), made a picture never to be forgotten.

CHAPTER XVII.

Mr. Damant—The Naga Hills—Rumours on which I act—News of revolt in Naga Hills and Mr. Damant's surrender—Maharajah's loyalty—March to the relief of Kohima—Relief of Kohima—Incidents of siege—Heroism of ladies—A noble defence.

In November, 1878, Mr. Damant removed the headquarters of the Naga Hills District from Samagudting to Kohima, and established himself there with his party, in two stockades. He had a very ample force for maintaining his position, but he had not sufficient to make coercing a powerful village an easy task. He was an able man, with much force of character, high-minded and upright, and had been greatly respected in Manipur, where he acted as Political Agent for some months after Dr. Brown's death. He was also a scholar, and was perhaps the only man of his generation in Assam capable of taking a comprehensive view of the languages of the Eastern Frontier, and searching out their origin. His premature death was an irreparable loss to philology.

With all this he had not had sufficient experience with wild tribes to be a fit match for the astute Nagas, and was constantly harassed by the difficulty in the way of securing supplies, which ought to have been arranged for him, in the early days of our occupation of Samagudting, by making terms with the Nagas as to providing food carriage. It was his misfortune that he inherited an evil system. We had been forced into the hills by the lawlessness of the Naga tribes, and we ought to have made them bear their full share of the inconveniences attendant on our occupation, instead of making our own people suffer.

Mr. Damant at first contemplated getting his supplies from Manipur, through the Durbar, but they objected, it being their traditional policy to prevent the export of rice for fear of famines, the distance and cost of transport making the import, in case of scarcity, an impossibility. I declined to put pressure, as I saw the reasonableness of the Durbar argument, and I objected to force the hill population of Manipur to spend their time in carrying heavy loads, to save the turbulent and lazy Angamis. In September, 1879, however, I heard a rumour from native sources that Mr. Damant was in great difficulties and straits for want of provisions,* and I wrote and told him that if it were true, I would make every effort to send him some supplies, and to help him in every way I could. I did not receive any answer to this letter, and subsequently ascertained that it had never reached him.

I knew the Angamis well, and was very anxious about Mr. Damant and his party, and felt sure that some trouble was at hand.

About this time my wife's health began to give me much anxiety; she had one or two severe attacks of illness, and was much reduced in strength. Who

* It will be seen later on that this rumour was not correct.—Ed.

that has not experienced it can imagine the terrible, wearing anxiety of life on a distant frontier, without adequate medical aid for those nearest and dearest to us. She was better, though still very weak, when an event occurred that shook the whole frontier.

Early in the morning of October 21st, I received a report from Mao Tannah, the Manipuri outpost on the borders of the Naga Hills, to the effect that a rumour had reached the officer there, that the Mozuma Nagas had attacked either Kohima, or a party of our men somewhere else, and had killed one hundred men. I have already mentioned my anxiety about Mr. Damant's position, and there was an air of authenticity about the report which made me feel sure that some catastrophe had occurred, and that he was in sore need. I said to Thangal Major, "We will take off fifty per cent. for exaggeration, and even then the garrison of Kohima will be so weakened that it is sure to be attacked, and there will be a rising in the Naga Hills."

I instantly took my resolve and detained my escort of the 34th B.I., which had just been relieved by a party of Frontier Police, and was about to march for Cachar. I also applied to the Maharajah for nine hundred Manipuris, and sufficient coolies to convey our baggage. He at once promised them, and I made arrangements to march as soon as the men were ready; but there was some delay, as the men had to be collected from distant villages. The next morning, before sunrise, Thangal Major came to see me, bringing two letters from Mr. Cawley, Assistant Political Agent, Naga Hills, and District Superintendent of Police. The letters told me that Mr. Damant had been killed by the Konoma men, and that he and the remainder were besieged in Kohima, and sorely pressed by Nagas of several villages. Immediately after this, the Maharajah himself came and placed his whole resources at my disposal, and asked me what I would have. I said two thousand men, and he replied that that was the number he himself thought necessary, and asked if he should fire the usual five alarm guns, as a signal to call every able-bodied man to the capital. I consented, and in ten minutes they thundered forth their summons. Coolies to carry the loads were the chief difficulty, as they, being hill-men, lived at a greater distance. I also despatched a special messenger to Cachar to ask for more troops and a doctor; and I made arrangements for assisting them on the road. I despatched two hundred Manipuris by a difficult and little-frequented path to Paplongmai (Kenoma*), to make a diversion in the rear of Konoma, as, from all I heard, it seemed that the astute Mozuma was not involved. I sent on a man I could trust to the Mozuma people, to secure their neutrality. I also sent my Naga interpreter, Patakee, to Kohima, to do his best to spread dissension amongst its seven different clans and prevent their uniting against me. I gave him a pony, and told him to ride it till it dropped under him, and then to march on foot for his life, and promised him 200 rupees reward if he could deliver a letter to Mr. Cawley before the place fell. In the letter I begged Mr. Cawley to hold out to the last as I was marching to his assistance.

* A different place from Konoma.—Ed.

One day, about a year before, a fine young Naga of Viswema, a powerful village of 1000 houses, a few miles beyond the frontier of Manipur and right on our track, had come to me and asked me to take him into my service. I did so, thinking he might be useful some day, and now that the day had arrived, I sent him off to his people to win them over, threatening to exterminate them if they opposed my march.

I had fifty men of the Cachar Police and thirty-four of the 34th B.I., including two invalids, one of them a Naik, by name Buldeo Doobey, who came out of hospital to go with me, as I wanted every man who could shoulder a musket. For the same reason I enlisted a volunteer, Narain Singh, a fine fellow, a Jât* from beyond Delhi, who had served in the 35th B.I., so he took a breach-loader belonging to a sick man of the 34th. I shall refer to him again. He carried one hundred and twenty rounds of ball cartridge on his person, three times as much as the men of the 34th. I sent off my combined escort with all the Manipuris who were ready under Thangal Major, and stayed behind to collect and despatch supplies and write official letters and send off telegrams to Sir Steuart Bayley, and on the 23rd rode out, and caught up my men at Mayang Khang, forty miles from Manipur. The rear-guard of the 34th had not come up when I went to bed that night at 11 P.M.

I left my poor wife still very weak and I was thankful that she had her good sister as a stay and support. Just before leaving, our youngest boy

* A Sikh.—ED.

Arthur held out his arms to be taken. I paused from my work for a moment and took him. It was the last time I saw him. Sad as was my parting, I rode off in high spirits; who would not do so when he feels that he may be privileged to do his country signal service! Besides, I hoped to find all well when I returned.

We left Mayang Khang on October 24th and marched to Mythephum, twenty miles along a terribly difficult mountain path, much overgrown by jungle. It was all I could do to get the 34th along, as they were completely knocked up. I had a pony which I lent for part of the way to one of my invalids and so helped him on. I was continually obliged to halt myself and wait for the stragglers, cheer them up, and then run to the front again. Narain Singh was invaluable and seemed not to know fatigue. We reached Mythephum after dark, but the rear-guard did not arrive till next morning.

At Mythephum I mustered my forces. The Maharajah had sent the Jubraj and Kotwal Koireng with me (little did I think of the fate in store for them and for old Thangal*) and found that very few Manipuris had arrived, and almost all of the force with me were so knocked up that, to my intense disappointment, I had to make a halt. I was too restless to sit still, so spent the day in reconnoitring the country. In the evening I had an interview with Thangal Major and afterwards with the Jubraj.

* The Jubraj, who afterwards reigned as the Maharajah Soor Chandra Singh, died in exile; Kotwal Koireng and Thangal Major were hanged in August, 1891, by order of the sentence passed upon them for resisting the British Government.—Ed.

Old Thangal was for halting till we could collect a large force as he said a large one was required, and he begged me to halt for a few days. I finally pointed out that a day's halt might cause the annihilation of the garrison of Kohima, and said that if the Manipuris were not ready to move, I would go along with any of my own men who could march. I appealed to the Jubraj to support me which he did,* and for which I was ever grateful, and we arranged to march next day. I found that the Nagas of Manipur were infected with a rebellious spirit, and not entirely to be depended on, and any vacillation on our part might have been fatal, and would certainly have sealed the fate of Kohima.

We left Mythephum at daybreak on the 26th, and marched as hard as we could, as I hoped to cover the forty miles to Kohima by nightfall. We stopped to drink water at the Mao river, which we forded, and to prevent men wasting time, I drew my revolver and threatened to shoot any one who dawdled. We ascended the steep hillside, and passing through one of the villages marched on to Khoijami, a village on the English side of the border. We had been so long, owing to the extreme badness of the roads, and the fatigue of the men, that we only reached it at 3 P.M., so I reluctantly halted for the night.

Here my emissary to Viswema joined me, and told me that he had induced his fellow-villagers to be friendly, and that presents would be sent. I sent him back to demand hostages, and the formal sub-

* In 1891, the Jubraj, then the ex-Maharajah, brought forward this fact in his appeal to the British Government, as a reason for his restoration.—ED.

mission of the village, as otherwise I would attack them on the morrow and spare no one. It was not a time for soft speeches, and I heard rumours that we were to be opposed next day.

Late in the afternoon some Mao Nagas brought in seven Nepaulee coolies who had escaped from Kohima the previous day, and wandered through the jungle expecting every moment to be killed. I gave the Mao men twenty rupees as a reward. The Nepaulees said that they had been shut outside the gate of the stockade by mistake, and had hidden themselves and so got away. They gave a deplorable account of affairs, and said that there was no food, and that the ammunition was almost all spent, and that two ladies were in the stockade, Mrs. Damant and Mrs. Cawley. They stated that Mr. Damant was taken unawares and shot dead, and fifty men killed on the spot, and that thirty ran away and hid in the jungles, some saving their arms, others not. Each man had fifty rounds of ball cartridge. Most of the rifles lost were breech-loaders. The men told me that early that morning they had seen smoke rising from Kohima, and thought it might have been burned.

All this made me very anxious, as the men said that Mr. Cawley was treating for a safe passage to Samagudting. Late in the evening I heard that a building inside the stockade had been burned by the Nagas, who threw stones wrapped in burning cloth on to the thatched roofs. The Nagas in arms were said to number six thousand, and they had erected a stockade opposite ours from which they fired. The fugitives were in a miserable state of semi-starvation, and ashy pale from terror, and seemed more dead than alive when they were brought to me. We slept on our arms that night, at least such as could sleep, and rose at 3 A.M. in case of an attack, that being a favourite time for the Nagas to make one.

When ready, I addressed my men, telling them the danger of the enterprise, but assuring them of its success, and urging them, in case of my being killed or wounded, to leave me and push on to save the garrison. I promised the Frontier Police that every man should be promoted if we reached Kohima safely that night. This promise the Government faithfully kept.

At sunrise I received two little slips of paper brought by two Nepaulese coolies who had managed to escape, signed by Mr. Hinde, Extra Assistant Commissioner, and hidden by them in their hair. On them was written :—

> Surrounded by Nagas, cut off from water
> Must be relieved at once. Send flying
> column to bring away garrison at once.
> Relief must be immediate to be of any use
> H. M. Hinde. A. P. A. Kohima. 25 x. 79.

and—

> We are in extremity, come on sharp
> Kohima not abandoned.
> Kohima not abandoned
> H. M. Hinde. A. P. A. 26 x. 79.

After getting these, I could not wait any longer, and, as the Manipuris were not all ready, I started off at once with fifty of them under an old officer, Eerungba Polla and sixty of my escort, all that were able to make a rapid march, and Narain Singh. We carried with us my camp Union Jack.

I obtained hostages from Viswema and placed them under a guard with orders to shoot them instantly, if we were attacked, and on our arrival at the village we were well received. At Rigwema, as we afterwards discovered, a force of Nagas was placed in ambush to attack us, but the precautions we took prevented their doing so, and we passed on unmolested, and soon had the satisfaction of seeing the stockade at Kohima still intact. A few miles farther, and on rounding the spur of a hill, the stockade appeared in full view and we sounded our bugles which were quickly answered by a flourish from Kohima.

We marched on with our standard flying, we reached the valley below, we began the ascent of the last slope, and forming into as good order as the ground would allow, we at last gained the summit and saw the stockade, to save which, we had marched so far and so well, before us at a distance of one hundred yards.

The garrison gave a loud cheer, which we answered, and numbers of them poured out. Messrs. Cawley and Hinde grasped my hand, and others of the garrison formed a line on either side of the gateway, and we marched in between them. I recognised many old faces not seen since I had left the Naga Hills in 1874, and warmly greeted them; especially Mema Ram, a Subadar in the Frontier Police; Kurum Singh, and others. I was told afterwards that when Mema Ram first heard that I was marching to their relief, he said, "Oh, if Johnstone Sahib is coming we are all right."

I at once told the officers of the garrison that

Colonel Johnstone, the Princes of Manipur, Thangal Major, the European Officers in Kohima, etc.

[Page 157.

there could be no divided authority, and that they must consider themselves subject to my orders, to which they agreed. I then saw the poor widowed Mrs. Damant, and Mrs. Cawley who had behaved nobly during the siege. While talking to the last, one of her two children asked for some water. Her mother said in a feeling tone, "Yes, my dear, you can have some now." Seldom have I heard words that sounded more eloquent.

The Manipuris now began to pour in, in one long stream, and were greeted by the garrison with effusion, and I gave them the site of a stockade that had been destroyed by Mr. Cawley, in order to reduce the space to be defended as much as possible, and told them to stockade themselves, which they did at once. After arranging for the defence of our position, I sent off a letter to my wife to say that I was safe, and that Kohima had been relieved, and telegrams to the Chief Commissioner, and Government of India, to be sent on at once to Cachar, the nearest telegraph office, informing them of the good news.

It appeared from what Mr. Cawley told me, that on the 14th of October, Mr. Damant had gone to Konoma from Jotsoma, to try and enforce some demands he had made. He had been warned several times that the Merema Clan of Konoma meant mischief, and several Nagas had implored him not to go, and finding him deaf to their entreaties, begged him to go through the friendly Semema Clan's quarter of the village. However, he insisted on having his own way, and went to the gate of the Merema Clan at the top of a steep, narrow path. The gate was closed, and while demanding an entrance, he was shot dead. His men were massed in rear of him, and a large number were at once shot down, while the others took to flight. Some of the fugitives reached Kohima that night, and Mr. Cawley at once, grasping the gravity of the situation, pulled down one stockade, and dismantled the buildings as already related, concentrating all his men in the other, and making it as strong as possible. The neighbouring villages had already risen, and were sending contingents to attack Kohima.

Mr. Cawley had just time to send a messenger to Mr. Hinde, the extra-Assistant Commissioner at Woka, a distance of sixty-three miles, ordering him to come in with the detachment of fifty police under him. These orders Mr. Hinde most skilfully carried out, by marching only at night, and on the 19th he reached Kohima, thus strengthening the garrison and making it more able to hold its own, for the number of the attacking party now greatly increased.

Most fortunately, owing to the zealous care of Major T. N. Walker, 44th R. L. Infantry, there were some rations in reserve for the troops, which were shared with the non-combatants and police. These he had insisted on being collected and stored up, when he paid a visit of inspection to Kohima some months before. But for this small stock the place could not have held out for two days, but must inevitably have fallen, as all supplies were cut off during the progress of the siege. The water was poisoned by having a human head thrown into it. The Nagas fired at the stockade continually, but made no regular assault. They seemed to have tried picking off every man who showed himself, and starving out the garrison. The quantity of jungle that had been allowed to remain standing all round afforded them admirable cover, and, as before stated, they erected another small stockade from which to fire. This they constantly brought nearer and nearer by moving the timbers.

At length, the garrison wearied out, entered into negotiations, and agreed to surrender the stockade, if allowed a free passage to Samagudting. This fatal arrangement would have been carried into effect within an hour or two, had not my letter arrived assuring them of help. What the result would have been no one who knows the Nagas can doubt; 545 headless and naked bodies would have been lying outside the blockade. Five hundred stands of arms, and 250,000 rounds of ammunition would have been in possession of the enemy, enough to keep the hills in a blaze for three years, and to give employment to half-a-dozen regiments during all that time, and to oblige an expenditure of a million sterling, to say nothing of valuable lives.*

Throughout the siege, Mrs. Damant, and Mrs. Cawley had displayed much heroism. The first undertook to look after the wounded, and went to visit them daily, exposed to the enemy's fire. Mrs. Cawley took charge of the women and children of

* The savage mode in which the Nagas conduct their warfare is vividly described by a correspondent of the *Englishman* writing from Cachar, January 28, 1880, after a raid on the Baladhun Tea Gardens by a band of the same tribe as those of Konoma. He ends with "The whole was a horribly sickening scene, and a complete wreck; and such surely as none but the veriest of devils in human form could have perpetrated."—ED.

the sepoys, and looked after them, keeping them in a sheltered spot. The poor little children could not understand the situation at all, or why it was that the Nagas were firing.

The casualties would have been more numerous than they were, but that the Nagas were careful of the cherished ammunition, and seldom fired, unless pretty sure of hitting. All the same, the situation was a very critical one, and not to be judged by people sitting quietly at home by their firesides. It is certainly a very awful thing, after a great disaster and massacre, to be shut up in a weak stockade built of highly inflammable material, and surrounded by 6000 howling savages who spare no one. In addition to that too, to have the water supply cut off, and at most ten days' full provision; for this was what it amounted to. It must be also remembered that the non-combatants far out-numbered the combatants, and that the two officers who undertook the defence were both civilians. Anyhow, the view taken of it by the defenders is shown by the fact that they were willing to surrender to the enemy, rather than face the situation and its terrible uncertainty any longer, as they were quite in doubt as to whether relief was coming or whether their letters having miscarried they would be left to perish.

Looking back, after a lapse of fifteen years, and calmly reviewing the events connected with the siege of Kohima, I think I was right at the time in describing the defence as a "noble one."

CHAPTER XVIII.

Returning order and confidence—Arrival of Major Evans—Arrival of Major Williamson—Keeping open communication—Attack on Phesama—Visit to Manipur—General Nation arrives—Join him at Suchema—Prepare to attack Konoma—Assault of Konoma.

Early on the morning of the 28th, I took out all the men I could collect and set to work to clear away the jungle in the neighbourhood of the stockade so as to give no covert to enemies. I also did my utmost to collect supplies. Kohima, with its twelve hundred houses, was able to give a little, and I sent to distant villages. I also sent to the head-man of Konoma to ask for Mr. Damant's body. The man at once sent in the head, but said that the body had been destroyed. A true statement, I have no doubt, as the head is all the Nagas value, and the body would have been given up instantly had it existed. His signet ring, and several other little articles were also sent. The head was buried with due honours, the Manipuri chiefs drawing up their men and saluting as the funeral procession passed. The Jubraj, Soor Chandra Singh, spoke very feelingly on the subject.

The watercourse, which formerly supplied the garrison, had been diverted, and the only other supply had been, as already stated, poisoned by a head being thrown into it. My first business was to see that the water communication was restored, to every one's comfort. Some of my old acquaintances among the Nagas began to come in, and there was a great disposition to be friendly.

The next day a sepoy of the 43rd, who had escaped the massacre and lived in the jungle, was brought in by some friendly Nagas. He was almost out of his mind, and nearly speechless from terror, and could not walk, so was carried on the man's back.

I made up my mind to attack Konoma as soon as I could, and the people knowing this, tried negotiations with my Manipuri allies. So great was the fear we inspired that at first I believe I could without difficulty have imposed more severe terms than were obtained later on after four months' fighting. With Asiatics especially, everything depends on the vigour with which an enterprise is pushed forward. The Nagas never expecting an attack from the side of Manipur, were at first paralysed. All the villages were without any but the most rudimentary defences, in addition to those which nature had given them from their position; not one of them could have stood against a well-directed attack.

I was in the midst of my preparations when, on the 30th October, Major (now Major-General) Evans, of the 43rd Assam Light Infantry, arrived with two hundred men, who had come with him from Dibroogurh. I also received a telegram saying that General Nation was coming up with one thousand men and two mountain-guns, and might be expected on the 9th November. I was also given strict orders to engage in no active operations till his arrival. These orders I at first disregarded, feeling the urgent necessity of instant action before the Nagas had time to recover from their surprise. However, next day the order was reiterated so strongly, and in the Chief Commissioner's name, that, believing that the Government had some special reason for the order, I accepted it, much to my disappointment, as I felt the urgent necessity of an immediate advance. Konoma was still unfortified, and a few days would have sufficed to capture it, and place the Naga Hills at our feet. As it was, the delay, not till November 9th, but November 22nd, owing to defective transport arrangements, gave the enemy time to recover, and when we tardily appeared before Konoma, we found a scientifically defended fortress, whose capture cost us many valuable lives. The order, it subsequently appeared, was not issued by Sir Steuart Bayley,* and was altogether due to a misapprehension.

* The order came in a telegram purporting to be from the Chief Commissioner, and by whom really transmitted is a mystery. The Deputy-Assistant Quartermaster General's Report of this Naga Hill Expedition states, that after Lieutenant-Colonel Johnstone's Kuki levies had attacked Phesama, and killed about two hundred of the enemy in consequence of the loss of some of their own men from an assault from this village, the Manipuri army performed no other operation in this war (except as coolies and bringing in supplies, and in this respect they were invaluable). But he adds, "Colonel Johnstone, it is understood, was anxious to attack Konoma on his own account without waiting for General Nation and the troops." Colonel Johnstone explained in a memorandum that no arrangements had been made by the military authorities for the carriage of the guns, and that up to the evening before the attack on Konoma he had received no request for coolies, but foreseeing some neglect of this kind he had kept over one hundred reliable Manipuris for the work, and without them the guns could not have gone into action. As to the rest of his levy, they had lost three hundred men by sickness, and like all irregulars, had been injured by the long delay and enforced idleness. They had also been already fired upon by our troops in mistake for Nagas, and he feared some unfortunate complication

As there was to be no immediate work, I urged Major Evans to take up his post at Samagudting, where a magazine containing 200,000 rounds of ammunition was very inefficiently guarded; he, however, left a subaltern, Lieut. (now Captain) Barrett with me, as I wanted another officer. On their way, some men of the 43rd had shot two Nagas, one a relation of the chief of the Hepromah clan of Kohima, a most unfortunate proceeding, and quite uncalled for, as the men were quietly working in their fields. I was already sufficiently embarrassed by the promises made by the garrison to the *so-called friendly* clans of Kohima, to induce them to be neutral during the siege, and which I felt bound to keep, and this additional complication added to my troubles. People situated as the garrison were should make no promises except in return for real help.

All this time troops and supplies came pouring in from Manipur in one long thin stream, and the greatest efforts were made to collect supplies on the spot. I also forced the unfriendly Chitonoma clan of Kohima to surrender six rifles they had captured, and to pay a fine of 200 maunds of rice. We had been expecting a force of Kuki irregulars from Manipur; these now arrived, and I had a talk with the chief, who said: "Our great desire is to attack

---

if he brought them again to the front. But one hundred and fifty at the request of General Nation were posted in the valley to intercept fugitives, and they did what they were told. Another force was also left to help to protect the camp at Suchema. Colonel Johnstone therein states that he felt confident he could have captured Konoma with his Manipuris alone, directly after the relief of Kohima. The Konoma men, in fact, offered to submit on harsher terms to themselves to Colonel Johnstone than were afterwards wrested from them by General Nation with the loss of valuable lives, and at a heavy pecuniary cost.—ED.

that village," pointing to Kohima, "and to kill every man, woman, and child in it!" He looked as if he meant it.

One day a cat was caught that had given great trouble stealing provisions, etc., we all wanted to get rid of it, but Hindoos do not like having cats killed, and I respected their prejudices when possible, and there were many Hindoos about us, so I said, "I won't have it killed, unless some one wants to eat it." A Kuki soon came and asked to be allowed to make a dinner of it, and then I gave my consent, and our scourge was removed. I once asked a sepoy of my old regiment why they objected to killing cats. He said, "People do say that if you kill a cat now you will have to give a golden cat in exchange in the next world as a punishment, and where are we to get one?"

To keep open communications, I established Manipuri posts in strong stockades at all the principal villages on the road to the frontier, and had daily posts from Manipur. To my great distress, I heard that my youngest boy, Arthur, was ill, and my wife in much anxiety about him; but I could not leave to help her.

Our forced inaction had, as I anticipated, been misinterpreted by the Nagas. Some decisive action was much needed, and I attacked the hostile Chitonoma clan of Kohima, and destroyed part of their village. On the 10th, as a party of men were bringing in provisions from Manipur, they had been attacked by some of the Chitonoma clan in the valley below our position. I heard the firing, and ran out of the stockade with a party to drive off the enemy.

At the gate, a man who had just arrived, put a letter in my hand. I read it anxiously, it told me that my child was dead. My wife and I had chosen a spot at Kang-joop-kool where we wished to be buried in case either of us died, and there she buried him.

We soon cleared out the Chitonoma men, and I found that with the troops escorting the provisions was Dr. Campbell from Cachar, whose arrival was very welcome. I remember in connection with him a striking incident showing the courage of Manipuris in suffering. A man who had been wounded in an encounter had to have an operation performed on his arm. Dr. Campbell wanted to give him chloroform as it would be very painful. But the man refused, saying, "I will not take anything that intoxicates," and at once held out his arm and submitted to the knife without flinching!

Every day the delay in the commencement of active operations made the Nagas more and more confident, and some vigorous action on our part was absolutely necessary. I heard from spies that our Manipuri post at Phesama was about to be attacked by the people of the village, who held nightly converse with emissaries from Konoma. I therefore determined to punish Phesama, which was not far from Kohima, and on November 11th, I sent a party of Manipuris and Kukis who destroyed the village in a night attack, and killed a large number of people. They brought in twenty-one women and children as prisoners whom the Manipuris had saved from the Kukis, who would have spared neither age nor sex had they gone alone.

The next day my old friend Captain Williamson arrived to act as my assistant, I having been appointed Chief Political Officer with the Field Force that was being formed. Having now a competent man to leave in charge, I determined to go to Manipur for a few days, and marched to Mythephum on the 13th, and rode thence on the 14th to Manipur, accomplishing the whole distance of over 100 miles in thirty-one and a half hours. I stayed one day in Manipur and then returned, reaching Kohima on the 17th.

On November 20th, General Nation having arrived at Suchema, ten miles from Kohima, Williamson and I left to join him. We were fired at on the road, but got in safely and found all well and in good spirits. The troops consisted of 43rd and 44th Assam Light Infantry and two seven-pound mountain-guns under Lieut. Mansel, R.A. Lieut. (now Major) Raban, R.E., was engineer-officer and Deputy Surgeon-General (now Surgeon-General, C.B.) De Renzy was in charge of the Medical Department. Major Cock, a well-known soldier and sportsman, was Brigade Major.

On the 21st, the guns arrived on elephants, and feeling sure that no proper carriage could have been provided for their transport, I had taken the precaution to bring one hundred Kuki coolies to carry them. The assault was to be next day. Mozuma remained neutral, and even gave us a few coolies and guides.*

* I also heard from an old Mozuma friend, Lotojé, that the enemy intended to concentrate all his fire on the officers, so as to render the men helpless. I told this to the General and Major Cock, and strongly advised them to do as I did, and cover their white helmets with blue turbans to

How well I remember the night of the 21st. Williamson and I dined with the General and all the staff, and poor Cock, great on all sporting subjects, told us in the most animated way, stories of whaling adventures when he was on leave at the Cape. He warmed to his subject and greatly interested us; he was a fine gaunt man of over six feet in height, and great strength and ready for any enterprise; some of the Mozuma Nagas knew him and liked him as they had, years before, been on shooting expeditions with him in the Nowgong jungles. Besides this we had a surgical address from Dr. De Renzy, who told us what to do if any of us were wounded. How we all laughed over it, he joining us. I knew we should have some hard fighting, but we all counted on carrying everything before us with a rush, and who is there who expects to be wounded? We are ready for it if it comes, but we all think that we are to be the exception. It is as well that it is so.

We were under arms at 4.30 A.M. on the 22nd. The first party consisting of two companies of the 43rd Assam Light Infantry and twenty-eight Naga Hills Police, under Major Evans and Lieut. Barrett, conducted by Captain Williamson, who knew the country, were directed to proceed to the rear of Konoma and occupy the saddle connecting the spur on which it is built with the main road, so as to cut off the line of retreat.

At 7.30 A.M., the remaining portion of the force

---

render themselves less conspicuous, urging the inadvisability of needlessly rendering themselves marks for the enemy's fire. The General refused, and Cock said he should do as the General did, so I said no more; admiring their dogged courage, but wishing that they would take advice.

marched off. We all went together to the Mozuma Hill, where Lieut. Raban, R.E., was detached with part of a rocket battery, to take up a position on the hillside and open fire on Konoma, simultaneously with the guns. A small force was left in Suchema, to which, on my own responsibility, I added one hundred and ten Kuki irregulars, as I thought it dangerously small for a place containing all our stores and reserve ammunition. At the General's request, I had posted a force of two hundred men in a valley to intercept fugitives, and cut them off from Jotsuma.

After leaving Lieut. Raban, we crossed the valley dividing Mozuma and Konoma, and when half-way between the hills, Lieut. Ridgeway (now Colonel Ridgeway, V.C.) was sent with a company of the 44th to skirmish up to the Konoma hill. The main body with the guns then gradually ascended to the Government Road. Just before reaching it, we found a headless Aryan corpse in a stream, it was probably that of a sepoy of the 43rd, who formed part of Mr. Damant's ill-fated expedition.

After going for a short distance along the road, we found a place up which the guns could go, and a party of fifty men under Lieut. Henderson, 44th Assam Light Infantry, was sent ahead to skirmish up the hill-side, the guns carried by my coolies following with the General and his Staff, including myself. As we ascended the hill, Colonel Nuttall, with the remainder of the 44th, exclusive of the gun escort, proceeded along the road, crossing the small valley that divides the Konoma hill from the ridge of the Basoma hill which we were ascending, a few hundred yards from where it joins the main valley, and halted at the foot. After incredible labour, we succeeded in getting the guns into position at about 1200 yards distance from the highest point of Konoma, and at once opened fire, while Lieut. Raban did the same with his rockets which, however, for the most part fell short over the heads of Lieut. Ridgeway's party, though once two struck the village. On being signalled, Lieut. Raban withdrew his rockets and joined us. Meanwhile, the guns had made little impression on the people, and none on the stone forts of Konoma, but the 44th were advancing gallantly to the attack up the steep ascent to the village, a brisk fire being kept up on both sides.

At about 2.30, the position of the guns was changed, and they were advanced to within eight hundred yards of the works, here one of my gun coolies was wounded by a shot from the village. The change of position had little effect, and Lieutenant Henderson's party which had skirmished along the hillside, effectually prevented the enemy from evacuating his strong position.

At this time we saw a body of men on the ridge above Konoma, and a gun and rocket fire was opened on them, but speedily stopped as the regimental call of the 43rd sounding in the distance, followed by a close observation with our glasses, led us to the conclusion that it was the party with Captain Williamson and not the enemy who occupied the point at which we had directed our fire. Subsequently it was discovered that the stockade there had been captured and occupied by the party of the 43rd. After firing a few shots from our new position, and imagining that the force under Colonel Nuttall was in full possession of the hill we unlimbered, and, crossing the small valley before mentioned, we followed Mr. Damant's path up the hill, entering the village by the gate where he met his death. As we neared the place where we had last seen Colonel Nuttall's party, ominous sights met our eyes, dead bodies here and there and men badly wounded, while sepoys left in charge of the latter told us that the Nagas were still holding out in the upper forts. After advancing a few paces further we had to pick our way over ground studded with pangees,* and covered with thorns and bamboo and cane entanglements, exposed to the fire of the enemy, and passing the bodies of several Nagas we ascended a kind of staircase, and after again passing under the Naga fire climbed up a perpenpicular stone wall and found ourselves in a small tower, which, with the adjoining work, was held by a small party of the 44th. I asked Colonel Nuttall where all his men were, and he pointed to the handful around him and said, "These are all." The situation was indeed a desperate one, and I felt that without some immediate action our power in the Naga Hills for the moment trembled in the balance. The needed action was taken as the guns had now arrived under a heavy fire, and they opened on the upper forts at a distance of eighty to one hundred yards, Lieutenant Mansel and his three European bombardiers pointing them, fully exposed to the fire of the enemy. I strongly urged on the General the necessity of making an attempt to dislodge him

* Sharp stakes of bamboo hardened in the fire.

before nightfall, and he was about to lead out a party to the attack when it was deemed more prudent to try the guns from another point first. After a series of rounds with such heavy charges that the guns were upset at every shot, the order for the assault was given, and we all rushed out in two parties, led by nine officers, viz., General Nation, Colonel Nuttall, Major Cock, Major Walker, Lieutenant Ridgeway, Lieutenant Raban, Lieutenant Boileau, Lieutenant Forbes, and myself, with all the men we could collect. The party I was with, which included the general, Colonel Nuttall, and Major Cock, attempted to scale the front face of the fort, the other the left, *i.e.*, on our right. The right column of attack led by Ridgeway and Forbes advanced splendidly; I seem to hear to this day Ridgeway's shout of "Chulleao," *i.e.*, "Come along," to his men as he dashed to the front, and I saw him mounting the parapet.

The Nagas met us with a heavy fire and showers of spears and stones. One of the spears struck Forbes, and Ridgeway was badly wounded in the left shoulder by a shot fired at ten paces, and Nir Beer Sai, a gallant subadar, shot dead. My faithful orderly, Narain Singh, was also killed. Unfortunately we had no force to support the assaulting parties and the men began to retire. While this was doing on the right, our column, the left, was scaling an almost perpendicular wall in front but unsuccessfully, as those of us not killed were pushed back by showers of falling stones and earth, and as we alighted at a lower level the remnants of the right column who were retiring met us. I tried to rally them, but I was a stranger to them and it was no use. Lieutenant Raban was equally unsuccessful, the men had acted gallantly, but our party was too small, and as I had before predicted the fire was concentrated on the European officers. Major Cock walked back leisurely to get under cover, and just before he reached it turned round to take a parting shot. I saw him thus far, and immediately after heard that he had been shot. Seeing that our only chance of safety lay in a retreat, I shouted to Mansel to open an artillery fire over our heads which he did, this saved us. In another minute, the general, Colonel Nuttall, myself and five sepoys were the only men left. I suggested to the former that we had better go too and retire, which we did over the embers of a burning house.

As I retired with the General we found Major Cock mortally wounded, laid under cover in a sheltered spot; a little farther on under a heavy fire we met Lieutenant Boileau bringing out a stretcher for him. As Cock was being carried in, a bearer was shot dead, and Dr. Campbell took his place and brought him into hospital.

It was a strange situation, as in our retreat we were alternately exposed to a fire, and quite sheltered. Luckily the place selected for a hospital was safe, and there a sad sight met my eyes. In the short period that elapsed between the commencement of the assault and my return, the hospital had been filled. Young Forbes was on his back, pale as a sheet, but cheerful. Ridgeway flushed with the glow of battle on him. "Certamis gaudia," I said, "I hope you are not much hurt." "Only my shoulder smashed," he said. Colonel Nuttall was slightly wounded, making four out of nine Europeans. Besides these were men of the 44th of all ranks, some almost insensible, others in great pain, some composed, others despondent. Outside lay a heap of dead. Twenty-five per cent. of the native ranks had fallen, killed or wounded. Some of my gun coolies were among the latter, besides one or two killed.

I remember a wounded Kuki who was supporting himself by leaning against a great vat of Naga beer prepared to refresh the defenders of the fortress, and by him lay a dead Naga. The Kuki had a dao (sword) in his hand, and every now and then he fortified himself with a deep draught of the grateful fluid, and thus strengthened made a savage cut at the body of his foe.

We had captured all but the highest forts, and a renewed attack with our small numbers was out of the question, as night was closing in, and we were very anxious as to the safety of our detached parties under Evans, Macgregor, and Henderson.*

It was determined to remain where we were for the night, and Lieutenant Raban represented to the General the necessity of fortifying our position. This duty he and Mansel and I undertook, I bringing my Kuki coolies to the work, which we accomplished by 7 P.M.

* The official medical report of this campaign gives a deplorable account of the sufferings of the wounded, and the gangrene which affected the wounds in consequence of the extremely insanitary condition of the Naga villages and stockades, where the Naga warriors had been congregated for weeks expecting the attack—an additional reason why the immediate pursuit into their strongholds which Colonel Johnstone had recommended after the relief of Kohima should have been carried out—failing the acceptance of the harsh terms of peace. See *ante*.—ED.

CHAPTER XIX.

Konoma evacuated—Journey to Suchema for provisions and ammunition, and return—We march to Suchema with General—Visit Manipur—Very ill—Meet Sir Steuart Bayley in Cachar—His visit to Manipur—Grand reception—Star of India—Chussad attack on Chingsow—March to Kohima and back—Reflections on Maharajah's services—Naga Hills campaign overshadowed by Afghan War.

General Nation had intended to capture Konoma and return to Suchema at once, but the stout resistance offered by the Nagas upset all calculations, and we were thus stranded without warm clothing or provisions on a bleak spot, 5000 or 6000 feet above the sea. I sent off some of my Naga emissaries, and induced the neutral men of Mozuma to go to Suchema and bring the bedding of the wounded men and some food which was done. With difficulty we got enough water to drink, but there was none for washing, and when at last we sat down on the ground to eat our frugal meal, the doctors had to eat with hands covered with blood, indeed, none of our hands were very presentable. At last, to our great relief, our detatched parties returned one by one. Lieutenant (now Colonel C. R. Macregor, D.S.O.), a most gallant and capable officer, had been out all day with only fifteen men, and inflicted some injury on the Nagas. He was Quartermaster-General of the force, and did good service throughout. The accession of numbers was a great relief, as we now had the means of renewing the attack next day, but ammunition and supplies were required, and Williamson and I volunteered to go to Suchema for them next day. The night was very cold, but we managed to sleep all huddled up together, the dead lying all round us.

Early next morning, Williamson and I started with all our coolies and an escort of fifty men. We saw no signs of the enemy, but came across several men of the 43rd who had strayed away from their detachments in the dark and hidden in the jungles. At Suchema we found all right, but before we got there, we saw our flag flying over Konoma, showing, as I had expected, that it had been evacuated during the night. This event immediately made our neutral friends of Mozuma, our allies, and they gave us hearty assistance, and we took back an ample supply of provisions. The Mozuma people told us that the Konoma men had never contemplated the possibility of being driven out, and that they had stored up 2000 maunds of rice which had fallen into our hands.

The enemy had retired into some fortified stockades called Chukka on the main range to their rear, a most difficult position to attack. I offered the General to carry the guns into position for him if he cared to assault them, but our loss, especially in officers, had been so great that he declined, and probably he was right, as the risk was very great if the enemy stood his ground, so the General decided to await reinforcements. All the same it was to be regretted that we were unable to deliver two or three blows in rapid succession.

We left a party at Konoma and marched to Suchema with the wounded, Ridgeway, with great courage, marching all the way on foot, rather than endure the shaking of an improvised litter. On the 27th, I joined a force, with which we attacked and destroyed the unfriendly portion of Jotsuma, a large and powerful village, and on the 29th, as there was nothing else to do, made a rapid journey to Manipur with Lieutenant Raban, that he might survey the road as I wanted the trace for a cart road cut. We returned on December 4th.

On December 6th, Williamson and I started for Golaghat, to meet Sir Steuart Bayley. At Samagudting I had a perfect ovation, all the village turning out to see me, and greeting me warmly as an old acquaintance. Alas! many were suffering from a disease we called Naga sores, and several had died. The once lovely place looked desolate and miserable, almost all the fine trees had been ruthlessly cut down by one of my successors, in a panic, lest they should afford cover for hostile Nagas. The place looked so sad that I could not bear to stay there as I had intended, and left again almost directly. We reached Golaghat on December 9th, and stayed with the Chief Commissioner and started again on the 12th, and rode fifty-five miles into Dimapur, but I was not at all well, indeed had been much the reverse for several days, bad food and hard work having upset me. We reached Suchema on the 14th.

Overtures for submission were made by some of the hostile villages, but I said that an unconditional surrender of all fire-arms must precede any negotiations. Meanwhile, I grew daily worse, and the doctors told me that I must go to Manipur for change and quiet, which, as there was nothing to be done just then, I did, leaving Captain Williamson in charge of the Political Department.

I reached Manipur on December 22nd, and a day or two's rest did me so much good that I left again on the 27th, and rode to Mythephum, sixty miles, but was taken ill on the road, and suffered most dreadful pain for the last twenty miles, arriving completely prostrated. The next day, being worse, I sent a message to Manipur, asking for the native doctor and a litter to be sent to meet me, while I got back as far as Mayang Khang on my pony, though hardly able to sit upright. I halted here for the night, but had no sleep, and in the morning started in a rough litter, but the shaking increased the pain, so that I again tried riding till I reached Kong-nang-pokhee, twenty miles from Manipur, where, to my intense relief, I found my doolai and our native doctor, Lachman Parshad. I reached Manipur at 11 P.M.

Next day, December 30th, I was no better, and as the doctor was very anxious, not understanding my case, which was acute inflammation, my wife wrote to Dr. O'Brien of the 44th, asking him to come and see me. I was laid up till January 17th, and only narrowly escaped with life, my suffering being aggravated by a deficiency of medicine in our hospital, and a week's delay in getting it from Cachar. One day I got out of bed to see Thangal Major on very important business connected with Konoma, of which some of the inhabitants had tried to open an intrigue with Manipur. Dr. O'Brien arrived about the 13th, and left on the 18th, and I was preparing to follow in a few days, when complications on the Lushai frontier detained me, and then as the Chief Commissioner was about to come up *en route* to the Naga Hills, to present the Maharajah with the order of the Star of India in recognition of his services, I waited till I could march up with him.

On January 30th, I heard that the Baladhun tea factory in Cachar had been attacked, and a European and several coolies killed by the Merema clan of Konoma. Knowing that Cachar was badly off for troops, I asked the Durbar to send two hundred men to the frontier, close to the tea factory, to aid the Cachar authorities, and this was done. On February 6th, I started for Cachar to meet the Chief Commissioner, reaching that place on the 7th, and marched back with him, arriving at Manipur on February 20th, where he was received with every demonstration of respect, the Maharajah turning out with all his court to meet him at the usual place, and escorting him to the spot where the road turned off to the Residency.

The Chief Commissioner's visit gave the greatest satisfaction to every one in Manipur. He stayed five days, during which he had several interviews with the Maharajah, and held a grand Durbar, at which he invested him with the star and badge of a K.C.S.I. He also attended a review held by the Rajah, besides seeing all the sights of the place, including a game of polo by picked players. In fact the visit was a thorough success, and the Manipuris often spoke of it with pleasure years afterwards.

Just before we started for the Naga Hills, I received the news of an attack by the Chussad Kukis on the Tankhool village of Chingsow, to the north-east of Manipur, forty-five people were said to have been killed or carried off; and the excitement was all the greater from the belief entertained that the attack had been instigated by the Burmese. I determined, after consultation with Sir Steuart Bayley, to proceed to the spot myself, and investigate the whole affair; and it was, therefore, decided that, after escorting him to Kohima, I should return to Manipur and take up the case. We marched to Kohima, which we reached on March 1st, and on the 2nd, I returned to Mao, *en route* to Manipur, where I arrived on March 5th.

Before leaving the subject of the Nago Hills, I ought to say, that, it is difficult to over-estimate our obligation to the Maharajah, for his loyal conduct during the insurrection and subsequent troubles. According to his own belief, we had deprived him of territory belonging to him, and which he had been allowed to claim as his own. The Nagas asked him to help them, and promised to become his feudatories, if only he would not act against them. The temptation must have been strong, to at least serve us as we deserved, by leaving us in the lurch to get out of the mess, as best as we could. Instead of this, Chandra Kirtee Singh loyally and cheerfully placed his resources at our disposal, and certainly by enabling me to march to its relief, prevented the fall of Kohima, and the disastrous results which would have inevitably followed. It is grievous to think that his son, the then Jubraj Soor Chandra Singh, who served us so well, was allowed to die in exile, and that Thangal Major died on the scaffold: while many others who accompanied the expedition, were transported as criminals, across the dreaded "black water" to the Andamans.

It was the misfortune of those engaged in the Naga Hills expedition, that they were overshadowed, and their gallant deeds almost ignored, by the Afghan war then in progress. Some of the English papers imagined that the operations in the Naga Hills were included in it, and the Government of India, which has only eyes for the North-West Frontier, showed little desire to recognise the hard work, and good service rendered on its eastern border, amidst difficulties far greater than those which beset our troops in Afghanistan. The force engaged, hoped that the capture of Konoma, which was achieved after such hard fighting and at so great a loss, would have been at least recognised by some special decoration, but this hope was disappointed, apparently for no other reason, than that the troops engaged, fought in the east, and not in the west of India. Kaye, the historian, once said that, "the countries to the east of the Bay of Bengal, were the grave of fame." Well did the Naga Hills campaign, prove the truth of his words. A bronze star was the reward of a bloodless march from Kabul to Kandahar, but not even a clasp could be spared to commemorate the capture of Konoma, and those who never saw a shot fired, shared the medal awarded equally with those who fought and bled in that bloody fight.

CHAPTER XX.

Visit Chingsow to investigate Chussad outrage—Interesting country—Rhododendrons—Splendid forest—Chingsow and the murder—Chattik—March back across the hills.

I HAD not fully recovered my strength after my illness, and besides there was much to do, so I did not start for Chingsow till the 11th, when I marched to Lairen, twenty-five miles distant. Near a place called Susa Kameng, where the hills approach each other very closely, from either side of the valley, a rampart connects them. It was built in former days as a barrier against the Tankhools, when they were the scourge of the neighbourhood.

After leaving Susa Kameng, the valley narrowed for some miles, and then we crossed a ridge about 1000 feet above it, and finally descended into a charming little upland valley, which, but for the Kukis, those terrible enemies of trees and animal life, would be the cherished home of wild elephants. After crossing this, we again made a slight descent, and found ourselves close to the camp on a lovely stream. There I found Bularam Singh, who was to be minister in attendance on me during my march, that part of the country being under his jurisdiction. The next day we went on to Noong-suong-kong over a most lovely country, often 5000 feet above the sea, and with hill villages in the most romantic situation; and—remarkable sign of the peace produced by the rule of Manipur—we met large numbers of unarmed wayfarers. This day we also saw terrace cultivation, in which the Tankhools excel, and rhododendrons in full flower, a splendid sight. The next day, after another most interesting march, we halted in a pretty upland valley, 5100 feet above the sea; the valley was long, and a stream meandered through it, the banks being clothed with willows and wild pear trees, covered with blossoms. The hillsides were well-wooded, the trees being chiefly pines with rhododendrons here and there.

On March 14th, we descended the Kongou-Chow-Ching, and in a village I saw for the first time shingle roofs. We passed the last fir tree at 5800 feet, and reached the watershed at 7300 feet. At the top of the pass in a slightly sheltered position, was a solitary rhododendron. The cold was so great that, though walking, I was glad to put on a thick great-coat; the winds were exceedingly piercing. Some of the hills round were denuded of trees, and the hill people said that it was the severity of the winds that prevented their growth. The view from the highest point was splendid, on all sides a magnificent array of hills and valleys. Near to us were some of the most luxuriant forests I have ever seen, the trees of large size, and many of them with gnarled trunks, recalling the giants of an English park. Under some of these trees was a greensward where it would have been delightful to encamp, had time allowed, but the difficulty of obtaining water limits one's halting place in the hills. Everywhere on the western face of the hills pines seemed to stop at 5800 feet; but on the east they rose to 9400!

Four villages, in the Tankhool country, apparently monopolised the bulk of the cloth manufactures, and different tribal patterns were made to suit the purchaser. Some of these cloths are very handsome and strong, and calculated to wear for a long time. But the superior energy of the Manipuris in cloth weaving, has greatly injured the trade in the hill villages; in the same way that Manchester and Paisley have injured the weaving trade in most of India. The Manipuris supply a fair pattern of the different tribal cloths at a lower price, and thus manage to undersell those of native manufacture, but the quality is not nearly so good as in the original. The prices in the hills are decidedly high. Every village has its blacksmith, but some devote themselves more especially to ironwork.

We reached Chingsow on March 15th, after a march of twelve miles that morning, chiefly made up of ascents and descents, some being so steep that it was with difficulty that we got along. Finally, after a direct ascent of 4980 feet, followed by a descent of 3600 feet, we reached our encamping ground below the village which towered above us. The next day I investigated the case, and found that, as reported, twenty males and twenty-five females had been murdered. I saw the fresh graves and dug up one as evidence, the bodies contained in it were those of a mother and child, and presented a frightful spectacle with half of the heads cut off, including the scalp, and both in an advanced state of decomposition. It appeared that a demand has been made by Tonghoo, the Chussad Chief, that the Chingsow Nagas should submit to him and pay tribute, but they, of course, refused as subjects of Manipur. They heard of nothing more till they were attacked on the morning of the fatal day. The people had just begun to stir, and some had lighted their fires, when suddenly they heard the fire of musketry at the entrance of the village. They ran out of their houses, and the Chussads fell upon them, and the massacre commenced. The assailants were about fifty in number, and the people in their terror were driven in all directions, and slaughtered, some being shot and others being cut down by daos.

While this was going on, some of the men assembled with spears and advanced on the Chussads, who then retreated firing the village, and carrying off all the pigs, spears and iron hoes they could lay hands on. Five Nagas of Chattik came with the Chussads and were recognised. The village of Chingsow was most strongly situated, even more so than Konoma, indeed, the same might be said of many villages in that part of the country, and is entered by long winding paths cut through the rock, by which only one man at a time could pass, so that well defended it would be difficult to take. But the fact was that Manipur having put a stop to blood feuds among its subjects, had rather placed them at a disadvantage, as they were not quite as well prepared for an attack as formerly.

After leaving Chingsow, we marched through a pretty country, part of our way lying along a high ridge with a precipice on one side, and a deep ravine on the other, and we finally halted in a stream far below our last camp. Every march was a succession of steep ascents and then equally steep descents into narrow valleys. It was most exasperating sometimes to see how needlessly an ascent was made over a high ridge, when a path of no greater length could have been made round it.

On the 17th, I encamped beside a river where I was visited by many Tankhools, including children, who crowded round me fearlessly. The people were a fine race, but almost inconceivably dirty, some of them seemed grimed with the dirt of years. There were plenty of fine pieces of terrace cultivation. It was very curious to find that among the Tankhools there seemed to be a universal belief that they originally sprung from the "Mahawullee," or sacred grove in Manipur.

On March 18th, we reached Chattik, a fine village on a ridge from which we had a splendid view, including the Chussad villages. As I had done all I had come for, and wished to see a new country, I determined to march back straight to Manipur across the hills. It was not the beaten track which lay by Kongal Tannah, and no one in my camp knew it, but I felt sure it could be found, and old Bularam Singh cheerfully agreed. We started on the 19th, and after passing a village that had been plundered by the Chussads, we halted after a sixteen-mile march, during which I was badly hurt by a bamboo which pierced my leg. On the march we passed some terrible-looking pits, 12 feet deep, and about 3 or 3½ feet wide with sharp stakes at the bottom. They are meant to catch enemies on the war path, or deer, and are placed in the centre of the roads and covered lightly. God help the poor man or animal who is impaled in these horrible pits and dies in agony, for no one else will.

On the 20th, we halted at Pong, after an interesting but tiring march, during which we crossed the summit of a high range at 7100 feet, covered with forest, and small and very solid bamboos. The descent was through a noble pine forest with trees that must have been two hundred feet high. It rained heavily, and when we halted I should have had a miserable night of it but for the care of the Manipuris, who built me a comfortable hut, and went away smiling and cheerful to cook their food, though they looked half drowned. Never did I see men work better under difficulties. Owing to them I had as nice a resting-place as a man on the march could want, and an hour after I had an excellent dinner.

We started early next morning, and made a gradual ascent till we reached Hoondoong, a Tankhool village 5200 feet above the sea. After that our road lay through a splendid fir forest, with here and there an avenue of oaks, but from time to time we came across large tracts of forest that had been laid low and burned. At Hoondoong I saw some curious graves, high mounds shaped like a large H.

They were outside the village. There were also

more and better-looking women and children than are to be seen in most Tankhool villages. The men of the Tankhool race are, in physique, quite equal to the Angamis.

In the main street of Hoondoong, there were two rows of dead trees about twenty feet high, planted in front of the houses, and orchids were growing on them. The people seemed happy and contented under the rule of Manipur, and their houses were large and commodious structures.

We reached Eethum Tannah in the valley of Manipur after a terrible descent, rendered all the more difficult by heavy rain, which made the narrow path so slippery as to be almost impassable. During the whole of my long march through a wild country covered with forest I had, with the exception of the Hoolook monkey (*Hylohete*) seen no wild animals, scarcely a bird!

I reached Manipur on March 22nd, having greatly enjoyed my tour in the hills, and had hardly arrived when Thangel Major came to see me and talk about the Chussad business. Soon after I sent to Tonghoo, the Chussad chief, to demand his submission. He did not come himself, but sent his brother Yankapo. The Manipuris thought this a grand opportunity to secure hostages, and begged me to allow the arrest of him and his followers. I severely rebuked them for making such a treacherous proposal.

I had several interviews with the young chief and his followers who spoke Manipuri fluently, and admitted that they were subjects of the Maharajah. This visit eventually led to a better understanding with the Chussads, and to the submission of Tonghoo himself, who subsequently became a peaceable subject. For the present, however, I had to exact reparation for the attack on Chingsow, and for some months the affair cost me much anxiety.

CHAPTER XXI.

Saving a criminal from execution—Konoma men visit me—A terrible earthquake—Destruction wrought in the capital—Illness of the Maharajah—Question as to the succession—Arrival of the Queen's warrant—Reception by Maharajah—The Burmese question.

About this time I heard one morning that a man had been convicted in concert with a woman of committing a grave offence, and that the woman had, according to custom, been sentenced to be exposed in every bazaar in the country, in the way already described. The man had been sentenced to death, and ordered to Shoogoonoo for execution. As the offence was not one which our courts would punish with death, I sent a friendly remonstrance to the Maharajah, and requested that he might be produced before me, that I might satisfy myself that he was uninjured. The Maharajah at once consented, and in a few days the man was brought before me safe and sound, and after having been exposed as a criminal in several bazaars, he was sentenced with my approval to a fitting term of imprisonment. I also asked the minister in future, to let me know for certain when a sentence of death was passed, that I might advise them, without appearing to the outer world to interfere, in case they inadvertently condemned a man to capital punishment, for a crime which our laws would not approve of being visited so severely. Realising that my object was to save them from discredit, they at once consented, and I hinted that I would never sanction the penalty of death for cow-killing.

As I have stated, it had been almost always the custom to refer death sentences to me. Often and often when I made a remonstrance to the ministers about any contemplated action of which I disapproved, I was told that I misapprehended the state of things, and that nothing of the kind was intended. Of course, I let them down easily, and appeared satisfied with their assurances. However, neither party was deceived, they accepted my strong hint in a friendly spirit, and knew well that I took their denial as a mere matter of form. The result was what I cared for, and it was generally achieved without friction.

One of the most unpleasant parts of my duty was the perpetual necessity of saying "No" to the ministers. My great object was to be continually building up our prestige. Colonel McCulloch had said to me, "Never make any concession to the Manipuris without an equivalent," and it is inconceivable how many times in our daily intercourse I had to refuse little apparently insignificant, but really insidious requests. The struggle on behalf of native British subjects was long kept up, but in the end I gained my point, and their rights and privileges were fully recognised.

Early in June, some men of the Merema clan of Konoma who were fugitives in a very wild part of the hills of Manipur bordering on the Naga Hills, came to me, making a piteous appeal for mercy, saying they would have nothing to do with the Naga Hills officials, but came to me as their old friend and master in the days when I was at Samagudting. As they came in trusting to my honour, I would not have them arrested, but sent them away, telling them that nothing but good and loyal conduct on their part could win my esteem, and that they must make their submission and deliver up Mr. Damant's murderers to the Political Officer in the Naga Hills, before I consented to deal with them. I also gave orders to the Manipuri troops on the frontier, to act with the utmost vigour against all Konoma men found within the territory of Manipur.

Soon after some Lushais visited me, and we settled up a long-standing dispute between them and Manipur.

The Konoma men continued to give much trouble, and to keep some check on them, I refused at last to allow any to enter Manipur, except by the Mao Tannah, and furnished with a pass from the Political Officer, Colonel Michell. I also arrested one of the supposed murderers, but the evidence against him was not considered quite satisfactory.

On the morning of June 30th, at 4.45, when we were at Kang-joop-kool there was a violent earthquake, the oscillations continuing with great force from north to south, and *apparently* in a less degree from east to west for some minutes. Plaster was shaken from the walls, and crockery and bottles thrown down, and furniture upset. Locked doors were flung open and the whole house, built of wood and bamboo, shaken as by a giant hand. Two Naga girls sleeping in my children's room next to the one my wife and I occupied, sprang up and ran outside, my two boys, not realising what was up, seemed to think it a good joke. We all got up and hurried on our things to be ready for an emergency, but I soon saw that all present danger was over. At 8.50 A.M., there was another sharp shock, and again about 2 P.M., besides several slighter ones.

In the valley, and especially at the capital, the shocks were of the utmost violence and the earthquake said to be the worst known with the exception of the terrible one of January 1869. Many houses built of wood and bamboo were levelled with the ground, the ruins at Langthabal greatly injured, and a peepul tree growing over a picturesque old temple torn off. The old Residency was greatly injured, part being thrown down, and the fireplace and chimney shaken into fragments, but still, strange to say, standing. Some houses in the Residency compound were rendered useless. The great brick bridge on the Cachar road was cracked and much damage done. The earth opened in several places. The new Residency, which was nearly finished, and was built in the old English half-timbered style, was intact.

During the next few days several more shocks occurred, causing much alarm among the people, who predicted something still worse. The earthquake was followed by the severest outbreak of cholera that I had witnessed since a dreadful epidemic in Assam in 1860. There were many deaths in the palace, and public business was at a standstill. I was unable to lay any question before the Durbar, as half the officials were performing the funeral ceremonies of relations. The great bazaar was closed at sunset, and even then many of the sellers went home to find their children dead or dying. Everywhere on the banks of the rivers, and streams, people might be seen performing the funeral obsequies of relations and lamenting the dead. Amid this trouble, the attitude of all classes was such as to excite admiration, there were no cases of sick being deserted and every one appeared calm and collected.

Later on, the cholera attacked my village of Kang-joop-kool, and ten per cent. of the population died.

Early in the autumn, the Maharajah was taken ill with an abscess behind the ear, and great apprehensions were entertained for his life. The whole capital was for weeks in a state of alarm, fearing a struggle for the throne in case of his death. The four eldest sons, and also some members of the family of the late Rajah Nur Singh, had their followers armed so as to be ready to assert their several claims immediately the Maharajah died, the former were constantly in attendance on their father night and day. The Maharajah was himself very anxious about the conduct of his younger sons. As suffocation might any moment have terminated the invalid's life, I made all necessary plans, with a view to acting promptly, if required, and, in conjunction with Thangal Major, arranged so as to secure the guns and bring them over to the Residency the moment that he died. I also desired the Jubraj (heir apparent) to come over to me at once, in the event of the death of his father, that I might instantly proclaim him and give him my support. I had a most grateful message from the Maharajah in reply, as also from the Jubraj, who promised to abide entirely by my instructions. However, the abscess burst, and the Maharajah recovered, and though a shot imprudently fired one evening led to a panic when the bazaar was deserted, things soon settled down again.

As soon as the Maharajah was again able to transact business, he begged me to write to the Government of India and request that the Jubraj should be acknowledged by them as his successor. I did so, at the same time strongly urging that the guarantee should be extended to the Jubraj's children, so as to preclude the possibility of a disputed succession on his death. The Jubraj earnestly supported this request, but the Maharajah preferred adhering to the old Manipuri custom, which really seemed made to encourage strife. If, for instance, a man had ten sons, they all succeeded one after the other, passing over the children of the elder ones, but when the last one died, then his children succeeded as children of the last Rajah, to the exclusion of all the elder brothers' children. All the same, if these could make good their claim by force of arms, they were cheerfully accepted by the people who were ready to take any scion of Royalty.

The consequence had always been in former days that to prevent troublesome claims, a man, on ascending the throne, immediately made every effort to murder all possible competitors. It is obvious that such a cumbersome system was undesirable, and I held that having once interfered we ought to set things on a proper and sensible basis, and that there was no middle course between this and leaving the people to themselves. Thangal Major, who always greatly dreaded the violent and unscrupulous disposition of Kotwal Koireng (afterwards Senapattee), agreed with me. The Maharajah, however, with a father's tenderness for his sons, would not advocate my proposal, but still, would have gladly accepted it. The Government of India judged differently, and only sanctioned my proposal so far as to allow me to say that they would guarantee the Jubraj's succession, and maintain him on his throne. This decision gave great satisfaction.

This year was unpleasantly distinguished by a great deficiency of rain in the valley, and a corresponding superfluity, though at irregular intervals, in the hills. For a long time there were apprehensions of scarcity, while in the hills the rainfall was so heavy that the Laimetak bridge was washed away and the river rose six feet above its banks. On one side, a large portion of its pebbly bed was hollowed out, and much widened, and 80 feet width of solid boulders carried away. The Eerung rose about 40 feet, and portions of the hill road were cut away, but the want of steady rain was felt.

By the end of September, the Maharajah was able to transact business, though, as he was not well enough to visit me, I visited him, that I might congratulate him on his recovery, and present him with Her Majesty's warrant, appointing him a Knight Commander of the Star of India. The papers bearing the Queen's signature were received with a salute of thirty-one guns, and the Maharajah rose to take it from my hand, and at once placed it on his forehead, making an obeisance. I then made a speech to all assembled, expressing my satisfaction at the Maharajah's recovery, and the gratification it gave me to be the means of conveying the warrant to him.

Nothing of great importance now occurred, but I was constantly occupied by the troubled state of the eastern frontier of Manipur where Sumjok (Thoungdoot) continued to intrigue with the Chussad and Choomyang Kukis, who were a ceaseless trouble to the Tankhool Nagas, about Chattik. These intrigues were conducted with a view to gaining over the latter as subjects. The chief difficulty of Manipur was, that the boundary had never been properly defined, so neither party had a good case against the other. Manipur was in possession, but otherwise everything was unsatisfactory, our failure to settle the Kongal case having encouraged the Burmese authorities to resistance.

CHAPTER XXII.

March to Mao and improvement of the road—Lieutenant Raban—Constant troubles with Burmah—Visit to Mr. Elliott at Kohima—A tiger hunt made easy—A perilous adventure—Rose bushes—Brutal conduct of Prince Koireng—We leave Manipur for England.

In November, I marched to Mao on the Naga Hills frontier, and arranged for the improvement of some of the halting places on the way. I also asked Sir Steuart Bayley, the Chief Commissioner, to allow Lieutenant Raban, R.E., to visit Manipur, with a view to laying out the line of a cart road from the Manipur valley to Mao. This arrangement he sanctioned, and Lieutenant Raban arrived in Manipur on December 30th, 1880. The line from Sengmai was bad throughout, and an exceedingly difficult one in many places. Thangal Major accompanied us, and I had induced the Maharajah to open out a narrow road, on being supplied with the necessary tools. We carefully examined the whole of the road in detail, and, after deciding on the line to adopt, cut the trace. It was a matter requiring great skill and patience, both of which Lieutenant Raban had. He was very ably seconded by the Manipuris, whose keen intelligence made them good auxiliaries. Often the line had to be cut along the face of a cliff, but fortunately the rock was soft, and the work was accomplished without accident. The way we turned the head of the Mao river, the descent to and ascent from which I had so often, so painfully accomplished, was a great success, and did not materially increase the distance, as we saved it by striking the main path at different points.*

In the village of Mukhel near which we passed, we saw a pear tree three or four hundred years old, and greatly venerated by the villagers. In the same village I saw a Naga cut another man's hair with a dao (sword). The operation was performed most dexterously and neatly, by holding the dao under the hair, and then slightly tapping the latter with a small piece of wood. The result was that the hair-cutting was as neatly accomplished as it could have been by the best London hair-dresser. I asked a fine young Naga why all his tribe wore a single long tuft of hair at the back? He at once replied, "To make the girls admire me," and added that without it, he should be laughed at. This is the only explanation I ever had of the curious fact that most of the Naga tribes wear a long tuft behind, like Hindoos. By the third week in January we had laid out the line of road. Thangal Major approved of most of it, but said, regarding the piece between Sengmai and Kaithemahee, "I will cut it as I promised, but who will ever use it?" I differed from him, as nothing could exceed the tortuous and hilly nature of the old road, running as it did across one succession of spurs and deep ravines, one of the most heart-breaking paths I ever went along.

* This was the road along which Colonel Johnstone had marched to relieve Kohima. The old route from the capital of Manipur to Cachar was easy enough in comparison.—Ed.

Within a month of its completion the old path was entirely deserted.

My health was beginning to break down entirely. I had been very ill during and immediately after the Naga Hills Expedition, and during the last march I was laid up one or two days. My wife had long been a sufferer, but she did not like to leave me, and I did not like to leave Manipur while the frontier was disturbed and the Kongal case unsettled. However, now I felt that we both must have change, and our children also were of an age to go home.

On my return from looking after the road, fresh complications awaited me. News came from Chattik of the Sumjok (Thoungdoot) authorities having again caused dissension and joined with another village in firing on a Manipuri piquet. This had led to reprisals on the part of the Manipuris, who attacked and drove out the enemy. All this was done without our relations with Sumjok being anything but strained, the act of hostility being unauthorised. The ill-defined nature of the frontier was such, that neither party could be said to be in the right or wrong. The Kuki, Chussad, and other frontier villages took advantage of the state of things to plunder the Tankhools, and the latter in their turn appealed to Manipur.

I felt that, until something was done to set things on a right footing, I could not leave. Sir Steuart Bayley was about this time appointed to Hyderabad, which added to my difficulties, as he was intimately acquainted with the situation, and of course a change in the administration necessarily means delay. The Burmese authorities, knowing what I now do, were always, as I then believed, favourably inclined to us; the ill-feeling was entirely on the part of Sumjok, whose Tsawbwa had influence at Mandalay, and was able to prevent justice being done in the case in which he was so discreditably concerned. He also took advantage of this influence to carry on the guerilla warfare he did through the Chussads, who disliked Manipur, on account of some treacherous behaviour on her part in former years.

As the spring advanced, of course the danger of hostilities became less. Cæsar said, "*Omnia bella hieme requiescunt.*" The reverse holds good in India, and on the eastern frontier the fiercest tribes keep quiet in the rainy season.*

In March, I heard that Mr. (now Sir Charles) Elliott, the new Chief Commissioner, was about to visit Kohima, where he wished to meet me, and I set off on my way there, arriving on the 19th, being well received all along the road by the people of the different villages. I had a long talk with the Chief Commissioner about the affairs of Manipur, and the necessity for a survey and delimitation of the boundary between it and Burmah during the ensuing cold weather, and then returned. The new road had been opened out to such a width, except here and there—I was able to ride the whole distance.

The weather was lovely, and the rhododendrons near Mao, and the wild pears, azaleas, and many other flowering trees along my route, made the long journey a most pleasant one. Let me say here, while on the subject of the road, that, notwithstanding all the criticisms passed on it and predictions of its

* All wars rest in winter.

uselessness, it proved of immense, nay, incalculable value during the Burmese War of 1885–86, and the sad troubles of 1891. It was throughout of an easy gradient, never exceeding one in twenty, and, had a bullock train been established, might have been used from an early date for conveying produce from Manipur to the stations of Kohima.

This was my last visit to Kohima, a place fraught with so deep an interest to me, and so many pleasant and painful associations. I shall always regret that the site chosen by myself and Major Williamson was not adopted for the new cantonment, which, with the larger space available, would have admitted of a greater development than is possible under present circumstances. Still the place will always possess an undying interest for me, filled as it is with the memory of events bearing on my work from the early triumphs of old Ghumbeer Singh, and my predecessor, Lieut. Gordon, to the day when I marched in at the head of the relieving party, and heard the fair-haired English child told by her mother that at last she could have water to drink!

On my return to Manipur, I intended to have started for England, and our passages were taken by a steamer leaving in April. But the unsettled state of the Burmese frontier forced me to stay till the rains had set in in the hills. During this spring we had a visitor, Mr. Hume, C.B., the well-known ornithologist, who spent three months in studying the birds of Manipur, with the result, I believe, that very few new species were found.

In April, we had a little excitement to vary the monotony of life, though to me my work was of such never-ending interest, that I needed nothing of the kind. On April 13th, the Maharajah sent to tell me that a tiger had been surrounded, and asked me to go out and help to shoot it. The place was about fourteen miles from the capital, and we started early and rode off to a spot a few miles from Thobal.

I took my sister and the two boys with me, my wife staying with the baby. The tiger had, according to Manipuri custom, been first enclosed by a long net, about eight feet high, and outside this a bamboo palisading had been erected, on which the platforms were built for the spectators. The space enclosed was eighty to a hundred yards in diameter, and contained grass and scrub jungle, and a log of wood tied to strong ropes was arranged, so that it might be dragged up and down to drive the tiger out of the covert. As soon as we were all in our places this rope was vigorously pulled, with the result that a tigress, followed by two cubs, sprang out with a loud roar. The Jubraj was present, and took command of the proceedings, courteously asking me from time to time what I wished done. After the first charge, the tiger was not very lively, and this being the case, several Manipuris, contrary to orders, jumped down into the arena with long and heavy spears in the right hand, and a small forked stick in the left. With the latter they held up a portion of the net, which had been allowed to fall on the ground to shield their faces, if necessary, and with the right hand poised the spear, shouting to irritate the tiger, whom others in the stockade tried to drive out by throwing stones.

Roused by this, the infuriated brute charged in earnest at one of the men on foot, the latter awaited her with the utmost coolness, and, as she approached, struck her with the spear; the tiger, however, made good her charge, but the net stopped her, and she rolled over, and when released, she retreated. This was repeated, both by the tigress and the cubs, and after a shot or two, the men on foot attacked them with spears and finished them off.

The whole scene was a very exciting one and a very fine display of courage and coolness on the part of the Manipuris.

We did not reach home till 10 P.M., but the weather was splendid, not unbearably hot as it would have been in India so late in the season. The day was a memorable one to the boys, and I well remember the astonishment they caused when, stopping at Shillong on their way home, some one jokingly said, "And how many tigers have you shot?" The boys gravely replied "Three."

The day was very nearly proving the last to some of us. The two boys were being carried in a litter, and my sister and I riding on ponies. On leaving the village where we had halted, we were riding down a narrow path with only room for one to pass at a time, when, suddenly, I heard a shout behind me and saw an elephant following me at a great pace, the mahout (driver) vainly endeavoured to stop him, he had been frightened by the tiger's dead body and was quite unmanageable. I called to my sister, who was in front, to ride at full speed, and I followed as quickly as her pony would allow. It was a race for life, as, had the elephant gained on us, I, at least, must have been crushed. Luckily, the mahout recovered his control, and managed to slacken the pace.

On our way home, we passed bushes of wild roses twenty feet in diameter and quite impenetrable.

Finally, the tiger was taken to the Maharajah, who had not been well enough to come, and, next morning, was brought to us and skinned.

I have already alluded to the turbulent character of Kotwal Koireng, the Maharajah's fourth son, and now, again, I was to have fresh evidence of it. Early in May, I heard of his having three men so severely beaten that one had died, and two were dangerously ill. On investigation, I found that the men had been tied up and beaten on the back, it was said, for two hours and slapped on the face at the same time. I questioned the ministers, and practically there was no defence, and, as I heard that the Maharajah was enquiring into the matter, I said no more, beyond a warning that a case of murder must not be passed over.

The Maharajah handed over the case to the Cherap Court* for trial, and, as might be expected, they acquitted Kotwal of the charge of causing death and found him guilty of injuring the other two. The Maharajah sentenced him to banishment for a year to the island of Thanga, in the Logtak Lake, and temporary degradation of caste. As a sentence of two years' imprisonment had been passed some years previously in our own territory, for death caused under similar circumstances, the sentence was not so lenient as might have been expected. I reported the matter to the Government of India, expressing

* Chief Court.

my approval of the sentence, under the circumstances, and my verdict was ratified. I intimated to the Durbar that, should such a thing occur again, I should insist on his permanent banishment from Manipur.

This I was prepared to carry out myself if necessary. I should have liked on this occasion to have procured his banishment, but, in dealing with Native States that in these matters are practically indepedent, it is not always well to press matters too far. In old days, under our early political agents, such an offence would have passed unnoticed. It was a point gained to have the case investigated and adjudicated on by the Maharajah, and anything approaching to an adequate sentence inflicted. Since the troubles in Manipur, I have seen it stated that the sentence was a nominal one; that it certainly was not, the prince was banished to Thanga, and if he surreptitiously appeared at the capital, he did not appear in public, and when I left Manipur on long leave, early in 1882, was still in banishment.

On May 31st, we all left Manipur on our way to England, and my children bade adieu to a most happy home. It was a sad parting for most of us, and though my wife's health and mine urgently required change, we left the valley with regret, and felt deep sorrow as we took our last look of it from the adjacent range of hills. We reached Cachar on June 8th, having halted as much as possible on high ground. The rivers were in flood, and sometimes there was a little difficulty in crossing. We left for Shillong on June 9th, and arrived there on the 15th, leaving again on the 21st for Bombay, from which, on July 5th, we sailed for England.

While at Shillong we were the guests of the Chief Commissioner, so that I had an ample opportunity of talking over affairs with him, and it was finally settled that I was to take Shillong on my way back, and see Mr. Elliott before leaving, to settle the knotty question of the boundary between Manipur and Burmah on the spot, in accordance with orders lately received from the Government of India.

CHAPTER XXIII.

Return to Manipur—Revolution in my absence—Arrangements for boundary—Survey and settlement—Start for Kongal—Burmah will not act—We settle boundary—Report to Government—Return to England.

I WAS really not fit to undertake any work in India till my health was re-established, but could not bear to leave the interests of Manipur in other hands until the boundary was settled. I felt that I alone had the threads of the whole affair in my hands, and that I could not honourably leave my post till I had seen Manipur out of the difficulty. Thus it came that I left England again on September 7th, and my devoted wife, far less fit than I was for the trials of the long journey, accompanied me, as she would not leave me alone.

We reached Shillong on October 18th, 1881, and, after arranging all matters connected with the boundary settlement with the Chief Commissioner, started for Cachar, and reached that place on October 25th, leaving again for Manipur next day, and marching to Jeree Ghât, where we were met by Thangal Major. We made the usual marches, and reached Manipur on November 4th, the Jubraj coming out with a large retinue to meet me at Phoiching, eight miles from the capital.

While I was away in the month of June, an

attempt at a revolution had occurred, the standard of revolt having been raised by a man named Eerengha, an unknown individual, but claiming to be of Royal lineage; such revolutions were of common occurrence in former days. In Colonel McCulloch's time there were eighteen. In this case there was no result, except that Eerengha and seventeen followers were captured and executed. The treatment was undoubtedly severe, but not necessarily too much so, as too great leniency might have led to a repetition, and much consequent suffering and bloodshed.

I had an interview with the Maharajah, who was ill when I arrived, as soon as he was well enough; and set to work to make preparations for our march to the Burmese frontier. I intimated my desire to the Maharajah that Bularam Singh, and not Thangal Major, should accompany me, as I wished the last to stay at the capital, and also not to let him appear to be absolutely indispensable.

I had been appointed Commissioner for settling the boundary with plenipotentiary powers, and Mr. R. Phayre, C.S., who was in the Burmese commission, and a good Burmese scholar, was appointed as my assistant. There was also a survey party under my old friend Colonel Badgley, and Mr. Ogle, while Lieutenant (now Major, D.S.O.) Dun,* came on behalf of the Intelligence Department. Mr. Oldham represented the Geological Survey. Dr. Watt was naturalist and medical officer, while Captain Angelo, with two hundred men of the 12th Khelat-i-Ghilzie Regiment, commanded my escort. Mr. Phayre arrived first, and I sent him off to Tamu to try and

* Major Edward Dun died on the 5th of June, 1895.—Ed.

smooth over matters with the Burmese authorities there. Then my old friend Dun came, soon followed by Dr. Watt, then the survey party arrived, and Captain Angelo with my escort, and last of all Mr. Oldham. Never had Manipur seen so many European officers. Some time was required for necessary triangulations before we could start.

On November 30th, just as the sun was rising, Thangal Major came to see me, and told me that the Maharajah was very ill and suffering great pain. While talking, two guns were fired from the palace, when the old man turned pale, evidently thinking that the Maharajah was dead. A few minutes after a messenger came to inform us that the guns merely announced a domestic event, but Thangal Major was nervous and soon took leave, running away to the palace at a pace that did credit to his sixty-four years.

On December 1st, Mr. Phayre returned from Tamu, having had a friendly but unsatisfactory interview with the Phoongyee. The Pagan Woon had been expected but did not arrive, and the Phoongyee had no authority to act.

Before starting, the Maharajah visited me in state, and I introduced all the officers of the party to him. He looked pale and haggard after his illness, but seemed in good spirits. At last, on December 16th, we made a move and marched to Thobal-Yaira-pok, and on the following day to Ingorok, at the foot of the hills. My wife accompanied us, as I was exceedingly anxious to show the Burmese my peaceful intentions, and felt sure that the presence of a lady would be a better proof of my *bona fides* than any other I could offer. I heard before leaving the frontier, that had it not been for this, a rupture would have been certain while our relations were in a state of great tension, but the fact of my wife being there, convinced the authorities in the Kubo valley, that I had no idea of hostile action.

I have already described the route to Kongal, and my escort were much tried by the severity of the marches over such a rough country. The men had only lately returned from Afghanistan, and were in fine condition, but they said that the country between Kandahar and Kabul, was nothing to that between Ingorok and Kongal Tannah. Every day many men were footsore, and reached camp, hours after me and my Manipuris. There can be no doubt that for some reason or other the Eastern hills and jungles are far more trying than those of the North-West frontier.

However, at last we arrived safely at Kongal, and though the Burmese and Sumjok officials, to whom I had written polite letters asking them to meet me, did not turn up, the survey work went on merrily.

On the 18th, Colonel Badgley, who had come by an independent route through the hills, joined my camp, and after a conference we came to the conclusion that at any rate I was right in claiming the country occupied by the Chussads and Choomyangs, as Manipuri territory. This was very satisfactory, as the day before I had been much annoyed by the Sumjok authorities having prevented some of the former *fears* coming to pay their respects to me. The attitude of the Sumjok people was passively hostile, they refused to join in making out the boundary, and threw every obstacle in the way of my doing so, but they were evidently not inclined to be the first to shed blood.

On December 19th, I sent out two unarmed parties to clear some ground for survey marks, but one of them was stopped by an armed party of Sumjok men. On hearing this the next day I ordered the Manipuri subadar in charge, to halt where he was, and I wrote to the Pagan Woon to complain, and to ask him to order the Tsawbwaa to interfere. On the 21st, I heard that another party had been stopped, and I asked with regard to them as I had done with the first. That afternoon I received a civil letter from the Pagan Woon brought by a Bo (captain), saying that he had orders to conduct negotiations at Tamu, and was not authorised to come to Kongal Tannah. I wrote a conciliatory reply urging him to visit us.

On the 22nd of December, I heard that my two parties had been forcibly driven out by large bodies of armed men. I therefore called in some Manipuri detachments lest there should be a collision, as the atmosphere was getting very warlike, and only required a spark to produce a conflagration. All the population of the Kubo valley were said to be arming. The Burmese we talked to frankly admitted if there was a rupture the fault would lie with Mandalay, for not sending a proper representative to meet me, in accordance with the request of the Government of India, conveyed months before.

Certainly one false move on our part would have provoked a rupture. However, everything comes to him who waits. We made every effort to keep the peace, and while the authorities were opposing us we kept up a friendly intercourse with all the individual Burmese and Shans near us, and I carried on negotiation with the Kukis. The Chussads were inclined to be friendly, but the Choomyangs were still under the influence of Sumjok. Fortunately Colonel Badgley found that he could dispense with the two points from whence our men had been driven, and we discovered a little stream that formed an admirable boundary line entirely in accordance with the terms laid down in Pemberton's definition of the boundary.

Further north, I knew the country well myself, and we had now no difficulty in laying down a definite boundary line about which there could be no doubt. This was done, and pillars were erected, and the line marked on the map. Manipur might, according to Pemberton's statement, have claimed a good deal of territory occupied by Burmese subjects, but this I refused to allow, as it would have been interfering with the "*status quo*," which I desired to preserve. I called all the Sumjok people I could to witness what I had done, and they all agreed that what I said was fair, and that the fault, if any, lay with the Burmese authorities, for not taking part in the arrangement. This was willing testimony, as none of the people need have come near me. Even Tamoo, the chief of Old Sumjok, or Taap, as the Manipuris call it, visited me, and expressed his satisfaction with what had been done. On Christmas Day, 1881, my wife and I had a party of seven at our table, an unprecedented sight, and probably the last time that nine Europeans will ever assemble at

Kongal Tannah. My friend Dun, who had been badly wounded by a pangee (bamboo stake) had to be carried in.

Before leaving Kongal, I went round all the pillars that had been erected, and saw that they were intact. Mr. Ogle's party went off to the north, escorted through the village of Choomyang by Lieutenant Dun. These people being under the influence of Sumjok, it was a very delicate business getting through their village without a rupture. This affair Dun managed with great tact. We left Kongal on our homeward journey on the 6th of January, but previous to starting I brought my long-standing negotiations with the Chussads to a successful conclusion. They agreed to negotiate with me but not with the Manipuris, and to abide by my decision entirely.

I sent a message to the Choomyangs and other Kukis who had given trouble, telling them that they were undoubtedly within Manipur, and that I gave them forty-two days in which to submit, or clear out, adding, that if at the end of that time they gave any trouble, they would be treated as rebels and attacked without more ceremony. Eventually they submitted and became peaceful subjects of Manipur. As to the great question—that of the boundary—I may here add that it received the sanction of the Government of India, and proved a thorough success. Though not noticing it officially, the Burmese practically acknowledged it, and it remained intact, till the Kubo valley became a British possession in December 1885.

My wife and I reached Manipur on the 9th of

January, having made the last two marches in one, and next day were joined by Mr. Phayre, who had come, *viâ* Tamu. He gave it as his opinion, that the Pagan Woon was greatly disappointed at having had no authority from Mandalay to negotiate with me, and described him as a sensible well-disposed man.

I had now to write my report of my mission, and having finished this, and handed over charge to my successor, I left Manipur with my wife on the 29th of January, reaching Cachar, where we met Mr. Elliott, the Chief Commissioner, on 5th of February. We left that evening by boat, and travelling with the utmost speed possible, with such means as we possessed, reached Naraingunge, near Dacca, and after waiting two days for a steamer went to Calcutta, *viâ* Goalundo, and thence to Bombay and England, where we arrived in March, both of us very much in need of a prolonged rest.

CHAPTER XXIV.

Return to India—Visit Shillong—Manipur again—Cordial reception—Trouble with Thangal Major—New arts introduced.

I LEFT for India again in August 1884. I had had but a sad period of sick leave, as my wife never recovered from her fatigue and illness, and died in 1883. I was obliged to prolong my leave to make arrangements for my children.

I took over charge of the Manipur Agency on the 1st October, 1884, at Shillong, and stayed a few days with the Chief Commissioner. I left again on 8th October and reached Cachar on the 15th, having made every effort to push on, and given my boatmen double pay for doing so. On my way to Cachar, I met people who complained to me of the way they had been treated in Manipur while I was away, and of the arrogance displayed by old Thangal Major, who, during my absence, had become almost despotic. Thangal was an excellent man when kept well in hand, but he required to be managed with great firmness. During the Maharajah's increasing illness, a good opportunity was given to a strong man to come to the front, and Thangal took advantage of it. On 20th October, I reached Jeeree Ghât, and was received with great effusion by the Minister Bularam Singh. At Kala Naga on the 22nd, I heard definite complaints against Thangal, a sure proof that something very bad was going on, as no one would have ventured to complain without grave provocation. Bularam Singh was Thangal's rival, so I asked him nothing, knowing well that I should hear as much as I wanted at Manipur. At Noongba, next day, there were fresh complaints, the charge being, that men told off to work on the roads were being used by Thangal to carry merchandize for himself.

At Leelanong, overlooking the beautiful Kowpoom valley, some Nagas (Koupooees) brought me a man of their tribe who had been carried off as a boy by the Lushais, and only lately redeemed. He was still in Lushai costume, and though shorter and fairer, he greatly resembled one of that tribe, showing what an influence dress has.

On 28th October, I arrived at Bissenpore, intending to march to the capital next day, but was delayed by an unpleasant circumstance. It was, as already mentioned, the custom for the Maharajah to meet me at the entrance to the capital on my arrival, but knowing that he was not well, I asked the minister to write and say that I did not expect him to do so, but I would invite the Jubraj to meet me at Phoiching, half-way between the capital and Bissenpore instead. I also wrote the same to my head clerk, Baboo Rusni Lall Coondoo, asking him to notify my wishes to the Durbar, as I felt it extremely likely that were Bularam Singh alone to write, old Thangal might intrigue and throw obstacles in the way to discredit him with me and the Durbar. The minister's letters were not answered, but I heard from Rusni Lall Coondoo, that he asked to see the Jubraj who had already heard from Bularam Singh, but he was told that he was ill. After a great deal of delay an interview was accorded, and though he appeared quite well, the Jubraj said he was too ill to come, but would send a younger brother. Feeling sure that there was nothing to prevent his coming, I sent a message of sympathy, also to say, that I would wait at Bissenpore till he recovered. I knew perfectly well that all this story had emanated from Thangal Major's brain, and that I was to be subjected to inconvenience and want of courtesy, in order to snub his colleague. He had suffered from a sore foot which prevented his coming to Jeeree Ghât to meet me and he could not forgive Bularam Singh for having taken his place. The Jubraj ought to have known better, but among natives any slight offered to a superior is an enhancement to one's own dignity, so from this point of view he would gain in his own estimation.

On the morning of October 30th, as soon as I was dressed, I saw Thangal Major outside my hut. I heard afterwards that, directly my decision had been communicated to the Durbar, he had volunteered to come out, and as he said, bring me in. When we had had a little friendly conversation, he with his usual bluntness, which I did not object to, asked me to go in, saying that the Wankai Rakpa * would meet me, the Jubraj being ill. I firmly declined, saying that I would wait till he recovered. He then assured me that the real cause was the critical state of the Jubraj's wife. I doubted the truth, but a lady being in the case, courtesy and good feeling

* Known as Regent during the recent troubles.

demanded that I should accept the statement as an excuse, and I therefore said I would leave, if the Wankai Rakpa and another prince met me on behalf of the Jubraj. This was at once agreed to, and I therefore marched off, being met in great state by the two princes, who rode by my side all the way. As I neared the capital, a vast crowd came out to meet me, the numbers increasing at every step, and I was received with every demonstration of respect and sympathy, many of those who knew my wife showing a delicacy of feeling that greatly moved me. Old Thangal, when I met him, spoke very kindly on the subject, saying, "It is sad to see you return alone, and we know what it must be to you." Numberless were the enquiries by name after all the children. At last I reached the Residency, where my old attendants were ready to do all they could for me. It was something like home, old books, furniture, children's toys, still here and there, and in a corner of the verandah my little girl's litter, in which she was carried out morning and evening, but the faces that make home were away.

I mention the foregoing incident regarding the Jubraj, as it is a good example of the small difficulties connected with etiquette, that one has to contend with in a place like Manipur. The question is far more important than it seems. Any relaxation in a trifling matter like this, seems to Asiatics a sign that you are disposed to relax your vigilance in graver questions. Indeed, to a native chief, etiquette itself is a very grave matter, and many terrible quarrels have arisen from it. I well remember a slight being offered to the Viceroy, because a Rajah fancied he had not received all the honours due to him.

I found a crop of small difficulties awaiting me in Manipur, the Durbar, and especially old Thangal, had got out of hand, and had to be pulled up a little. There were numberless complaints from British subjects of petty oppression which had to be listened to, and I felt it rather hard having this unpleasant duty to perform just after my return; but it was duty, and had to be done, and by dint of firmness, combined with courtesy, I soon set things right, but Thangal Major rather resented the steady pressure which I found it necessary to apply.

Before leaving Manipur in 1881, I had sent off some Manipuris to Cawnpore to learn carpet making and leather work. When I returned, these men had long been making use of their knowledge in Manipur, and I found that first-rate cotton carpets and boots, shoes and saddles of English patterns, had been manufactured for the Maharajah, the workmanship being in all cases creditable, and in that of the carpets most excellent.

I tried to send men to Bombay to learn to make art pottery, and the Maharajah was at one time anxious about it, but the correspondence with the School of Art was conducted in so leisurely a manner on their side, extending over nearly a year, that he got tired of it, and declined to send the men. I had a little pottery made in Manipur, which I brought home with me, the only existing specimens of an art that died out in its infancy.

I had several pieces of silver work made to try the mettle of the Manipuri silversmiths, one bowl, a most perfect copy of a Burmese bowl with figures on it in high relief, was beautifully executed, and still excites the admiration of all who see it.

The Mussulman population of Manipur, was descended from early immigrants from India, Sylhet, and Cachar, who had married Manipuri wives; they numbered about 5000, and were rather kept under by the Durbar, but to nothing like the same extent that Hindoos would have been under a Mussulman Government. Formerly, they had to prostrate themselves before the Rajah like other subjects, but they having represented that this was against their religion, Chandra Kirtee Singh excused them from doing it, allowing a simple salaam instead. They, (probably owing to their dependent position), were not such an ill-mannered and disagreeable set as their co-religionists of Cachar, and were generally quiet and inoffensive. The headman of the sect received the title of Nawab from the Rajah. These men had a grievance to bring forward when I returned, and I procured them some redress.

I visited the Maharajah in due course, and found him better than I expected, and I took an early opportunity of announcing my return to the Burmese authorities in the Kubo valley, receiving civil letters in return. Unfortunately, I found that great soreness still prevailed in Manipur on account of the non-settlement of the Kongal case, and I was constantly on the alert lest evil results should follow, as I always suspected old Thangal of a desire to make reprisals.

When I had a day to spare, I went to see my experimental garden and fir wood, at Kang-joop-kool, finding everything in a flourishing state, the wood a tangled thicket, with foxgloves and other English flowers growing in wild profusion. One morning when walking out, I saw some prisoners going to work, and as they passed me, one or two looked as if they would like to speak. I accordingly passed by them again to give them an opportunity, when a man ran up and complained that he was imprisoned without any definite period being assigned, a common practice in Manipur. Another man, whom he called as a witness, spoke good Hindoostani, and on my enquiring where he learned it, he said he was a Manipuri from Sylhet. I sent for him directly I got home, and he came with Thangal Major, and, as he was a British subject, and the Durbar had no right to imprison him, I sent for a smith, and had his irons struck off in my presence. I spoke quietly, but firmly to the Minister, but showed him plainly that I would not stand having British subjects imprisoned except by my orders. The man's offence was not paying a debt for which he was security, and the punishment was just, according to the laws of Manipur, and would have been in England before 1861.

CHAPTER XXV.

A friend in need—Tour round the valley—Meet the Chief Commissioner—March to Cachar—Tour through the Tankhool country—Metomie—Saramettie—Somrah—Terrace cultivators—A dislocation—Old quarters at Kongal Tannah—Return to the valley—A sad parting.

On the 26th of November, my old friend Lieutenant Dun (now Major Dun, D.S.O.), joined me. Knowing I wanted a friend to cheer me in my loneliness, he had very kindly accepted the permission of his department to accompany me on a tour through the hills to the north-east of Manipur. No European was more deservedly popular of late years among all classes in Manipur, where he had visited me once or twice before. I felt his kindness deeply, he was always a charming, genial and highly intellectual companion, and many a long and tiring march was cheered by his society. On the 2nd of December, we started on a preliminary tour round the west and south of the valley, visiting the Logtak lake, with its floating islands, its island-hill of Thanga, with its orange gardens and place of exile, and large fishing establishment. When I first arrived in Manipur, oranges were a rarity. Now, owing to the enterprise of the Maharajah in planting trees, they were fairly common, and here we were able to gather them. The orange tree is capricious and all soils will not suit it, and up to the fifth or sixth year it is always liable to be attacked by a grub that kills it, after that it becomes hardier. I never was very successful with orange trees, though I took great pains with them. From the Logtak lake, we marched to a place called Thonglel, in the hills, where we were met by all the representatives of the Kukis in that direction, thence to a place called Koombee, a settlement of Loees, low-caste Manipuris. Afterwards we marched to Chairel on the main river into which all the rivers of Manipur flow before it enters the hills to the south of the valley. After visiting Shoogoonoo, a frontier post, we returned to the capital, on December 11th, after a very pleasant tour of one hundred and forty-six miles in nine marching days.

We next marched up the road to the Naga Hills, meeting the Chief Commissioner, Mr. Elliott, at Mao, and returning with him to Manipur, where the usual visits were exchanged. After a day or two's halt, the Chief Commissioner set out for Cachar and I accompanied him to the frontier at Jeeree Ghât, returning to Manipur by forced marches. The bridge over the Mukker had been broken by a fallen tree, but the river, so formidable in the rains, was easily fordable. A short time before reaching the summit of Kala Naga, a pretty little incident occurred, which I have never forgotten. Some of my coolies were toiling up the steep ascent with their loads, when two young Kukis met us with smiling faces as if something had given them great pleasure. They immediately made two of the men with me put down their loads, and took them up themselves to relieve the wearied ones. On my enquiry who they were, they said they were friends of my coolies and had come to help them. It was one of the prettiest sights I ever saw, the pleasure the two men seemed to derive from doing a kind act. Dun and I reached Manipur on the 10th of January. Soon after my return, in fact before the evening, a Lushai was brought to me who had been found in the jungle with his hands tightly fastened together by a bar of iron fashioned into a rude pair of handcuffs. He appeared to be mad, but harmless, and had probably been kept in confinement by his own people and had escaped. I had the irons taken off, and ordered him to be cared for, but he soon ran off in the direction of his own country.

On the 21st of January, Dun and I set off on our tour through the Tankhool country. We marched *viâ* Lairen and Noongsuangkong, already described. The country had been surveyed, but the surveyors had taken names of villages given by men from the Naga Hills district, and they were unrecognisable to the native inhabitants. Much of my march, after leaving Noonsuangkoong, was through a new country, and a very interesting and lovely country it was. The benefits of being under a strong government were evident in the peace that reigned everywhere. The Manipuri language also had spread, and in some villages seemed to be used by every one, while in others even children understood it. It was evidently the common commercial language.

On the 26th, we halted on the Lainer river, the large village of Gazephimi being far above us at some miles distant. It was late in the afternoon but

Dun wanted to see all he could, and accompanied by some hardy Manipuris started. They all returned in a suspiciously short space of time, just at nightfall, Dun having astonished every one by his marching powers. He described the villagers as a surly, morose set, the description always given of them.

On January 28th we reached Jessami, a fine village of the Sozai tribe; they much resembled the Mao people. They crowded round us and were much pleased when we showed them our watches, and allowed them to feel our boots and socks. Some of the houses were large and well stocked with rice. One old man took us into his house and showed us a shield carefully wrapped up in cloth that bore the tokens of his having slain fifteen people. The village contained no skulls, and our friends told us that they obeyed orders and killed no one. We enquired about the snowy peak of Sarametttie, which was visible from some point not far dis ant, but the people assured us that they had never heard of it.

On the 29th, some Metomi men came in with a young man who acted as interpreter, he having been captured, and then kept as a guest in Manipur for some time, to learn the language, by Bularam Singh, who was the Minister accompanying me. He seemed quite pleased to see his old host. The Metomi people were a strange set, quite naked, except for a cloth over the shoulders in cold weather. They are slighter built than the Angamis and Tankhools. They could count up to one hundred, and three of their numerals, four, six and seven, are the same as in the Manipuri language. They wear their hair cut across the forehead like some of the tribes in Assam. Their patterns of weaving rather resembled those of the Abors and Kasias, but were finer. They wore ear-rings of brass wire very cleverly made, the wire being imported through other tribes.

On the 31st, having heard that I should be well received, Dun and I started for Metomi, with an escort of Manipuris. We first made a descent of 2000 feet to the Lainer, which we forded, the water being knee deep; there were the remains of a suspension bridge for use in the rainy season. We then ascended for about 1000 or 1500 feet, till near the village, when I halted my men and sent on my Angami interpreter, and one of the Metomi men, to ask that a party might come down to welcome us, as I had reason to think that the villagers were undecided as to what they should do, and I feared to frighten them. After waiting a long time, we heard a war-cry, and we all started to our feet and seized our arms, in case of an attack; the next minute, however, there was another cry, showing that the people were carrying loads. Soon after a long line of men appeared, each carrying a small quantity of rice, and the heads of the village came forward, presenting us with fowls, and heaped up the rice in front of me. We then walked on to the village, distant about a mile and a quarter, along an avenue of pollarded oaks, backed by fir trees. At last, after passing a ditch and small rampart, we reached the outer gate, then passed along a narrow path, with a precipice to our right, and a thick thorn hedge to our left for about eighty yards, as far as the inner gate, on entering which we found ourselves in the village. We were then led along a series of winding streets till we came to the highest part.

This was the most picturesque Naga village I have ever seen, and reminded me of an old continental town, the ground it covered, being very hilly, and the houses, constructed of timber with thatched roofs with the eaves touching one another, built in streets. Sometimes one side of a street was higher than the other, and the upper side had a little vacant space railed in, in front of the houses.

The houses were more like those of the Tankhools than the Angamis, and contained round tubs for beer cut out of a solid block of wood, in shape like old-fashioned standard churns. The village contained pigs and dogs, and the houses were decorated with cows' and buffaloes' horns. We were welcomed in a friendly way, but our hosts did not seem to like the idea of our staying the night, of which we had no intention. Our watches and binoculars greatly interested them. We tried in vain to induce the women to come out, the men saying they feared lest we should seize them. This seemed very strange, as it was the only hill village I ever saw where the women had the slightest objection to appear. As the Manipuris always respect women, it could not be due to their presence, even had they had experience of them, which was not the case. On leaving the village, we passed through a splendid grove of giant bamboos, and then turned into our old path again. Metomi was said to contain seven hundred houses, but that seemed to me a very low estimate. We reached our camp near Jessami at 7 P.M., narrowly escaping a severe scorching, as some torch-bearers who came to meet us, set fire to the grass prematurely, and we had to run hard to escape the flames. I wanted to make a vocabulary of the Metomi language the next day, but the whole village had a drinking bout, and every one was incapacitated during the rest of our stay.

We marched to a place called Lapvomai on Febuary 3rd, and next day, wishing to explore the country beyond, Dun and I, with a picked party of Manipuris, crossed the ridge above the village, and descending to the stream below, began the ascent of the great Eastern range, encamping in a most lovely spot in a pine forest. Every one was too tired to search for water, so the Manipuris went supperless to bed. Dun and I had brought a supply, which we shared with our few Naga followers, the Manipuris being prevented from doing the same, by their caste prejudices. Early next morning we started up the hill again, leaving the bulk of our party a mile or two in advance of our halting place, to search for water and cook. We, with two or three plucky Manipuris, whom hunger and thirst could not induce to leave us, pursued our upward path. At last we came on patches of snow, and in a hollow tree found the remains of a bear which had gone there to die. After a toilsome ascent, often impeded by a thick undergrowth of thorny bamboo, we, having long passed the region of fir trees, reached the summit at 8000 feet, only to find, to our great disappointment, a spur from the main range blocking our view. As this range might have taken another day to surmount, and after all be only the precursor of another, we reluctantly traced our steps backwards, and reached our party who found water and cooked their food. We witnessed some amusing instances of rapid eating, on the part of our hungry followers, who had well deserved their dinner. We then descended to the stream, and encamped on its banks after being on foot for eleven hours.

Next day, we marched to our old encampment at Lapvomai. On Febuary 7th, we marched to Wallong, passing through lovely scenery, a series of deep valleys and ravines and high hills, with a splendid view down the valley of Thetzir and Lainer, and beyond, the junction of the latter with its north-eastern confluent, we finally encamped close to a very remarkable gorge. On the 8th, we had another march to the village of Lusour, where I greatly pleased a woman and some children, by giving them red cloths, the former would have denuded herself to put hers on, had I not prevented her. Next morning, before starting, we had our breakfast in public, and ordered some boiled eggs; the hill people are supremely indifferent to the age of an egg, and even seem to think the richness of flavour enhanced by age, so that almost all brought to us were either addled or had chickens in them. At least two dozen were boiled before we found one that we could eat, and as soon as an egg was proved to be bad, there was a great rush of Tankhools to seize the delicacy, and our bad taste in not liking them gave great satisfaction.

On February 9th, we reached Somrah, a most interesting but severe march of eighteen miles. We first crossed a ridge 8000 feet in height, where among other trees we found a new species of yew—

Cephelotaxus. After reaching the summit, we made a gradual descent along an exceedingly steep hillside, where a false step would have landed us in the stream 2000 feet below. After this we descended more rapidly, and, crossing a stream, followed a beautifully constructed watercourse through some recently cleared land. We traced our way along its windings for some miles, and then, after another ascent, at last came to a lovely undulating path through a forest of firs and rhododendrons, the latter just coming into flower. The path at length, after an ascent of 200 feet, brought us to the village, a finely built one of the regular Tankhool type, with over two hundred houses, built with stout plank walls, and having an appearance of much comfort.

The next day we went to Kongailon, one of the Somrah group, making a descent of 2000 feet to cross a river, and again ascending 5600 feet. We passed many skilfully constructed watercourses and much terrace cultivation, indeed, the Somrah villages have the finest system of irrigation I have ever seen, and the long parallel line of watercourses on a hill-side present a most remarkable appearance. At Kongailon, we halted a day to explore the country, and receive deputies from various villages. From the ridge behind the village, at a height of from 7000 to 8000 feet, there was a fine view of the Somrah basin—valley it cannot be called; it is a huge basin, the rim of which consists of hills, having an average height of over 8000 feet, the villages being on the inner slopes or on bold spurs.

On February 12th, a very severe march took us to

Guachan, a miserable-looking village full of very dirty people, many of whom were naked, their bodies being covered with a thick coating of dirt. We had to halt next day to rest the coolies, and to have a path cleared ahead. On February 14th, we again started, halting on the Cherebee river, at a height of 4400 feet. On our way, while passing along a lovely ridge, covered with rhododendrons in flower, we had a fine view of Sarametti, with its snow cap.

Next day, we marched over Kachao-phung, 8000 feet high, and encamped on its slopes at 7600 feet. So perverse are the ways of the hill-men, that the road, a well-used one, was carried within fifty feet of the summit, though it would have been easy to cross at a much lower level. We encamped in a primeval forest of huge trees, the branches of which, moved by the fierce wind that blew all night, waved to and fro with such a threatening noise as to preclude sleep for a long time.

On the evening of the 12th, one of our coolies was brought to me, who had dislocated his shoulder. We had no doctor of any kind with us, and no one who understood how to reduce it. Dun and I tried our utmost, and I put the poor fellow under chloroform, to relax the muscles and spare him pain, but, alas! with no result. I tried to induce him to go to Manipur, and be treated by my native doctor there; but he objected, and preferred going to his home; so I gave him a present and let him go, and very sorry we were to see him relinquish his only chance of getting right again. Every one ought to be taught practically to reduce a dislocation; I had often heard the process described, but never seen it done, and my lack of experience cost the poor Naga the use of his arm. It is one of the saddest parts of one's life in the wilds of India to meet cases of sickness and injury without the power to give relief. Simple complaints I treated extensively, and with great success, but it was grievous to see such suffering in more complicated cases, and to be unable to do anything. A skilful and sympathetic doctor has a fine field for good work in such regions. A sick savage is the most miserable of mortals.

The good points of the Manipuris, as excellent material for hardy soldiers, were brought out very prominently on these long marches. No men could have borne the fatigue and hardships better or more patiently than they did. It quite confirmed me in the opinion I had long since formed that, taken every way, the Manipuris were superior to any of the hill-tribes around them. I remember that when at Jessami, one of the Manipuris, at my suggestion, challenged any Naga, who liked, to a wrestling match, none would come forward, though the villagers were a fine sturdy set. It was impossible, also, to help noticing, as we went along, the very remarkable aptitude the Manipuris possess for dealing with hill-tribes. The Burmese tried in vain to subdue the Tankhools, and in one case a force of seven hundred men, that they sent against them, was entirely annihilated. However, as the Manipuris advanced, the different tribes, after one struggle, quietly submitted, and on both occasions when I marched through the north-eastern Tankhool country, the people were in admirable order, and behaved as if they had always been peaceful subjects of Manipur.

Next morning, though the thermometer was at thirty-six degrees, the Manipuris felt the cold so severely from the terrible wind that had been blowing all night, that they did not attempt to cook before marching, but started off and hurried down the hill to get to a warmer region. I never knew the hardy fellows do this before, and it shows the influence of a piercing wind in making cold felt, as I have often seen them quite happy on a still night with the thermometer at twenty-six degrees or lower.

Five more marches brought us to Kongal Tannah, where I encamped on the ground we occupied in 1881–1882 when I was Boundary Commissioner. On our way, we received a visit from Tonghoo, the redoubtable Chussad chief, now a peaceful subject of Manipur, a man of the usual Kuki type, imperturbable and inscrutable. Next day, I inspected the boundary pillars I had set up, and found them intact, a satisfactory proof that the settlement was not unacceptable to either Manipur or Burmah.

We marched back by the old route, encamping as we had done more than four years before in the deep valleys of the Maglung and Turet. On the 24th, from the crest of the Yoma range, we saw the valley of Manipur once more at our feet, and in the evening encamped at Ingorok. Next day, I parted from my friend, I riding into Manipur, and Dun going north for a few days' more survey of the country. He rejoined me on March 2nd. Thus ended one of the hardest, but, at the same time, one of the pleasantest marches I ever made, all the pleasanter for the society of such a clever and charming companion. We spent one more week together, and then Dun went back to his appointment in the Intelligence Department, to my great regret, and I settled down to my usual routine work, constantly varied by interesting little episodes.

CHAPTER XXVI.

More troubles with Thangal Major—Tit-for-tat—Visit to the Kubo valley—A new Aya Pooiel—Journey to Shillong—War is declared—A message to Kendat, to the Bombay-Burmah Corporation Agents—Anxiety as to their fate—March to Mao.

DURING the spring of 1885, I had constant trouble with Thangal Major; the old man was perpetually doing illegal acts. He had lost his head during my absence in England, and though treated with every courtesy, he greatly resented being called to order. Some Mussulmans had complained to Mr. Elliott about the oppression exercised towards them, and in my absence Thangal was foolish enough to imprison them. Of course, I heard of it, and insisted on their release, and this weakened his authority. Again, he, as "Aya Pooiel," *i.e.* Minister for Burmese Affairs, greatly resented our not having settled the Kongal case, and insisted on the authors being punished. We were very good friends privately, though I always expected further trouble with him. The Maharajah's ill health also gave me anxiety, as he was no longer the active man he once was, and was daily falling more and more under Thangal's influence.

At last matters came to a crisis. On May 23rd, I received a letter from the Burmese authorities at Tamu, brought by a deputation reporting that some murders had been committed by Manipuri subjects, and the next day when the visitors came to see me, they openly accused the Mombee Kukis of having done the deed. I felt sure that the outrage had been carried out at the instigation of Thangal Major, as a set-off against the Kongal case, and I sent for him. He came to see me on May 25th, and, when I opened the subject, he assumed rather a jaunty air. I spoke very gravely, and told him that it was a very serious business, and that an investigation must take place, and that I wished him, as Aya Pooiel, to accompany me. He replied in a very unbecoming manner, and began to make all sorts of frivolous excuses, the burden of his speech being that, as justice had not been done in the Kongal case, there was no need to investigate a case brought by the Burmese. I was very calm, and remonstrated several times, but seeing that it had no effect, I requested him to leave my presence, which he did. I then wrote to the Maharajah asking him to appoint Bularam Singh to aid me in the investigation, also reporting Thangal's conduct, and saying that I could not allow him to attend on me till he had apologised. The worst of Thangal's behaviour was, that he spoke in Manipuri, and in the presence of the Burmese messengers, who understood it, instead of in Hindoostani which no one but myself understood. Thinking carefully over the matter, I wrote to the Maharajah on May 26th, requesting him to replace Thangal in the Aya Pooielship by another officer, suggesting Bularam Singh, as I did not consider it safe to leave him in charge of the Burmese frontier.

There was the greatest opposition offered to my request, and the Maharajah made every effort to evade it. It was currently stated by people in the Court circle that it would be easier to depose the Maharajah himself, but I remained firm. Meanwhile, Bularam Singh was appointed to accompany me, and, on June 8th, I left for Moreh Tannah, near Tamu, halting the first day at Thobal. Before leaving, I received an apologetic letter from Thangal, and later he called on me, and made an ample apology, speaking very nicely. I accepted the apology personally, quite reciprocating his friendly sentiments, but told him that, having acted in the way he did, I could not trust him as Aya Pooiel.

I reached Moreh Tannah on June 13th, and was visited by some Burmese. The next day, I proceeded to the scene of the murder, and exhumed two headless bodies, and took evidence regarding the raid. Before reaching Manipur, I heard through some Kukis the most convincing proofs that the Mombee people had committed the raid, and at Thangal Major's instigation. I obtained all the necessary details later on, but the Burmese war prevented my undertaking an expedition for the release of some Burmese captives who had been carried away and sold, though I accomplished it later on.

At Moreh Tannah, I obtained some excellent mangoes, the only ones free from insects that I ever saw on the eastern frontier, those in Assam and Manipur being so full of them as to be uneatable when ripe, though beautiful to look at. Here also I had most unpleasant evidence of the existence of a plant that has the smell of decomposed flesh. I imagined that a dead body had been buried under the temporary hut I lived in, till a Manipuri explained matters to me, and showed me the plant in question.

I reached Manipur on June 20th, and a day or two after wrote to the Maharajah, calling to mind my letter respecting the Aya Pooielship, and again requesting Thangal's removal. The next day the old fellow called, and we had a very friendly interview, and I explained my reasons for acting as I had done. He seemed convinced, and rose and seized my hand, and said, "You are right. I understand thoroughly." He then said he would cheerfully submit, and went away in an apparently excellent frame of mind. It is said that after this, his son, Lumphél Singh, a very bad young man, talked him over and urged him to resist, but, anyhow, he soon after went to see the Maharajah, and recanted all he had said to me. However, I was determined to persist, and told the Maharajah plainly that he must choose between me and Thangal, with the result that he consented, and the Aya Pooielship was given to another.

This struggle caused me great regret, as Thangal had many good qualities, and but for his having had his own way too much during my absence in England, would never have lost his head as he did. However, there was one good result, as I established very friendly relations with the Burmese authorities, who saw that I wished to be just, and this stood me in good stead when the war broke out.

During the whole time that the dispute was going on, I had the support of the Jubraj, who said I was in the right, and most people, I believe, thought likewise. All the same it was painful to gain a victory over one who had worked well with me for years, more especially as I felt that the weakness of our own Government in not insisting on justice being done in the Kongal case, had given him some justification in his own eyes, though this was a plea that I could never admit.

In October 1885, I went to Shillong to see the Acting Chief Commissioner, Mr. Ward, and as he was intending to march through Manipur on his way to the Naga Hills, I stayed with him, and we all left Shillong together on November 4th. We left Cachar on November 12th, and halted that evening at Jeeree Ghât, I on the Manipuri side of the river, the Chief Commissioner and his following on the British. A short time before dinner—we were all Mr. Ward's guests—I received a note from him, directing my attention to a telegram, and asking me to act on it. The telegram was a startling one, and was to the effect that war with Burmah was to commence, and that our troops would pass the frontier on a certain date; that there were nine European and many native British subjects in the employ of the Bombay-Burmah Corporation in the Chindwin forests with whom it had been impossible to communicate, and to ask me to make every effort to let them know the facts, and to do anything I could to assist them. The matter was extremely urgent, as, if I remember rightly, the 25th was the day for the troops to enter Upper Burmah, and every moment was of the utmost importance.

I thought it over for five minutes, and determined on a course of action, and set to work at once to follow it out. I knew perfectly well that with the frontier and all roads so carefully guarded, as I had seen those in the Kubo valley to be, there was absolutely no chance of a secret messenger advancing ten miles on Burmese soil, and I therefore resolved to send my letter through the Kendat Woon (Governor of Kendat), the great Burmese province of which the Kubo valley was part. I wrote a letter to the European employés of the Bombay-Burmah Corporation, giving the message I was asked to transmit, and urging them to make every effort to accept my hospitality and protection in Manipur. To this letter I appended Burmese and Manipuri translations, and put them in an open envelope addressed in the three languages, hoping and believing that, seeing that the contents were the same in both languages, which they had the means of understanding, the Burmese authorities would, on the principle of the Rosetta stone, assume that I had said the same in English.

This done, I enclosed the envelope in a letter to the Kendat Woon, in which I told him exactly how matters stood, and that in a short time Burmah would be annexed, and urging him, as he valued the goodwill of the conquerors, to make every effort to protect and aid the British subjects in his province. I asked him to deliver the letter, to which I had appended translations that he might read what I said, and to bear in mind that any service he might render would be richly rewarded and never forgotten, while he might rely on my word as his well-wisher; that a terrible punishment would befall any one who injured a hair of the head of a British subject. In addition to this, I wrote letters to the Burmese authorities at Tamu, with whom I was on friendly terms, begging them, as they valued their lives, and my goodwill, to forward the letter to the Woon with all possible speed.

This done, I went to dine with the Chief Commissioner, and when he asked if I had received his note, I told him I had acted on it. Feeling that I had done all that I could for the best, I took no further steps at the time than to issue orders to the Manipuri frontier stations, to give all aid requisite to fugitives from Burmah, and to make arrangements for their being entertained in Manipur, should they arrive in my absence.

I heard afterwards that there was great anxiety in Burmah when it was known that I had communicated with our isolated countrymen through the Burmese authorities, it being regarded as likely to seal their fate.

I marched to Mao on the Naga Hills frontier with the Chief Commissioner, and then returned to Manipur, arriving on the 4th, and on the 5th heard from Moreh Tannah that a European was being kept a prisoner at Kendat. I wrote at once to the Tamu Phoongyee, asking him to use his influence to release him, saying that I was in a position to march to his aid in case my letter had no effect.

On December 9th, I heard that all the Europeans at Kendat had been murdered, the Queen of Burmah's secretary having arrived with one hundred regular troops on a steamer and ordered their execution, and that forty of the Bombay-Burmah Corporation's elephants and all their native followers had been arrested.

On December 10th, the news of the capture of Mandalay arrived. It gave immense satisfaction, and it was said that many of the old people, who knew what Burmah was, were so pleased that they could not eat their dinners. The Jubraj visited me to offer his congratulations, and a salute of thirty-one guns was fired.

CHAPTER XXVII.

News from Kendat—Mr. Morgan and his people safe—I determine to march to Moreh Tannah—March to Kendat—Arrive in time to save the Bombay-Burmah Corporation Agents—Visit of the Woon—Visit to the Woon.

ON December 17th, I at last received a letter from Mr. A. J. Morgan, the chief agent of the Bombay-Burmah Corporation at Kendat, acknowledging my letter of November 12th. He told me that three Europeans, Messrs. Allan, Roberts and Moncur, had been murdered on the River Chindwin by the Queen's Secretary; that he and Messrs. Ruckstuhl and Bretto had been protected by the Kendat Woon, and four others by the Mengin Woon. He said the Chindwin valley was filling with dacoits, *i.e.*, brigands, and that their position was very precarious. I at once wrote to the Woon thanking him warmly for the protection he had accorded to my fellow-subjects, and sent him a pair of handsome double-barrelled guns, one of them a rifle, as a present, also five hundred rupees, which I asked him to give to Mr. Morgan.

Feeling certain of the dangerous position of the British subjects at Kendat, if they were surrounded by disbanded soldiery who had turned brigands, I determined to march to the frontier, so as to be ready to give aid, if necessary. I accordingly asked the Maharajah to lend me 400 Manipuris, and 500 Kukis, and one mountain gun. With these, and fifty men of my escort of the 4th Bengal Infantry, under Subadar Baluk Ram Chowby, I marched off on December 19th.

My escort consisted of sixty men of all ranks, but I weeded out ten as not likely to stand the severe marches we might have to undertake. I then paraded the remainder and addressed them, saying that any man who felt himself unfit for service might fall out, and I should think none the worse of him. All stood fast, and then I said, "Now, I will not take you, unless you promise me not to fall sick, till you have escorted me back safely to Manipur." The men gave a shout of acclamation, and I gave the order to march, and never had I better, braver or more devoted men under me, or men who bore hardship and want of all the little comforts of life more cheerfully.

We reached Moreh Tannah, where I had intended to halt and watch events, on December 23rd, and there I received a letter from Mr. Morgan, who described the state of things at Kendat as daily getting worse, and expressed his conviction that if the dacoits reached Kendat, the Woon would be unable to hold his own; he therefore hoped I might be able to afford them the aid they so sorely needed, as, unless a force marched to their assistance speedily, their lives would not be safe. On hearing this, I determined to march for Kendat at once, and by the rapidity of our movements overcome all resistance; indeed, not to allow the Burmese time to think of it. Accordingly we marched to Tamu, where the authorities at once submitted, and I declared the country annexed, and reappointed the old officials, pending further orders, promising my protection to all classes, and calling on the people to complain at once if any of my followers injured them.

All this done, we marched to Mamo, some miles beyond Tamu, where we halted in the rice fields attached to the village which was very strongly stockaded. My camp was at once filled with men, women and children, all disposed to be friendly and all willing to receive little presents. It was a pretty feature of the Kubo valley, as of Upper Burmah generally, and as in Assam formerly, that immediately on leaving the village cultivation you plunged at once into forest.

My party was not so numerous as I could have wished. The Minister, Bularam Singh, accompanied me, but the nine hundred men all told, that I had asked for, were not there, and the supply of provisions was scanty. I made all my escort take ten days' food per man, with orders not to touch it, without my direct permission, and I procured supplies where-ever I could, as we went along. I also took a large supply of money.

As Bularam Singh was holding the appointment formerly held by Thangal, he had not the knowledge to help him in all petty details that the other would have had. However, realising more keenly than ever from my experience at the relief of Kohima, the extreme value of time, and of rapid strokes, I pushed on at all hazards, trusting to have my numbers made up.

I had a few first-rate Manipuri officers with me, and my old orderlies, Sowpa, Thutot, and Sundha.

I took my excellent hospital assistant, Lachman Parshad, and my Manipuri secretary and interpreter, Chumder Singh, and most of my old chuprassies, who were invaluable. My head clerk, Rusni Lall Coondoo, was unfortunately on leave, marrying his daughter, and I greatly missed him.

On the morning of December 24th, we started from Mamo, determined to reach Kendat next day, though the Burmese said it was *absolutely impossible* to do it. I had with me my escort of fifty men of the 4th B.I., and between three hundred and four hundred Manipuris, the Kukis not having arrived. The old road had been disused, and our path was a perfect zigzag. We halted long after sunset at Pendowa on a small stream, the Nunparoo. The mountain gun did not arrive, and half our force was not up till midnight. When all the coolies had arrived, I told them that if we reached Kendat next evening, they should have buffalo to eat.

The country through which we had passed was not naturally a difficult one, but there had been no attempt to make it good, and in places it was very bad, all the more so from the unnecessary number of times that we crossed the same river. I was much interested to see large numbers of bullock carts in the villages, such not being used in Manipur.

Next morning, we started early, and soon began to ascend the Ungocking hills. This seemed endless, one range succeeded another, here and there we saw coal cropping out of the hillside. After about 12.30 P.M., the path was alternately along the bed of a stream and over high ridges, one of those meaningless, winding roads that seem made expressly to irritate people with no time to spare. At last, in the far distance, we saw a scarped hill, that was said to be close to Kendat, and cheered by the sight, we pressed on, but it was hours before we reached the goal. About 4 P.M., I met a Burmese, who spoke Hindoostani, and gave me a letter from Mr. Morgan, telling me that he and his party were all well, and earnestly longing for our arrival. The man told me that he was the "Hathée Jemadar," *i.e.*, the man in charge of the elephants, and he accompanied us.

At last, just after sunset we reached the Chindwin river, even then, in the dry season, six hundred yards wide. We gave a loud cheer and hoisted the Union Jack; and the "Hathée Jemadar" went over to tell the Europeans we had come to save, of our arrival. All my escort and most of the Manipuris marched in with me; every man had done his best and hearty were the congratulations that passed between us.

We had marched sixty-five miles over a terribly rough country, the last thirty being quite impassable for even laden mules, in thirty hours. A havildar of the 4th said, "Sahib, is not our march one of the greatest on record?" I told him that it was. It was pleasant to think that we had arrived on Christmas Day. How little my children in England realised the way I was employed.

In less than an hour Mr. Morgan, who had seen our arrival, came over accompanied by Messrs. Ruckstuhl and Bretto, his subordinates, all dressed in Burmese costume, everything they had having been plundered in the Woon's absence. Mr. Morgan brought over a message from the Woon to me, saying that he submitted to my authority, and would come over to-morrow, and tender his formal submission.

Next day he appeared with Mr. Morgan and made his submission. He was a dignified old man, with a pleasant face expressive of much character. I thanked him on behalf of Government for his services in protecting British subjects, and told him that, while assuming charge of the country on the part of the British Government, I wished him to remain in office, and conduct the administration pending definite instructions. I told him that I expected him to maintain order, and quiet down the country, and promised him any assistance which he might require to aid him in the endeavour.

After this, I set to work to secure supplies with Mr. Morgan's aid, so as to be ready for any emergency, and then crossed the river and called on the Woon and inspected the stockade, a huge enclosure, 420 yards long and 163 wide, with a wall of solid teak logs, 18 feet high, and none less than a foot square, with strong heavy gates. I returned to my camp before nightfall, and the mountain gun arrived under the escort of Gour Duan Subadar. Next day, I heard that the Mengin Woon had absconded, finding his position untenable.

Had I had a trained levy at my disposal, as would have been the case had my advice been followed, I could have easily sent a force to occupy Mengin, and might indeed have marched to Mandalay. As it was, commanding only irregulars, my position was one of daily anxiety.

The site of Kendat was very picturesque, situated on the high left bank of the Chindwin, up and down which a view of many miles is obtained, the reach being there a long one. The stockade contained the greater part of the official residences, and a good proportion of the inhabitants, but there were many houses outside, and temples and phoongyes' residences. Below the town was a large Manipuri village, inhabited by the descendants of captives taken in the war of 1819–25.

In the rainy season, when the Chindwin is at its height, and 1200 yards wide, with the long ranges of the Manipuri Hills in the background, the view is said to be very beautiful. For many miles round Kendat, to the east of the Chindwin, the country is flat, but studded here and there with strange-looking hills with scarped sides, that rise abruptly out of the plains, calling to mind the hill-forests of Central India. Kendat was well supplied with boats, many of them being most elaborately carved.

It was a great misfortune that none of the men of my escort understood the management of boats, a most useful accomplishment on the eastern side of India, where rivers abound, and one in which the men of the old Assam regiments used to be proficient.

CHAPTER XXVIII.

People fairly friendly—Crucifixion—Carelessness of Manipuris—I cross the Chindwin—Recross the Chindwin—Collect provisions—Erect stockades and fortify our position—Revolt at Kendat—We assume the offensive—Capture boats and small stockades—Revolt put down—Woon and Ruckstuhl rescued—Steamers arrive and leave.

THE Burmese were fairly friendly to us, though they did not display any love for the Manipuris, and the latter showed rather too plainly that they thought the tables were turned, and that they now had the upper hand of the Burmese.

In many of the villages along our line of route in the Kubo valley, we had observed crosses ready for the crucifixion of malefactors, especially dacoits. These were also to be seen here and there, on the banks of the river at Kendat, but the Woon afterwards told me that he rarely crucified offenders and disliked employing torture; indeed he had the reputation of being a merciful old man. However, the people at large seemed quite to approve of strong measures, and knowing what Burmese dacoits are capable of, I hardly wonder. After I left, the man who introduced himself to me as "Hathée Jemadar" incautiously surrendered to some dacoits, who first broke the bones of his legs and arms inch by inch, and then ripped him up!

On the 28th December, I crossed the river with my

whole force, and entrenched myself on the sandbank of the Chindwin. That evening, I heard from Mr. Morgan, that there was a strong party opposed to the Woon, and greatly dissatisfied with him for having submitted. Troops had been expected up the river from the British force at Mandalay, and their delay encouraged the Burmese to hold up their heads. Next day, December 29th, the air was full of rumours, and some of the Burmese Manipuris, I have just alluded to, plied my Manipuris with all sorts of stories, of a rising against us, on the part of the Burmese. These stories had a great effect on the Manipuris, and they displayed so much unsteadiness, and at the same time such gross carelessness, that I determined to recross the river. I heard too that six men coming to join me, had been killed, and three wounded on the road, report said, by Burmese. I laughed at the idea, as I was sure that the assailants were wild Chins, as the Burmese would not show their hand prematurely. However, the news spread, and served to dishearten the men.

On the 30th I transported my whole force to the opposite bank, it cost me incredible trouble, and I had to superintend the most petty details myself. I sent over a party to construct a stockade into which the Manipuris could be penned like a flock of sheep for the night and which I could enlarge afterwards, and I insisted on the work being finished that day. It *was* finished, and last of all I crossed the river with my escort.

Next day, Mr. Morgan told me that things had quieted down very much among the Burmese; we did all in our power to collect provisions, and I enlarged the stockade, improving it from day to day, till it at last became a commodious and strong defensive building, scientifically constructed. I occupied a small stockade on a hillock above it, whence I had a good view, and could overlook the Manipuris. I had a circle of outlying pickets supplied by the Kuki irregulars with me, and these were a perpetual safeguard against surprise during the long dark nights. We cleared the jungle from round our stockade, and did all we could to make our position secure.

Still the Manipuris were a constant anxiety, illustrating the well-known saying, "Fools rush in, where angels fear to tread." Their carelessness was astonishing. I had the utmost difficulty in getting them to take the most ordinary precautions. The bravest and best-disciplined troops in the world would never think of neglecting every rule of warfare in the way that they did. Fire was a constant danger, and having no warm clothes, the Manipuris could hardly be prevented from lighting fires at night, thereby incurring a double danger, viz., that of setting fire to the stockade, also lighting up our position and enabling an enemy to fire at us. I was as a rule eighteen or nineteen hours on foot out of the twenty-four, and during the five or six allotted to sleep, I generally got up three times, to see that all was right.

Provisions began to come in, and on the last day of the year, I sent off 400 coolies to Moreh Tannah for provisions, so as to reduce the useless mouths, and to lessen the danger from fire. I rebuilt all the huts of green grass, as less inflammable than dry materials.

On January 1st, evil rumours were again afloat, and I asked the Woon if he were sure of his position. He replied that he was, and had perfect confidence that he could keep every one in hand. However, I went on collecting provisions, and while hoping for the arrival of the troops expected up the river, prepared for any eventuality. On January 3rd, large supplies of rice came in. The Issekai, an officer holding the rank of major, came twice to see me, and all seemed well. Mr. Morgan was with me all day helping with the rice sellers, but left about 4 P.M. About an hour afterwards, he reappeared with Mr. Bretto, saying that they had been shut out of the stockade, but that Mr. Ruckstuhl was detained there. They suspected a rising throughout the country, as a rumour had just been spread that a Royal prince was about to arrive at Kendat with 3000 men.

This was bad news, and I begged Messrs. Morgan and Bretto to stay the night with me. There was no time to be lost; I felt certain that the country had risen, and that in a few hours our communications would be cut, so I wrote to Manipur asking the Maharajah to send me 1000 men under Thangal Major at once to Moreh Tannah, to await events, and 500 to join me at Kendat, also a good supply of provisions. I telegraphed also to Government saying what had happened, and that I had taken every precaution, and that they might rely on my doing all that man could. I asked for no help, feeling that, if, with my present resources, I could not retrieve my position, I should soon be past help. I also wrote a few lines home, explaining matters in case I was killed, with a few last words to my children.

These letters I sent off by swift and trusty men well armed, with orders to push on with all speed. Having done this, I prepared for a life-and-death struggle next day.

As the morning broke and the heavy mist began to rise earlier than usual, we speedily saw the changed aspect of affairs. We had secured two boats under a guard the night before, but all besides had been taken from our side of the river. All the people had left a neighbouring village, but just below us we saw one boat after another leaving, heavily laden with the inhabitants and their portable goods. The opposite sandbank too, was occupied in force by the Burmese, who held our former entrenchment, and one or two small stockades. By this time also the country in our rear had risen, so we were completely cut off. The opposite bank was crowded with large boats, giving every opportunity to the enemy to send a strong party over to attack us by night, were he so disposed.

Immediate action was necessary, if only to save the British subjects, and the faithful Woon who had suffered in our cause. The good old Minister, Bularam Singh, quite lost his nerve, and begged and implored me to make terms and retreat, as the only means of saving ourselves. I told him that my very children and friends would despise me, if I, for a moment, contemplated such a course, and that there was nothing for it but to fight it out.

"Which man should you respect most?" I said, "one who cringed at your feet, or one who boldly struck you?" "The man who struck me," he replied. "Exactly so," I said; "and it is the same with the Burmese. I intend to strike a hard blow."

I had an ultimatum written in Burmese, demanding the surrender of the Woon, and his officers, and of all British subjects within two hours, under pain of my attacking the stockade; this I did, to run as little risk of injury to the captives, as possible. I had the ultimatum tied to a bamboo, and sent in a boat to a shallow part of the river, and I called to a Burmese to take it. This was done. I looked at my watch, and when the time expired, opened fire on the stockade.

For the first time in my life, I laid a gun. I judged the distance from the high bank where we stood, to the great stockade, to be 1250 yards, and the first shell went over it. I lessened the range by 50 yards, and again fired, and this time struck the stockade fair and well. We saw and heard the shell explode, and our men raised a loud shout of triumph. This little success gave the Manipuris renewed confidence. I lined our bank with picked shots of the 4th B.I., and under cover of these and the gun, sent two parties across in the boats, with orders to attack and destroy all the small stockades, and to capture some boats to convey more of our men across, and to burn all the rest, so as to prevent the enemy assuming the offensive.

Mr. Morgan, eager for the fray, went as a volunteer and assumed the natural position of leader. We kept up the fight all day. Shot after shot struck the great stockade, all the small ones were captured and burned, the enemy driven from the shore and every boat within sight either brought over to our side, or sent burning down the river.

Meanwhile, the Burmese had not been entirely passive, they had opened an artillery fire on us, and one or one-and-a-half-pound shots began to fall on our side. Old Bularam Singh walked up and down, notwithstanding this, with the greatest indifference, having now recovered his spirits, and behaved very well.

By sunset, nothing remained to be captured but the great stockade, and many were the volunteers, both Hindoostanis and Manipuris who begged to be allowed to cross once more and attack it. However, I would not consent, only two men, Messrs. Morgan and Bretto, knew all the turns and windings of the place, and one false move might convert our success into a disaster. All the same, I felt terribly anxious as to the fate of the Woon and of the British subjects.

I went to my hut in the evening, feeling that we had done all we could. As I passed through the stockade, I was surprised to see the clever way in which the coolies remaining with us had strengthened it, by digging deep trenches sufficient to afford a man perfect protection against rifle fire, even without the stockade.

I rose early on January 5th, after an anxious night, having given orders for a party to be ready to cross the river with me, to attack the great stockade; but, just as I left my hut to make a start, I was met by Mr. Ruckstuhl with irons on his ankles—he had got rid of the connecting bars—who told me that it had been evacuated. The facts I learned were as follows.

On the evening of January 3rd, incited by the near approach of three thousand men and the promised support of the Tsawbwas of Thoungdoot, Wuntha, Kubo, and six other districts, the bad spirits in the town rose against the Woon, and put him and his family and chief officials, with Mr. Ruckstuhl, in irons. It was only by a mistake that Messrs. Morgan and Bretto were shut out of the stockade and not arrested.

When my ultimatum arrived, the Burmese laughed at the idea of my doing anything, and when our fire opened on them they were just about to crucify the Woon and Ruckstuhl. When, however, our attack began to make an impression on them, and shells burst in the stockade, especially one in a room where the chief men were deliberating, they retreated, leaving their prisoners. Mr. Ruckstuhl had hidden under a hedge, and the Woon and his family were taking refuge in a Phoongye's house. This was good news and an immense relief to every one; we felt we had done our work.

I immediately took a party across the river and rescued the Woon, and took possession of the huge stockade, which would have cost us many a life to capture, had it been well defended. We took sixteen guns and a large number of wall pieces, all said to have been wrested from Manipur in former days.

The Woon's house was apparently intact, but empty, and the town was deserted. In a house we found a hen on a brood of chickens, unmoved apparently by all the firing and commotion. I made over the Woon's house to him again, and I established a Manipuri guard for his protection. With reference to the guns, I should say that I did not take them from the stockade on my first arrival at Kendat, not wishing in any way to lower the prestige of the Woon who had done us such good service, and who professed himself quite able to account for them, and to keep the people in order. As events proved, we were quite able to take them when necessary.

Just as we had finished our work, and Mr. Morgan and I were taking some food in the afternoon, two steamers came in sight far down the Chindwin. These proved to be the party sent to rescue the British subjects at Kendat, under Major Campbell, 23rd Madras Infantry; and consisted of a company of the Hampshire Regiment and some blue jackets, and some of the 23rd Madras Infantry, and great was their disappointment to find that the work had been done before they arrived. However, had we waited for them, there would have been no one to rescue on their arrival.

To my intense surprise, I heard that Kendat was to be abandoned, but no arrangements had been made for carrying away the Native British subjects. Mr. Morgan would not abandon these and the valuable property of the Bombay-Burmah Corporation, and elected together with Mr. Bretto to stay with me. I strongly urged Mr. Ruckstuhl (whose brother, one of the refugees from Mengin, had been brought up by Major Campbell) to leave for Rangoon with the steamers, as I thought, after twice narrowly escaping a violent death, he had better run no more risks. He took my advice. The steamers left on January 8th.

CHAPTER XXIX.

Mischief done by departure of steamers—Determine to establish the Woon at Tamu—The Country quieting down—Recovery of mails—Letter from the Viceroy—Arrive at Manipur—Bad news—I return to Tamu—Night march to Pot-tha—An engagement—Wounded—Return to Manipur—Farewell—Leave for England.

We had gained immense prestige by the vigorous way in which we had put down the revolt, and the people from the neighbouring country began to come in and make their submission, but the departure of the steamers was a great blow to it. Of course, the natives attributed it to fear. Had they stayed, all trouble would have been at an end, and the country would have quietly settled down. As it was, this unfortunate retreat again upset the minds of all.

The Chindwin, and the route to it through Manipur, had not been considered when the campaign was decided on. No part of a country that it is intended to annex can with safety be neglected, and the Chindwin valley was a very important part of Burmah.

As I have said before, a properly organised Manipur Levy would have solved all difficulties at the outbreak of war; failing that, a force specially devoted to the Chindwin valley, and entering through Manipur, and aided by local knowledge acquired during many years on that frontier, might have occupied the province of Kendat before any time had been given for the spread of lawlessness. It is almost incredible that, considering the part taken by Manipur, and troops moving through Manipur during the war of 1885–6, showing the immense facilities offered by that route, that no inquiry whatever was made regarding it before the outbreak of hostilities.

I saw plainly that without the certainty of troops and one steamer at least arriving to reinforce us, it would be unwise to attempt to hold Kendat so far from our base at Manipur, therefore I made preparations for escorting all British subjects and property to Tamu, within the Woon's jurisdiction, advising the latter to establish himself there for the present, and from that point gradually reconsolidate his authority. He greatly approved of the suggestion, and I made arrangements with a view to carrying it into effect.

It was not till the 10th of January that any post arrived from Manipur. The Kubo valley had risen, it was said, in obedience to orders received from the Kulé Tsawbwa and a man called the Lay Kahiyine Oke, and it was reported that we had been annihilated; but the sight of all the captured guns, which I at once sent to Manipur, told the people a different tale, and they soon subsided and returned to their allegiance. I sent out a party to attack and destroy the house of a hostile chief, east of the Chindwin, and it was successfully accomplished.

Several letter bags which had been stolen were now given up, and I issued proclamations to all the neighbouring chiefs calling on them to remain quiet, and keep their people in order.

Two hundred of the troops I had sent for from Manipur, arrived at Kendat, and 300 more I ordered to be stationed at different points on the road. The 1000 men under Thangal Major were directed by me to return to Manipur. Before leaving Kendat, I sent on the Woon, with his family and 250 native British subjects, *en route* to Tamu, with a strong escort. The road had been much improved during my occupation of Kendat, and was now passable for lightly laden elephants.

I left some Burmese officials at Kendat with orders to report regularly to the Woon, and collect taxes due, and having made all arrangements that I could for the peace of the country, I quitted it, with the remaining portion of my force, on January 14th, encamping at a place called Méjong. We reached Tamu on the 17th, where the Woon was well received.

I had written to the Thoungdoot (Sumjok) Tsawbwa, asking him to come and see me, but he was nervous, and sent his Minister instead. The man arrived on the 19th, with a very civil letter from the Tsawbwa, making his submission. I explained to him that I should hold his master responsible for the good behaviour of his people, and sent him to pay his respects to the Woon, which he did. About this time I received some very complimentary telegrams from Government, thanking me for what I had done; these being followed by an autograph letter from the Viceroy, Lord Dufferin.

Being completely worn out with the work and anxiety I had gone through, so much so, that I could not sleep without a dose of bromide of potassium,

I set off for Manipur, to get a little rest, on the 20th of January, and reached it, by forced marches, on the 22nd. Mr. Morgan came with me, and my escort followed two days after. The men had kept their promise, and not one man had "gone sick" for a day, and they had always been ready for work; often, since the outbreak on the 3rd of January, living for days on rice fresh cut from the enemy's fields by the Manipuris.

I left a strong guard of Manipuris in a stockade at Tamu as a help to the Woon, and let the Minister Bularam Singh and all the rest of the party return with me.

Before leaving Tamu, I handed over one or two men, supposed to be rebels, to the Woon, and gave him authority to execute them, should he consider it necessary, as an example, saying, however, that he must, in that case shoot, hang, or decapitate, as we could not allow painful modes of putting to death.

I found, on arrival at Manipur, that another detachment of the 4th B.I. had arrived, and I very soon found use for them.

I had hoped to have had some much-needed rest, but on the 24th I received a letter from the Woon telling me that two of the leading rebels in the outbreak of the 3rd, who had fled towards Wuntho, had returned, and were leading about bands of brigands. I heard from another source that the men I had delivered into his hands had been released on paying heavy fines, and had joined the rebel leaders. The Woon had an ample force at his disposal, but, as I saw that another storm was brewing, I sent off the new detachment of the 4th, towards Tamu, on the

26th, and followed myself (Mr. Morgan having preceded me) on the 28th; and on the 30th we marched into Tamu together.

I met the poor old Woon ten miles within the Manipur frontier; he had evidently lost his nerve and had fled, the ill-treatment he had undergone, and the narrow escape from crucifixion, were too much for him. I at once sent him on to Manipur, with orders that he should be my guest, and marched on.

As we crossed the frontier, the Burmese left the jungles where they had hidden from the dreaded dacoits, and returned with us to their villages. Tamu was quiet, the Manipuri guard had stood firm at their posts, and held the stockade intact, a work Manipuris are admirably fitted for, and thoroughly to be trusted with. My arrival seemed to quiet down the valley for many miles, indeed all the inhabitants for miles round were by the next day pursuing their ordinary avocations, and the only fear was from the dacoits.

On January 31st, at about 6 P.M., I received a report that a party of the enemy had hoisted the white flag (the Burmese Royal Standard), and taken up their quarters at Pot-tha, a disaffected village twenty miles from Tamu. This was an opportunity not to be lost, and I prepared to strike a decisive blow. We left Tamu about midnight, the force consisting of myself and Mr. Morgan, fifty of the 4th B.I., seventy Manipuris, and fifty Kuki irregulars. We had to march in single file through the forest, carrying torches to light us, and a most picturesque sight it was, the long line winding in and out under the tall trees, which the blaze of the torches lighted up, producing a very weird effect. We took with us guides from Tamu, and marched in deep silence, every now and then passing a village opening, though we generally avoided them, if possible.

At last, just after daybreak, we heard the sound of a musket shot; our Shan guides said: "This is the place," and instantly evaporated. I can use no other term; I saw them one moment, the next they had gone, where I know not. We went on, and after a hundred yards, passed fortifications just evacuated, and soon after entered the village, the enemy retiring before us without firing a shot; we rushed on, and searched the houses. I saw the white standard planted outside a large house on a platform; I ran up and seized it, close by was a tree called in Bengali, "Poppeya," the papaw, I believe, of the West Indies, with a soft trunk. A minute after, while I was looking about to see if I could observe any of the enemy, a volley was fired, evidently intended for me, the royal standard in my hand making me a conspicuous mark. I was not struck (probably just at the moment I moved), but the tree was, and fell, cut in two by at least twenty musket balls.

I then saw some of the enemy strongly posted, under a house, built like all in those parts on strong posts, affording excellent cover. I sprang down from the platform, calling to my scattered men to follow. One man was ahead of me, and was shot down mortally wounded; another minute, and I myself was struck by a shot on the left temple, and almost stunned. I was able to rise, but with the blood streaming down, not fit to pursue. I called to Mr. Morgan and asked him to head a party of the 4th B.I. and clear the village, which was done with great gallantry, the men, when they returned, greatly applauding Mr. Morgan's courage and dash. Having driven out the enemy who, we subsequently ascertained, lost seven killed and twenty-five wounded, we set fire to the village and 10,000 maunds of rice stored there, *i.e.*, about 360 tons, which, of course, we could not carry away, and marched back to Tamu which we reached about nightfall carrying our wounded with us. Besides myself, we had one mortally wounded, one severely and one slightly. I was able to march back. We took three prisoners and heard that the enemy, who did not stop till he had crossed the Chindwin, had a force of 400 to 500 men engaged, commanded by Boh Moung Schway Lé.

On February 6th, all the principal chiefs of the Kubo valley came in and made their formal submission to me, promising to remain quiet and obey the orders of the Tamu Myo Thugee, whom I appointed to administer the valley till further orders. Next day, I made them all go to the Pagoda, and swear allegiance to the British Government, the oath being most solemnly administered by the Phoongyees. I gave definite instructions to all, and urged them to keep the peace, and buy, sell and cultivate as usual.

I proclaimed the passes into Manipur open to traders, which gave great satisfaction to all, and having satisfied myself that everything was quiet I set out for Manipur to consult Dr. Eteson, the Deputy Surgeon-General, who was passing through, about my wound. I arrived by forced marches on

February 9th, and found that the sepoy mortally wounded on February 1st, had died on the 8th.

Dr. Eteson urged me to go to England on sick leave, and I very reluctantly determined to follow his advice. But, before leaving, I had the satisfaction of seeing the whole of the Kubo valley in a state of profound peace for a month and a half. Provisions were no longer a difficulty. They were freely brought in, and the little luxuries that Hindoostani troops require over and above what can be bought on the spot, were taken down by traders. So great was the energy of the latter, that 2000 buffaloes were exported through Manipur to Cachar during this short period, and when I finally bade adieu to my friends at Tamu, Mr. Morgan and I both expected that war was at an end, and that perfect peace would prevail. It was not our fault that it did not.

Let me here offer a tribute to one who stood by me nobly in the hour of need, but who, unfortunately, died of cholera at Kulé, after his return from well-earned leave in England. Morgan was a thoroughly good fellow all round, a devoted servant of the Bombay-Burmah Corporation, and one who put their affairs before everything. As gentle and kind as he was brave, he was a great favourite with the Burmese, and had evidently much influence with them. He was always in favour of mild measures, unless strong ones appeared absolutely necessary.

While still in Burmah, I had sent in my despatches to General Sir H. Prendergast, K.C.B., who commanded the army of invasion, in which I strongly commended to his notice the admirable services of my escort, mentioning specially several men whom I thought particularly deserving of it, though all had done so well, and shown such devotion to duty and soldier-like spirit, that it was a difficult task to select any one in particular. General Prendergast forwarded my recommendation to the Commander-in-Chief, and it was a great satisfaction to me when I heard afterwards that Baluk Ram Chowby, then Subadar Major of his Regiment, had received the Order of British India, with the title of "Bahadur," and that other decorations and promotions had been bestowed. The detachment of the gallant 4th Bengal Infantry, took with them, as trophies to their regiment, a standard they had captured, and also one of the sixteen guns taken at Kendat.

I left the old Woon at Manipur, having strongly recommended him to the favour of Government. He stood by our people in a dark hour, and saved them from torture and death. He was of high family, and had fought against us in 1852. He had the air of a thorough gentleman, and was, with all his family, most amiable in conversation and demeanour.

Before leaving, I paid one last visit to Kang-joop-kool and saw my child's grave,* and the peaceful

* "The Senaputtee seemed determined to wipe away all signs of British connection with the State. Not only were the charred remains of the Residency still further demolished, but every building in the neighbourhood, and the very walls of the compound and garden were levelled, and the graves of British officers were desecrated. The Kang-joop-kool Sanatorium, twelve miles from the capital, built by Sir J. Johnstone, was burnt, and his child's grave dug up." — *Times*' telegram, May 3, 1891.—ED.

It appears by the official correspondence that the Senaputtee sent seven Manipur sepahis to open the child's grave, and scatter the remains, out of

ARTHUR JOHNSTONE'S GRAVE. [*Page* 268.

scenery and lovely views over the hills and the broad valley, thinking of the past and its many memories connected with the place. I paid my last visit to the Rajah, when I told him that I had strongly urged the restoration to him of his old possession, the Kubo valley. I visited all the familiar spots round the capital. I said good-bye to old Thangal, Bularam Singh, and all my old followers, and, on the 19th of March, bade adieu to Manipur, which I felt I had raised out of the mire of a bad reputation.

I left it as it had been of yore, a faithful and devoted, though humble, ally of the British Government to whom it had done transcendent service. Alas! little did I think of the fate that would befall it before a few short years had passed by.

My escort turned out to salute me as I left the Residency gate, and I gave them an address, thanking them for their services. Then the Subadar Baluk Ram Chowby insisted on their accompanying me for some distance. When time for them to return, he halted his party, drew them in line by the side of the road, and presented arms, and as they did it they gave a loud shout of "Colonel Sahib Bahadûr ke jye," *i.e.* "Vive Monsieur le Colonel Victorieux;" we have no equivalent for it in English. My heart was too heavy to say much; I said a few words, and we parted.

As I crossed the summit of the Lai-metol range I

spite to Sir J. Johnstone, whom he knew had wished him to be banished, and who (on account of the Senaputtee's exceptionally bad character) would never admit him into the Residency. For this act the British military authorities had the sepahis flogged. — Nos. 1–11, East India (Manipur) Blue Books.—ED.

gave a last look at the valley, and saw it no more.

I passed through Shillong, where I was hospitably entertained by the Chief Commissioner, Mr. Ward, and on reaching Calcutta received a command to visit Lord Dufferin at Benares. He received me very kindly, and under his roof I spent a most enjoyable day. I left Bombay on the 9th of April, and reached home on the 28th, thus practically finishing my active Indian career, after nearly twenty-eight years' service.

CHAPTER XXX.

Conclusion.

The Events of 1890 and 1891.

When I first began this book it was my intention to have given a connected account of the Palace Revolution of September 1890, and that of 1891, against the British Government. Being probably the only living person in full possession of the whole facts connected with the startling events that then took place, and the circumstances that led up to them, and having, moreover, a strong conviction that it is best for all parties that the truth should be known, I felt that a fair and impartial statement could do no harm, and might act as a warning. Further reflection has led me to alter my determination, and to ask myself the question, "*Cui bono?*" The Government of India has shown no desire to make more disclosures than necessary, and it is not for me, a loyal old servant, to lift the veil.

"Let the dead past bury its dead."

However much, therefore, I may wish to see the right horse saddled, I shall for the present, at any rate, avoid criticism as far as possible, and confine myself to a few general remarks.

Nothing that I can say will undo the past, and all that remains is to hope for the future.

After I left Manipur fresh disturbances broke out in the Kubo valley, where I had left all peaceful, prosperous, and contented, and a considerable strain was put on the resources of Manipur. Had I been ordered to return I would gladly have done so, but my health was too bad to make it advisable for me to volunteer my services.* I regret that I did not, as I might in that case have again urged the claims of Manipur to have the Kubo valley restored to her, as she had a right to expect that it would be; substantial hopes having been on at least one occasion held out to her, and her many good services and constant loyalty entitling her to consideration.

However, it was not to be; and in the summer of 1886 another misfortune befell her, in the death of Maharajah Chandra Kirtee Singh. Perhaps, like his father, Ghumbeer Singh, he was happy in the hour of his death, as he did not live to see the disgrace of his country, and the ingratitude of our Government to his family.

Now was the grand opportunity for the Government and an able Political Agent to step in and make the many needful reforms, and introduce necessary changes, and instil a more modern spirit in keeping with the times, into the institutions of the country. Did we take advantage of it? Of course we did not; but, true to our happy-go-lucky

* "Oh! for a moment of Colonel Johnstone's presence at such a crisis," wrote a British official from Manipur, to the *Pioneer*, in 1891. "One strong word with the ominous raising of the forefinger, would have paralyzed the treacherous rebel Koireng (Senaputtee) from perpetrating this outrage."—ED.

traditions, let one precious opportunity after another pass by unheeded. Year after year during my period of office had I struggled hard, and carried on a never-ending fight for influence and prestige, with the strong and capable old Chandra Kirtee Singh, gaining ground steadily; but realising that, while I worked, the full advantage would be reaped by that one of my successors who might chance to be in office when my old friend closed his eventful life. At such a time, in addition to the result of my labours, a weaker occupant of the throne would afford many opportunities such as were not vouchsafed to me, and now the time had arrived when we might have worked unimpeded for the good of all classes.

Soor Chandra Singh, the former Jubraj, or heir apparent, succeeded his father, a good, amiable man, with plenty of ability, but very weak. He was loyal to the British Government, and had on several occasions given strong proof of it, and he was much respected by his own people. Had he been taken in hand properly all would have been well, but the Government of India seems never to have realised that excessive care and caution were necessary. The records of the past plainly showed that the appointment of a Political Agent was always a difficult one to fill satisfactorily, but no pains seem to have been at any time taken to find a suitable man; if one happened to be appointed, it was a matter of chance, and the post seems generally to have been put up to a kind of Dutch auction. On one occasion I believe that an officer, who was at the time doing well, and liked the place, was taken away, and another, who did not wish to go, sent up, to die within a month of a long-standing complaint. For all this, of course the Foreign Office must be held responsible, as it had a long traditional knowledge of Manipur; and though its powers were delegated to the Chief Commissioner of Assam, it should have ascertained that that officer was capable of making a good selection, and had an officer under him fit for the appointment. The work may not have been of a nature requiring the very highest class of intellect, but it certainly did require a rather rare combination of qualities, together with one indispensable to make a good officer, namely, a real love for the work, the country, and the people. My immediate successor had these latter qualities, but he died of wounds received within six weeks of my leaving.*

It is to be regretted, also, that the Government of India acts so much on the principle that the private claims of some of its servants should be considered before the claims of the State generally, and the people over whom they are put, in particular. It seems to be thought that the great object, in many cases, is to secure a certain amount of pay to an individual, quite irrespective of his qualifications, rather than to seek out an officer in every way competent to administer a great province, and satisfy the requirements of its people. I say this especially with reference to Assam. Few provinces of India require more special qualities in its ruler, containing, as it does, many races of different grades of civilisation; the situation being further complicated by the

* Major Trotter. He received wounds from an ambuscade, and died of their effects, July, 1886.—Ed.

presence of a large European population of tea-planters. These, by their energy and the judicious application of a large amount of capital, have raised it to a great pitch of prosperity, and they naturally require to be dealt with in a different way to their less civilised native fellow-subjects.

An officer may be an admirable accountant, or very well able to decide between two litigants, or, may be, to look after stamps and stationery; but without special administrative experience, or those abilities which enable a genius to grasp any subject he takes up, he cannot be considered fit to be trusted with the government of a great and flourishing province. His claims as regards pay should not be allowed to weigh at all with the Government of India; it is unjust to the people, and would be cheaper to give an enhanced pension than ruin a province. Yet it cannot be denied that the considerations I have referred to, do prevail, and that the Manipur disaster was, in a great measure, due to the system, and that with proper care it could never have happened.

When I was in Manipur no European could enter the state without obtaining the permission of the Durbar through the Political Agent, and the Maharajah, very wisely, did his utmost to discourage such visitors, unless they were friends of the latter. Orchid collectors, and such like, were rigorously excluded, wisely, again I say, considering the havoc wrought by selfish traders with these lovely denizens of the forests of Manipur and Burmah, and when the Burmese war broke out, very few were those of our countrymen who had visited the interesting little state. As for myself I quite sympathised with the Maharajah and I even said a word on behalf of the Sungai (swamp deer) peculiar to Manipur and Burmah, and advised him to preserve it strictly. I fear it must be extinct in Manipur by this time. The Burmese war changed all this; troops poured through the country, and European officers were constantly passing to and fro, much to the annoyance of the Durbar. Of course, a stay-at-home Englishman will hardly understand this, but to anyone knowing natives of India well, it is self-evident, a European cannot go through a state like Manipur where suspicion reigns rampant, and where people are wedded to their own peculiar ways, without causing a great deal of trouble. All sorts of things have to be provided for him, and though he pays liberally, some one suffers. The presence of one or two Europeans constantly moving about would no doubt in itself be a source of annoyance to the high officials of Manipur, who would always suspect them of making enquiries with a view to an unfavourable report to Government. All natives of India are suspicious, and this remark applies with tenfold force to Manipuris.

It cannot, I fear, be denied, that as a race we are a little careless of the feelings of others. It is possibly due in a great measure to our insularity; but, whatever be the cause, it is an undesirable quality to possess. With a regiment of Native Infantry stationed at Langthabal to support our authority, our prestige ought to have rapidly increased; apparently the reverse was the case, and from time to time incidents occurred, which indicated how events were drifting. On one occasion some sepoys of the Political Agent's escort were hustled and beaten by some Manipuris at a public festival, and on another the man carrying the Government mail bag between Imphal and Langthabal, was stopped and robbed of the mails. Everything seemed to show that our position was not what it had been. In former days such things could not have happened.

Kotwal Koireng had always been a bad character, and had for years been under a cloud. Had I remained in Manipur I should have turned him out when the Maharajah his father died, and reported the matter to Government. He was allowed to remain, and proved the ruin of the state. His bloodthirsty nature soon showed itself, and he half-roasted two men after a most cruel flogging, the Maharajah was asked to turn him out of the state, and would probably have consented, but just at the time a European sergeant shot a cow, the sacred animal of the Hindoos, an outrage far exceeding any that our imagination can paint, and the Rajah in his wrath flatly refused to punish his brother, while such a fearful crime as cow killing, was allowed to pass unnoticed. Of course the last was an untoward event, that should never have occurred. We ought not to allow uncultured Europeans likely to be careless of native feeling and susceptibilities to enter a state so full of prejudice and suspicion as Manipur.

Thus events followed one another in rapid succession, signs every now and then appearing which showed that all was not as quiet as it seemed. I heard from time to time things that made me uneasy, as I gathered that Kotwal Koireng, now become Senaputtee or Commander-in-Chief, had much power and influence, and I felt sure that he would soon make an attempt to oust his brother, the Maharajah.

At last the attempt was made. In September, 1890, the Maharajah Soor Chandra Singh was attacked in his palace at night, and driven out. He fled to Cachar and having petitioned the Government of India for his restoration, proceeded to Calcutta. The case was a simple one, a palace revolution had occurred and our nominee whose succession and whose throne we had guaranteed, had been deposed. The course to be adopted by Government was as clear as the day, Soor Chandra Singh should have been restored at once and the usurper severely punished for insulting the majesty of the British Government. Nothing of the kind was done. It was decided, on what grounds I know not, to break our pledged word; the Maharajah was to be exiled with a pittance for his support; his stupid boorish brother who had been set up as puppet by the Senaputtee was to be Rajah; while the evil genius of Manipur, the treacherous Senaputtee, was to be exiled. The Government of India then ordered the Chief Commissioner of Assam to proceed to Manipur and carry out their decision, including the Senaputtee's arrest.

It is difficult to say which showed the greatest want of wisdom, the Government in issuing such an order, or the Chief Commissioner in accepting such a mission, quite derogatory to one of such high rank. We all know how it ended. The less said about it the better, it reflects no credit on us.*

* "The general history of the Manipur incident," wrote the *Times* in a leading article, Aug. 14, 1891, "must inspire mingled feelings in the

With one or two things, however, I am concerned, and one of these is the sentence on Thangal Major, or General as he was called; in the correspondence usually ignorantly referred to, as "The Thangal General," a misnomer, Thangal being a name and not a title. This old man seventy-four years of age had long almost retired into private life. He was a devoted follower of Soor Chandra Singh, and hated the Senaputtee whose evil influence he always feared would wreck Manipur. This probably made the latter recall him to public life, so as to keep him under his eye; anyhow, he was by force of circumstances obliged, however unwillingly, to act as a loyal subject of his own *de facto* chief.

I have said so much about the old man, that his character will be well understood. He was a strong, able, unscrupulous man, not likely to stick at trifles, and, like most Asiatics of his type, capable of

breasts of most Englishmen. The policy in which it originated, cannot be said to reflect credit on the Government of India, while the actual explosion itself was precipitated by a series of blunders which have never been explained. There seems to be little doubt that had the Government of India made up its mind promptly on the merits of the dynastic quarrel between the dethroned Maharajah and his brothers, the Senaputtee would hardly have been able to commit the crimes which have cost him his life. But for five months the Government of India seemed to accept the revolution accomplished last September in the palace of Manipur. That revolution was notoriously the work of the Senaputtee, although he chose, for his own reasons, to place one of his brothers on the throne. The Government did not indeed assent to the change, but their local representative does not appear to have taken marked steps to express his disapproval. He is said to have tolerated and condoned it to this extent, that he kept up friendly relations with the new ruler as with the old. On the deplorable mistakes which led up to the massacre, and made it possible, it is unnecessary to dwell. They are still unaccounted for, and so many of the chief actors in that fatal business have perished, that it is more than doubtful whether we shall ever know exactly to whom they severally were due."—Ed.

anything. This does not, however, mean that he was worse than his neighbours, our characters are made by our surroundings, and in Manipur the surroundings are not of an elevating nature. Thangal was in many ways kind hearted, in others ruthless, and for the moment cruel, his wrath flared up and, except when kept aglow for policy's sake, soon burned itself out.

When first I heard of the outbreak I made two predictions, both proved to be true. One of these was that, whoever was guilty, Thangal Major would be accused. I never did think him guilty by premeditation, but I knew that, as for so long a time he was the strong head of the executive, he was not loved, and that to save the Senaputtee, whom I of course at once pitched upon as the "*fons et origo*" of the rebellion, and who like all of the blood royal was looked upon as semi-divine, he would be accused. I read the evidence published, which I can quite understand appeared conclusive to the tribunal before which he was tried; reading between the lines, however, with a thorough knowledge of Manipur as I was able to do, it gave me quite a different impression. Knowing the old man so intimately as I did, his way of talking and his way of acting, I am convinced that he was in no way a willing accessory to the rebellion, that he in no way connived at the invitation to our officers to enter the palace at night, and further that he never suggested or consented to their murder! The whole proceeding was so totally opposed to his policy that he would never have sanctioned such an act of folly, to say the least. The Senaputtee richly deserved all he got and more.

An unscrupulous and selfish butcher by nature he played his cards badly and when he lost, determined to involve his whole family and loyal dependents in the ruin which his own insensate folly had brought on him. I quite acknowledge old Thangal's many faults, but I also remember his good qualities, and shall ever regret that he came to such an untimely end.

As regards the disposition of the throne I have a word to say. Recognising as I do the necessity of maintaining the firmness of our rule and prestige to the utmost, a rule that is of incalculable benefit to millions, I quite approved of a heavy punishment being exacted as a terrible warning to all time, when we re-conquered Manipur. It cannot be denied that we showed unseemly want of nerve when the news of the disaster arrived. There was no necessity to place Assam under a military ruler, nor was there any need for such a formidable muster of troops, at a vast expenditure of money and suffering, to retrieve a disaster brought about by such an extraordinary want of courage, nerve, forethought and common-sense.* Our position in Manipur had never been a dangerous one, and even after the murder of the Chief Commissioner's party the troops in the Residency might easily have held their own till daybreak, when all opposition

* Three columns (one alone numbering 1000 strong), were marched at once on Imphal, which was found deserted. The Regent was the last of the princes who fled. He released the surviving English prisoner, and sent him to the British camp to ask for an armistice; but this was refused until he delivered up the Englishmen already dead. The Manipuris, then expecting no mercy, opposed the march of the troops.—ED.

would have collapsed, and the rebels would bave fled, leaving our people masters of the situation.

I have expressed my opinion as to the mistake we made in not restoring the Rajah *before* the outbreak of March, and now I ask the question, why, after the rebellion was put down, we did not do our best to repair the evil by restoring Soor Chandra Singh to his own? He, or his infant son, might have been restored, and have been kept in a state of tutelage as long as necessary, and good government would have been secured and our pledge to Chandra Kirtee Singh have been maintained intact. Instead of this, an obscure child, a descendant not of Ghumbeer Singh, but of Nur Singh, was selected, and the old line cut off from the succession, and yet three generations had been faithful to us. Ghumbeer Singh, Chandra Kirtee Singh, and Soor Chandra Singh all served us loyally, and yet we suffered the last to die of a broken heart in exile. Well might he exclaim, "And is this the reward for so many years' service!" For my part I say emphatically, *let us beware, we have not heard the last of Manipur!*

My sense of right and justice make me record facts as they strike me, and yet I cannot help acknowledging as I do so, that the Government of India is the best government in the world. When has India been so governed, and what country in Europe has such an able and just administration? Surrounded by difficulties, material, financial and political, badgered by ignorant members of the House of Commons, for ever asking foolish questions and moving foolish resolutions; the stately bureaucracy plods steadily on with one object in view, the good of the people. If at times it makes mistakes, who does not? The greatest General is he who makes fewest mistakes, and, judged by this standard alone, the Government of India has the first rank among governing bodies. It has, however, a title to honour which no one can assail. It is the only instance in history of a body of foreigners who govern an Empire, not for their own benefit, but for the benefit of the races committed by Providence to their charge. May Providence long watch over it!

INDEX.